FULL VALUE
Cases in Christian Business Ethics

FULL VALUE

Cases in Christian Business Ethics

Oliver F. Williams
University of Notre Dame
Department of Theology

John W. Houck
University of Notre Dame
Department of Management

Published in San Francisco by
Harper & Row, Publishers
New York, Hagerstown, San Francisco, London

To Leo V. Ryan, C.S.V.

His support of value education in the
business world made this book possible.

FIRST EDITION

Library of Congress Cataloging in Publication Data

Williams, Oliver F
  Full value.

  (Case study series)
  Bibliography
  Includes index.
  1. Business ethics—Case studies. I. Houck, John W.,
joint author. II. Title.
HF5387.W54   241'.6'44   78-3143
ISBN 0-06-069515-3

78 79 80 81 82 10 9 8 7 6 5 4 3 2 1

CONTENTS

Acknowledgements

We would like to thank the many people who have assisted us in the preparation of this volume. The faculty of the Department of Theology of the University of Notre Dame provided invaluable assistance at two department colloquia where early drafts of the manuscript were discussed. We are particularly indebted to Edward A. Malloy, C.S.C., Stanley Hauerwas and David B. Burrell, C.S.C. of the Department of Theology. Vincent R. Raymond, Associate Dean of the College of Business Administration, C. Joseph Sequin, Chairman of the Department of Management, University of Notre Dame, and Katharine Terry Dooley, St. Mary's College, Notre Dame, Indiana, all deserve acknowledgement for their counsel and assistance. James W. McClendon, Jr., a member of the faculty of the Church Divinity School of the Pacific of the Graduate Theological Union, Berkeley, California, was an invaluable colleague and friend. Donald B. Rice, President of the Rand Corporation, gave generously of his time in discussing the project. James F. Rainey, Associate Dean of the Graduate School of Business Administration of Michigan State University, offered helpful suggestions and criticisms. Fred K. Foulkes, Professor at the Harvard University Graduate School of Business Administration, provided assistance in researching material for the book. Jerry B. Handspicker of Andover Newton Theological School and the staff of the 1977 Case Study Institute Summer Workshop at Cambridge, Massachusetts offered many valuable suggestions for the manuscript. Robert A. Evans of the Hartford Seminary Foundation and Louis Weeks of Louisville Presbyterian Seminary were the series editors of our volume, and their untiring efforts are deeply appreciated. We also wish to thank Roy M. Carlisle, Editor at Harper & Row, for his careful attention to our work, and for his friendship.

We must give special recognition to the writers of the cases we have included, for theirs is a unique contribution to learning and understanding. One of the pleasantest tasks in preparing this volume was thumbing through *The New Yorker,* looking for appropriate cartoons. Cartoonists have a genius that we have drawn on with appreciation in this volume.

Our thanks would be incomplete without special mention of Father Theodore M. Hesburgh, C.S.C. He encouraged the project from its inception in the fall of 1975 when we first started teaching in this area, and he graciously offered to write the preface to our work. Finally, we are especially grateful to Brother Leo V. Ryan, C.S.V., Dean of the College of Business Administration at the University of Notre Dame, and the person to whom this volume is dedicated. Brother Leo's leadership has been an inspiration to all of us who are striving to discover creative ways to integrate value education with professional excellence in the business world.

A grant from the Vilter Foundation provided for much of the typing expenses of our work. The time to research and write the final draft of this book was made possible by generous leaves of absence from the University of Notre Dame. We are most grateful.

Oliver F. Williams, C.S.C.
John W. Houck
University of Notre Dame
Notre Dame, Indiana, 1978

Series Preface
Experience and Reflection:
Theological Casebooks

The series, Experience and Reflection, seeks to consolidate methodological gains from experimentation with the case method in theological education. It offers a variety of actual cases together with interpretive materials which aid in the study. Some of the writings are expressly designed for development of one particular aspect of theological education—Bible study, for example. Others are more generally focused to assist persons and communities in their process of religious maturation.

In the decade of the 1970's, the use of inductive educational methods has increased dramatically. In North American theological education this impact has proven most forceful, as use of the case method has become a primary mode of instruction for many. Now, the publication of case-centered works in various areas of theological education will provide resources for teaching in seminaries, in congregations, and in other learning situations. The books will also serve those studying religions and ethical traditions in colleges and universities.

Series Editors:
Robert A. Evans, Ph.D.
Hartford, Connecticut

Louis B. Weeks, Ph.D.
Louisville, Kentucky

Preface

The Rev. Theodore M. Hesburgh, C.S.C.
President, University of Notre Dame

This volume has as its theme the interpenetration of biblically based images and values with those of professional management and business leadership. While this theme is novel and ambitious and therefore risky, I believe that the authors have achieved what they set out to do. And I believe the exploration and integration of these important convictional bodies of belief—business and Christian—is critical to contemporary humankind's efforts to make sense out of the world in which we live.

It has become a truism that modern life is terribly complex and changeable. Since 1945, we humans have changed (and improved in many cases) our material, scientific, and technological bases more than in all our prior history. For example, we have published twice as many books and journals in these three decades as in all the centuries since Gutenberg. We can travel faster and to more places (including outer space) than even our more imaginative predecessors could have dreamed. Our growth in the uses and misuses of energy have been well documented, but it suffices to point out that we have used more energy in these three decades than in all of our prior history. No doubt, we will use in the next two decades more energy than in the prior three decades. This record-setting and record-breaking is the story of our recent history, whether it be in material goods or services, science, technology, education, or medicine.

But all this activity takes leadership, and since much of it occurs in the business world—whether in petroleum, transportation, manufacturing, or whatever—business must continue to develop a large cadre of successful managers to staff our huge business firms and multinational corporations. This task of training and testing leaders is the most important challenge facing business today, for while our problems have changed, the need for people of competence and creativity to deal with them remains the same. This volume recognizes the factor of leadership as necessary for today and tomorrow's world.

This volume also raises a question—leadership for what purpose? —and suggests that the answer could be affected by images and values growing out of a profound study of the Christian story. The authors share the conviction that Scripture still has a role to play in informing and making the world better. But this Christian commitment to social action must be matched by a zeal that is not afraid of the hard work necessary to master the complex technologies of large-scale organizations. Goodwill and piety are no substitute for competence. That is why the authors have included some very long and difficult exercises (cases) to demonstrate the role of competence, (i.e., knowledge, identifying choices, setting priorities, etc.) as a corequisite to being "men and women of goodwill."

For instance, one of the stories presented in the volume is the career of John Caron, a person I know and respect. He emphasized the role of competence when he stated: "There is nothing to me less inspiring than a person who talks Christian values and ethics, but who is a failure in his or her profession or work." He goes on to ask: "A person can talk, but can he or she act? Can he or she accomplish anything?" From my personal observations as a member of many boards and commissions, I can attest that failure too often in a worthwhile, ethically justified project was the result of incompetence. Many times needed reforms were delayed or lost altogether because of the absence of that essential quality of competence.

But competence must be balanced by values, whether intellectual or moral, and I am afraid that I have to report that values are often lost in the rush of day-to-day events and routine. Values are the constants of our existence; those qualities that over time and with much testing we have learned to cherish. Values are like navigational aids, or fixed points of reference, that keep our human journey from aimless wandering, or worse, frantic mindless rushing from one crisis to another. The debate about values give us our best hope for mastering and transcending the change and turmoil of our times. We would all admit in the quiet of our consciences that justice is better than injustice, love better than hate, integrity better than dishonesty, compassion better than insensitivity, beauty better than ugliness, hope better than despair, faith better than infidelity, order better than chaos, peace better than war, life better than death, knowledge better than ignorance, and so on and on and on. The authors have given us a set of values growing out of their study of Scripture, and I commend their efforts to you.

This volume, with its images, values, and exercises, challenges its readers to create a new kind of world, characterized by quite different social, economic, and political arrangements. The emphasis will be on the interdependence rather than the independence of nation states. Readers will be challenged to be world citizens as they seek solutions to problems of human rights, ecumenism, food, fuel, shelter, health care, urbanization, pollution, crime, terrorism, development, and education. None of these problems has a purely national solution. No longer can geographic prejudice decree that being born in the Northern Hemisphere promises an infinitely more human and humane existence than being born in the southern half of the earth. No longer can the affluent and powerful view the world as if everything important runs on a line between New York, London, Paris, Moscow, and Tokyo. Better than two-thirds of humanity lives far south of that line, and it is their earth, too. Readers will become increasingly conscious of the possibility of creating a better world than the one they are inheriting, one with liberty and justice for all, not just Americans; with liberty, equality, and fraternity for all, not just Frenchmen. Indeed, all of us are significant in the eyes of the Father.

Introduction

What does the Christian tradition have to say to a person intent on being a success in today's business world? Is it possible to be a Christian and a competent business leader at the same time? The authors claim that it is, and that a career in business can be a challenging and exciting vocation for persons of talent and integrity. The book can be used profitably by undergraduate and graduate students, as well as informed lay persons interested in Christianity and the business world. Because of its flexible format, adult education discussion groups and college classes, as well as individual readers, may find the volume useful.

The Chairman of the Securities and Exchange Commission, Harold Williams, made a statement in 1977 that sums up the mood of our times: "The public is convinced that big business is ripping everybody off to get what it wants for itself. The public believes the charges leveled at corporations and does not trust those who speak for corporations."[1] This lack of trust is the subject of one of the chapters of the book, which deals with the giant, multinational Gulf & Western Industries, Inc. In 1975, and for two years after, a stockholder resolution was prepared for the annual meeting of Gulf & Western criticizing the corporation for not paying sugar workers in the Dominican Republic a decent wage. The resolution was introduced in 1975 and 1976 by the National Council of Churches, the Jesuits' Maryland Province, and the Dominican Sisters of Adrian, Michigan, and asked for a full disclosure of Gulf & Western activities in the Dominican Republic. Although the corporation had provided stockholders some information on its operations in the Dominican Republic, the proposal clearly implied that stockholders didn't believe they were getting the full truth.

Probes made by the Securities and Exchange Commission in recent years have uncovered numerous violations of United States income tax laws and other government regulations by scores of companies. Major corporations such as General Tire and Rubber Company and Westinghouse Electric have admitted making payoffs to officials and customers in foreign countries. In the famous Gulf Oil Corporation case of 1976, the board of directors ousted its chairman and three other top executives for making illegal political contributions. That same year the president of Lockheed Aircraft Corporation resigned after admitting that he paid $12 million in bribes to Japanese political leaders and businessmen to secure airplane sales.

There is much written these days about the crisis of the business profession; like most other professionals, business people are increasingly losing the confidence of the public. The causes of this loss of confidence generally fall into two categories:

1. numerous violations of legal codes that have come to the attention of the public, such as price fixing, tax law violations, and bribery.

2. breaches of the professional code of ethics for business persons, such as deceptive advertising, selling company secrets, and dishonesty in expense accounts.

A professional code of ethics sets high standards for a whole range of issues. Violations of this code are not necessarily against the law, but they do rupture the *trust* between consumer and supplier, and the *honor* among business persons themselves. The public seems to feel that business has abandoned the ethics serving this trust and honor in favor of a "bottom line" ethic single-mindedly focused on the profit figure in the annual report.

The authors have not set out to propose new federal legislation for business or to develop a more comprehensive professional code of ethics. Before formulating rules, there is a need to develop a consensus on just what values ought to be promoted and protected. Therefore, drawing from the Bible and the best of the Christian traditions, the book examines the basic vision of the Christian business person and how that vision and its values might inform a life in the complex world of business.

The objective of this text, then, is to provide an opportunity for Christian persons to become more aware of the implied effect of Christian convictions on their speech and actions in the business world. For this reason, the book will stress some central values and principles explicitly advocated in the Bible and the Christian community. The focus of the volume is not "Why be religious?" although in passing there are some answers suggested for that question. Rather the operative assumption is that readers have an interest in Christianity, which has been fostered by a life in, or some contact with, the Christian community. There is no intent to say that people who are not Christian cannot be ethical. Some of the most morally sensitive persons today are secular humanists; a Christian ethic and a more broadly based humane ethic have much in common. Non-Christians may adhere to many of the same values and principles as Christians do, only for rational ethical reasons rather than religious reasons. Most of the positions taken in this book for religious reasons could also be justified by a secular humanist for rational ethical reasons. This is a fruitful area for further discussion in a future book. The point of this book is that if one calls oneself a Christian, then Christian images and concepts should play a role in viewing the world and analyzing situations. Unfortunately, Christians often become all too comfortable with the established system, and see their role as simply solving problems within that system. This posture completely neglects the task of challenging institutions and life-styles in light of the biblical way of life. The latter task is highlighted here.

The book uses cases and it focuses on a person's "story" and the character traits that endure over time, rather than a person's decisions, to display what it means to be a Christian in the business world. Christian beliefs give shape to a person's lifetime story. The assumption is that the Bible not only mediates the Christian experience of God, but that it also reveals certain values and principles for a Christian way of life. The business community, too, has a set of convictions and shared understandings that go into shaping life stories. These convictions are often in serious conflict with those of the Judeo-Christian Scriptures. A key issue to consider is whether a Christian story and a business story are mutually exclusive, compatible, or synonymous. The skills to be developed concern how to relate these two stories, and how to live a life that integrates key images from both these stories, under "master images" from the Judeo-Christian Scriptures.

Part I of the book includes three chapters and prepares the reader to see the magnitude of the challenge of living with a Christian vision. The text opens with a consideration of the hierarchy of values and various world views that are prevalent in our time. Unfortunately many people do not take sufficient time to consider the values embodied and revealed in the actions of their lives. Nor do they think much about where they are going with their lives, what story they are writing with words and deeds over a lifetime. Although they may participate in church services and call themselves Christian, many persons fail to reflect on the claims of the Christian tradition on their business and public life. One of the goals of the first chapter is to remind us of the many competing world views and value systems that may influence us much more than we are aware. It is designed to prepare the way for the deliberate and thoughtful integration of Christian convictions into the life of the business world.

The second chapter deals with what it means to live the Christian story, and how principles and values for the Christian way of life can be gleaned from the Bible. Seven contemporary values are examined critically in the light of values advocated in the Scriptures. These values are discussed in relation to some Biblical stories and images. Living as a Christian is seen to be living with a central biblical image (Servant of the Lord, Heir to the Kingdom of God, Pilgrim People of God, for example) as a controlling force in one's life. Although the dominant images controlling a life story may change as one advances through the various stages of life, a Christian will continue to draw on the Bible for these master images.

Chapter 3 focuses on how images guide life stories, and, in particular, how a business person might lead his or her life with a master image from the Bible. The chapter provides some examples of how images play a central role in determining how one evaluates a situation and plans a strategy for action. The question of the relation between biblical images and the doctrines of the Christian faith is also considered.

Part II of the book is devoted to "exercises" designed to develop skills required for the Judeo-Christian business person. Living in two convictional communities (business and Judeo-Christian) involves gaining some complex skills. Skills are best learned by doing. It is hoped that these exercises—consideration and discussion of ten cases that focus on important issues—will foster growth in a business person. The first nine of these cases are followed by a section called "Reflections on the Story." These reflections include a discussion of some key issues raised in the situation portrayed, an analysis of the case, an application of biblical images to the case and an annotated bibliography. The final chapter, and in many ways the most important exercise of the book, is called "Writing Your Own Story."

The first case tells the story of Harold Geneen, the top executive of International Telephone & Telegraph Corporation from 1959 to 1977. The case focuses on the style and manner of his leadership and offers an opportunity to reflect on how organizations can foster the growth of some character traits and capacities while inhibiting others. The reader might begin to ask, "What sort of person do I want to become, and what organizations will assist me in developing certain traits and capacities?"

"Walnut Avenue Church," the second case, presents an opportunity to examine the role of Christian images and concepts in all dimensions of life, personal as well as social. The case is designed to develop skill in "discernment," seeing the import of Christian convictions for action. Likewise the case can point to the indispensable role of participation in the liturgical and religious life of the community in order to acquire this skill.

The third case, "Agenbite of Inwit," is titled after a theme made popular in James Joyce's *Ulysses* and refers to "the again-biting of conscience" experienced by a middle-aged businessman. James P. Landis tells us that he is troubled about padding his expense account, and the reader is asked to reflect on the Landis story and come to some constructive resolutions. Each reader will also have an occasion to reflect on how he or she will fare with similar problems.

The fourth case, "Caribbean Corporate Strategy," deals with corporate social responsibility and affords the reader an opportunity to see the various points of view on the question. Pastor Dave Hopkins asks three corporate leaders for some assistance on a project in Jamaica. By deciding how the case might be resolved, the reader may begin to organize his or her hierarchy of values and set a thrust and direction for a personal story.

"Give Us This Day Our Daily Bread" focuses on the world hunger problem and how the value of distributive justice might take shape in the political arena. The lingering question for the reader is, "What do I do about the dilemma of limited resources in a growing world?"

"The Eli Black Story" is an account of a brilliant economic genius who was also a deeply spiritual person. As president of the conglomerate, United Brands, Eli Black was known both as a devout and compassionate member of the Jewish faith and as a corporate leader. His tragic death posed a difficult question for a writer in the *Wall Street Journal,* as well as for a young woman doing a research project, and the reader is asked to consider it: "Can a sensitive person, a person with high moral standards, survive in an uncompromising financial world?" Answering this question, a reader may begin to reflect explicitly about how he or she "puts it all together" in such a world.

"Bankers Trust" deals with a relatively new concern in American life, the humanization of work. Christians celebrate the dignity of the human person, and the case examines what that value might mean for the organization of work in the latter part of the twentieth century.

"The National Council of Churches vs. Gulf and Western" concerns a huge, multinational corporation. The case highlights at least two very important issues: (1) the secondary effects of economic decisions on the political and social life of a nation; and (2) the responsibility of stockholders for the policies of management.

The ninth case tells of a small businessman who is faced with the difficult decision of whether or not to send a letter to the local newspaper protesting what he takes to be racist housing policies in his suburban community. "The Bill Clark Story" is concerned with "the exit phenomenon," that is, at what point does one draw the line and refuse to compromise personal values for career advancement. The case portrays a situation that may be similar to ones many readers will encounter in their professional lives, and it can foster growth in the analysis of the many factors involved in deciding to leave a company or jeopardize a business for ethical reasons.

The last case is written about the president of Caron International Yarns and Leisure Products. "The John Caron Story" tells of a top business executive who is clearly a success in the business world and has consciously appropriated some central images from the Bible as a guide for his life. The story is offered as an example of one way of integrating the two worlds of business and Christianity and of how Judeo-Christian business persons might shape their lives. There is no "Reflections" section for this case, for the reader is asked to analyze it critically in the light of the presentation in the first three chapters. This case is placed last in order to help prepare readers for the final exercise of the book.

The last chapter is titled "Writing Your Own Story." This final chapter brings together the principles of the book to prepare the reader to write an imaginary projection of his or her own story as it might unfold in the next twenty to thirty years, or is now unfolding. Writing a personal story not only helps reveal the many little self-deceptions that we erect to avoid the painful truth, but also enables us to embrace our values and make them our own in a fuller way. The very process of putting our values into words can help make them a genuine part of our life patterns.

Notes

1   Quoted in "Honesty, Ethics: Let's Do What's Overdue," *The Wall Street Journal,* November 10, 1977, p. 19.

Part I
Life as a Story

"We all have a part to play in life, Meredith, and your part is being a yes man. There are lousier parts."

Is it possible to be a success in the business world and still remain a Christian? That question may seem inappropriate, if not downright insulting, to a significant number of business people who profess the Christian faith. Yet if Watergate or the recent scandals in corporate business have taught us anything, it is that decent people, just "doing their jobs," can find themselves doing things that otherwise they might not have even considered, had their "roles" not seemed to demand it. And so to bolster a faltering presidential administration or to keep a firm safely in the black, a whole host of executives did "what had to be done"—they played their roles well. Although they may have led exemplary Christian lives at home or in their church communities, when they came to their business offices, they often seemed to check their Christian values at the door.

Where does Christianity fit into all of this? How do the simple stories of the Bible apply to the complex problems of contemporary economic life? One of the obvious difficulties is that most dilemmas in business ethics are never directly addressed in the Scriptures. If we go to the Bible for direct assistance with a problem in decision-making, if we are looking for a couple of verses from Scripture to clarify a situation, we most likely will look in vain. For the Bible has few, if any, passages explicitly directed to the specific issues of today's business world.

Yet this does not mean that the Bible has little to say to the Christian in the business world. While the Bible may not often directly shape business decisions, it can and does do something much more significant, it shapes business decision makers. The Bible in the Christian community forms the values, attitudes, and intentions and shapes the vision of a person; it thus provides a stance for business people that colors their perspective and influences their decisions and actions.

The whole thrust of a life, the "story" a person is writing with the words and deeds of his or her life, can take its orientation from the Bible. Part I of the book is designed to explore this thesis.

Chapter One
A Christian Perspective

A popular type of Christianity holds that faith in Jesus Christ is primarily a private affair. One belongs to a church and prays with a community of believers, perhaps even participates in church social events and gives money in the collection for the poor. The Gospel message is taken to be a call for a change of heart, for a new trust and love, yet for many this conversion plays itself out solely in churchly activities and family life.

Although the major portion of each week for many Christians is spent in the business world, this world may be insulated from the values of the Gospel. The business world has its own criteria for what constitutes good and bad performance. Good performance in the business world is taken by some to be any "just and fair" behavior that enhances company goals. Company goals are frequently meant to satisfy customers while covering costs and making a profit; the rules of business are geared towards accomplishing this task as efficiently as possible.[1] Although business may get involved in protecting some values of society and assuming some social responsibility, this involvement is generally accepted only to the extent that it furthers the primary objective of the enterprise.[2] It is often assumed that the values of the Gospel have little application to the world of business. "There is no need to mix the oil of religion with the water of business."

It is often taken for granted that Christian faith is not really meant to change the world, and certainly not the business world. This may result from a sober judgment that, after all, business is business, and its rules and ethos must hold sway in its domain if an enterprise is to survive. The business world is a highly complex phenomenon, and some very competent people suggest that it is not at all clear that the simple stories of the Bible are relevant to twentieth century economic life. The authors reject that suggestion and accept the burden of demonstrating the opposite.

In order to prepare the way for a thoughtful and intelligent integration of Christian values into the business world, it is first necessary to take a fresh look at some central motifs of the Bible. The purpose of this chapter, then, is to examine one understanding of what it means to be a Christian, and to discover how the belief and the actions of Christians are intimately related.

HOW WE USE THE BIBLE

Christians believe that the Bible is Scripture, that is, it is more than good literature or interesting history. The authors take the Bible to be the revelation of the living God and his intentions for humankind. As such, it ought to have a decisive influence in the shaping of personal and community life.[3] In this perspective, the Bible presents models of the sort of person that one ought to become, and it provides visions of the way of life that should prevail in the Christian community, the Church. Through liturgy, preaching, and teaching, the Bible forms the identity of the Christian and the Church.

The character and conduct of a Christian ought to display the dispositions, intentions, and general orientation provided by the biblical witness. While no one biblical story and set of verses is a normative source for these values, there are dominant chords and recurring themes found throughout Scripture that are decisive for Christians.

The primary influence of the Bible is in shaping the vision of Christians, in forming the enduring characteristics of the person, such as overarching vision, dispositions, and intentions.[4] The Bible gives a person a perspective on life—a place to stand—and, when consistent, all the words and deeds of a life flow from this standpoint. When we see the Bible as forming the person in this fashion, it becomes clear that one comes to the decision-making process with certain presuppositions. There is always a vision and set of intentions that are carried through the many choices and actions in the various times and places of decision.

Being imbued with the biblical perspective means that in decision-making certain choices are ruled out from the start as inconsistent with biblical values, while others are given added weight in that they advance the biblical vision. While emphasizing the role of the Bible as primarily a shaper of the decision maker, we do not intend to overlook the assistance that Scripture might provide directly in decision-making.

It may be helpful to review the decision-making process and indicate some points of possible biblical influence. The following is one of the various ways to outline the process:[5]

1. Investigate the case and discern the relevant data.

2. Interpret the data, that is, determine and clarify the *meaning* of the facts. Often further reading is helpful here.

3. Evaluate the data, that is, determine what is valued in the situation, and the consequences of the various possible actions.

4. Consider the various alternatives and decide what to do.

The Bible could function indirectly in steps 1 and 2 because, by shaping the decision maker's vision, it has a decisive influence on what data are seen as significant and what factors appear to be critical and are to be taken into account. For example, in any personnel problem, the dignity of the human being would loom large for a Christian decision maker, because he or she has been formed in the Christian community to regard and promote this value. On the other hand, *blind* loyalty to the boss would have little positive effect, because it would not be perceived to be a desirable trait in the light of the values and vision of the Bible.

The Bible could function directly in step 3, for here there is a need for explicit values or standards in order to have a basis on which to evaluate the situation and the alternatives. There are instances where the Bible can directly provide a value. A number of them can provide both a guide for action (step 3), and a desirable character for the person (steps 1 and 2). In Chapter 2 we develop seven such values from the Scriptures to illustrate how the Bible provides guides for the Judeo-Christian way of life. The values have reference to:

1. how we use power over individuals;

2. how we understand our use of nature and natural resources;

3. how we understand wealth and property;

4. how we hope to achieve happiness;

5. how we understand justice;

6. how we respond to our drive to gratify material wants;

7. how we understand time.

These seven values do not necessarily capture *the* Christian character, or exhaust all the principles of the Christian way of life, but they help illustrate what it means to follow the Christian way of life. Accepting these norms means that there are boundaries within which decision-making can occur. Some other norms will therefore be automatically disqualified as inappropriate, outside the Christian framework.

Often biblical materials that do not directly address the business problem at hand can be most helpful in decision-making because they serve as a stimulus to the imagination to widen the vision and broaden the context for decision. For example, the story of Jesus washing the feet of the disciples gives us a new angle of vision on power, that is, power as service. This new perspective could lead to fresh insights on a personnel problem or policy, for instance, within the business firm.

THE CHRISTIAN LIFE:
NOT EARNING FAVOR BUT PRAISING GOD

One of the greatest pitfalls in describing what it means to be and live as a Christian may be the assumption that the Gospel is a rule book of correct behavior, and that following the rules will assure one a good place in God's eyes. The Gospel tells us that salvation is a gift given us by a loving God; it proclaims the boundless love of God and spurs us on to imitate that love in our own unique way. God's intentions for humankind are sketched in the Bible and, according to the Bible, the most acceptable motive for following these intentions in our life is the love that flows from our thankfulness.[6] We can never earn God's favor; salvation is always beyond our reach and can only come as a gift. This was a difficult lesson for the disciples of Jesus, and it is no easier for people today.

We can learn the way of life that Jesus taught by doing just what the first followers did: taking Jesus' teaching to heart, and joining the community that proclaims his name (the Church). For most of us, a key skill may be to rediscover what have become all too familiar and impotent, the values and principles taught by the Bible stories. Consider the parable of the Prodigal Son.

He also said, 'A man had two sons. The younger said to his father, "Father, let me have the share of the estate that would come to me". So the father divided the property between them. A few days later, the younger son got together everything he had and left for a distant country where he squandered his money on a life of debauchery.

'When he had spent it all, that country experienced a severe famine, and now he began to feel the pinch, so he hired himself out to one of the local inhabitants who put him on his farm to feed the pigs. And he would willingly have filled his belly with the husks the pigs were eating but no one offered him anything. Then he came to his senses and said, "How many of my father's paid servants have more food than they want, and here am I dying of hunger! I will leave this place and go to my father and say: Father, I have sinned against heaven and against you; I no longer deserve to be called your son; treat me as one of your paid servants." So he left the place and went back to his father.

'While he was still a long way off, his father saw him and was moved with pity. He ran to the boy, clasped him in his arms and kissed him tenderly. Then his son said, "Father, I have sinned against heaven and against you. I no longer deserve to be called your son." But the father said to his servants, "Quick! Bring out the best robe and put it on him; put a ring on his finger and sandals on his feet. Bring the calf we have been fattening, and kill it; we are going to have a feast, a celebration, because this son of mine was dead and has come back to life; he was lost and is found." And they began to celebrate.

'Now the elder son was out in the fields and on his way back, as he drew near the house, he could hear music and dancing. Calling one of the servants he asked what it was all about. "Your brother has come" replied the servant "and your father has killed the calf we had fattened because he has got him back safe and sound." He was angry then and refused to go in, and his father came out to plead with him; but he answered his father, "Look, all these years I have slaved for you and never once disobeyed your orders, yet you never offered me so much as a kid for me to celebrate with my friends. But, for this son of yours, when he comes back after swallowing up your property—he and his women—you kill the calf we had been fattening."

'The father said, "My son, you are with me always and all I have is yours. But it was only right we should celebrate and rejoice, because your brother here was dead and has come to life; he was lost and is found" '(Luke 15:11-32).

One important lesson that we might learn from the parable is that the Father is merciful, forgiving, and compassionate to a degree beyond our wildest imaginings, and that we ought to try to imitate that sort of love in our lives.[7] Telling this parable Jesus created the possibility of seeing the world in a whole new way. The very point of the parable was to talk about the familiar secular world in an unfamiliar way, and thus reveal God the Father. Jesus tried to crack the logic of the everyday world and offer a new logic with which to lead one's life. The parable of the prodigal son tells of a rascal who squandered his inheritance and then decided to return home. One would naturally expect the father to be angry and perhaps even insist on some form of retribution. And yet, perhaps to our dismay, the son is the honored guest at a great feast prepared by the father.

Through the story Jesus suggests to his disciples what his Father is like, and how they might model their lives after God the Father. We might imagine Jesus asking the disciples after telling the parable: "And what story do you live? Are you like the father who lavished his love on the fallen heir, or are you part of another story with a different logic?" Jesus' use of the image of the Forgiving Father teaches us to allow the Father's love to overflow into our lives, to have a new set of priorities and values. The Scriptures may provide us with a set of images that give us a new vision of our life and circumstances. We "see" with new eyes after being drawn into the parable of the Prodigal Son.[8]

The Bible may have a decisive influence on a Christian in that it shapes the sort of person he or she is becoming, that is, it has a hand in forming the overall vision of life, the attitudes or dispositions, the convictions, and the intentions of a person. In this light some of the lessons of the parable of the Prodigal Son might be outlined as follows:

Vision of Life: All humankind is a family and each individual is to be considered as a unique person with his or her distinct contribution. The challenge is to love and care for each other.

Attitudes: The above vision of life disposes us to extend forgiveness to those who have failed. Attitudes of compassion and concern for the downtrodden are engendered.

Convictions: We are confirmed in our fundamental belief that just as our Heavenly Father cares for us, so we must care for each other.

Intentions: We can deliberately choose not to make friends simply for "good contacts," people who will assist in our own personal advancement, but to be present to those who need us and ever alert and ready to extend a hand.

These elements of character formation are not appropriated with one reading of the parable; Christians grow in this way of life by living in the Christian community and being nurtured by the Bible in liturgy, preaching, and teaching.

One strength of the parable is that it employs the drama of human conflict to symbolize man's relationship to God. Jesus told the story of a father and his wayward son to dramatize and bring home the way God relates to humankind. Some fiction writers have a similar gift of revealing the truth about human life through stories. Flannery O'Connor was an articulate believer known for her Christian convictions expressed through literature. Some of her work is clearly marked by a literary form similar to the New Testament parable. She tells one story about a young man named Ruller who is playing in the woods and spies a wild turkey.[9] He gives chase with all his might, running through thicket and dense forest in quest of the turkey. Through all of this strenuous and sometimes stoic perseverance he is kept going by the thought of the lavish praise he will have earned from his parents. "He guessed they'd be knocked out when they saw him; he guessed they'd talk about it . . ."[10] He almost had the turkey once, but it got away. He was deeply disappointed and set out for home. Then, unexpectedly, while on his way home he stumbled on the turkey again. O'Connor tells us: "The picture of himself walking in the room with it slung over his shoulder came back to him. Look at Ruller with that turkey! Lord, look at Ruller! . . . Ruller gets our turkeys for us. Ruller got it in the woods, chased it dead. Yes, he's a very unusual child."[11]

The turkey was finally Ruller's; it lay dead on the path before his eyes, shot by a hunter's bullet. Ruller was jubilant, and he could not wait to get home and show his prize. He knew now that God was showing him favor, and he slung the bird over his shoulder and proudly marched through town on his way home. All the way he accepted the accolades of the townsfolk who admired his feat. He was indeed proud, and he resolved to repay God for his good fortune—he would give his only dime to a poor beggar.

Just when it seemed that he had all but delivered the big bird to his parents, unexpected trouble developed. Some "country boys" came by, grabbed his prize, and left him standing there empty-handed. O'Connor leaves us feeling that maybe the loss was not so bad after all. Life is like that, but life is still rich and full. Ruller had lost his earned reward. Maybe rewards are not earned, and losses can be turned to gain. Ruller was trying to live out a "false story," a story that had no place for God's generous and *mysterious* love.

The term "story" here means one's sense of reality, encompassing vision of life, dispositions, convictions, and intentions discussed above. "Story" is a very helpful word to describe the way we spontaneously structure our experiences (the images that comprise our vision, dispositions, convictions, etc.), and our understanding of what life is all about (our goals and intentions). In this sense, we are all living some "story." The "story" concept is helpful in focusing on the key issues at stake in the basic question of this book: "Is it possible to be a Christian in the business world?" Further discussion of this concept will prepare us for the chapters that follow.

STORY: A PATTERN OF MEANING

"Mother, tell me a story." All of us can remember hearing or even saying those words any number of times. At root we are all searching for a way to put order and meaning in our lives, for a pattern that helps us make sense of our experience. A child knows this, even if only dimly, and a child's (or adult's) love for a good story may be an expression of humankind's need to put form and focus into life. To have a "story" that you are living out means that you have some sense of what your life is all about. It has a beginning, a middle, and an anticipated ending.

The form and focus of our lives is provided by putting together or appropriating a number of stories. Some of the stories that provide a pattern and unite our experience we freely choose—husband, wife, parent, business person, active Christian. Other stories we have come to terms with and are not our own doing—Irish Catholic, German Lutheran, United States citizen, naturally talented female. The challenge is to weave our stories together in a way that is both fulfilling and true.

Our belief is that there is one story that sets the backdrop for all the others, provides the context and the coherence for all of the events of a life. We are suggesting that the Bible, God's revelation to us, provides the master story, the basic story that is to shape and limit the way all the other stories are to be appropriated into our lives. We will say more about this assertion later; for now, we ask you to follow us on our journey.

The theme of this book is business and its focus is on two stories: How to put together the Christian story and the business story. The focus in this first chapter is on our understanding of the Christian story. The New Testament declares that Jesus, in effect, holds the key that helps us discover who we are and who we ought to be. He provides the story that humankind was meant to live. Everyone puts his or her life together by picking and choosing from the stories available to the times, but there is one story that forms the backdrop or context for each life. Who are we, what have we done, what can we do now, and what can we hope for? What is power? Who has it and who does not? What is wrong? The answers to all of these questions are found in various stories competing for our attention in the twentieth century. Stories, then, are not a set of rules or a code of laws but the context that provides meaning to the rules; they are the unexamined presuppositions underlying a code or guidelines. Many of us want to be a "certain sort of person" and a story provides a model to follow.

A story provides shape for our lives; it gives us a way to pull together all the events of our lives, events not only in the past but also in the present and the future. The form and focus provided by the story we are living enables us to give an account of who we are. To say that "I am a Christian business person" means that I take as my own the logic and patterns of both a Christian story and a business story. Other people will only understand why I do what I do and why I say what I say if they can fathom what story I am living out. My story gives plausibility to my life.[12] In order to feel our way into a story of the Christian business person, it is important to focus on one perspective of what it means to be a Christian.

STORIES: SOURCE OF VALUES AND PRINCIPLES

If you ask a Christian, "What are the principles of the Christian life?" he or she may have a little difficulty in providing a summary list. "Love your neighbor, forgive your enemies, be faithful to your vocation as a child of God, and always be trusting of the mercy and love of God," might be a good response. Yet when we teach children how to be Christian, usually without thinking much about it, it seems very important to read the Bible stories. It is not enough just to pass on the principles or values. We do not just tell children to love one another or respect the value of community. These principles are themselves an abstraction from the Bible stories, a kind of "skeleton" of the stories. Just as a human skeleton could never convey the beauty of a complete person, so a principle could never capture the complexity of human action.

The actions of a Christian do not really flow from *principles*; rather they flow from *stories*, and in particular the story of Jesus as portrayed in the New Testament. The "story" concept helps us see that our principles ("Love your neighbor") and values (community, honesty) acquire a definite sense from their context. For this reason the Christian values revealed in the Bible are usually set in the context of a story or event that Jesus used to teach his disciples. This text will recount some of those Bible stories and also provide some new stories for our time.

The early Christian community continued Jesus' practice of using stories to help pass on the faith. For example, consider how Paul shares with the Philippians some basic values that came to be considered Christian. Paul, first of all, judges that the important values to be stressed for the Philippians are community, harmony, humility, and concern for others. He provides a more precise meaning for these values by quoting an early liturgical hymn that tells the story of Christ's life.

His state was divine,
yet he did not cling
to his equality with God
but emptied himself
to assume the condition of a slave,
and became as men are;
and being as all men are,
he was humbler yet,
even to accepting death,
death on a cross.
But God raised him high
and gave him the name
which is above all other names
so that *all beings*
in the heavens, on earth and in the underworld,
should bend the knee at the name of Jesus
and that every tongue should acclaim
Jesus Christ as Lord,
to the glory of God the Father (Phil 2: 6-11).

This story of Jesus tells of God's boundless concern for us, ("accepting death, death on a cross"), and of a humility almost beyond belief, (he "emptied himself to assume the condition of a slave"). Some scholars have suggested that Christ is offered by Paul as the model to follow in implementing the values; he is the "sort of person" one ought to become. If Paul had just said, "Be humble," or "Be generous and concerned," the Philippians would have had little idea of the way of life that they were being called to live. As it turns out, this story of Jesus tells us more about actions and values than we could ever learn from a principle; the story provides a model to follow in fleshing out and giving vitality to the principles. Paul makes this point in the same letter to the Philippians when he enumerates some of the principles of the Christian life. He lists the principles and then gives them a model.

If our life in Christ means anything to you, if love can persuade at all, or the Spirit that we have in common, or any tenderness and sympathy, then be united in your convictions and united in your love, with a common purpose and a common mind. That is the one thing which would make me completely happy. There must be no competition among you, no conceit; but everybody is to be self-effacing. Always consider the other person to be better than yourself, so that nobody thinks of his own interests first but everybody thinks of other people's interests instead. In your minds you must be the same as Christ Jesus . . . (Phil. 2:1-5).

Although principles can never convey the fullness of the quality of a life, they can clarify and bring precision to a story. If we read all the accounts of Jesus in the Gospel and try to analyze the stories for a fundamental principle, we might come up with a summary statement something like: "Life comes through death," or "By renouncing ourselves, we find ourselves." That might be our principle. Yet the story cannot be reduced to a principle, for it says more. Indeed a pattern of life emerges from this story; from a state of dignity, to a giving of self in service of others, to a final state of life in its fullest. Following this pattern is part of what it means to follow Christ.

STORY → VALUE → PRINCIPLES → RULE

Appropriating the Christian story with its set of images leads one to experience life, perceive events, imagine possibilities, and understand and act in the world in a whole new way. Key images from scripture, such as Servant of the Lord, Heir to the Kingdom of God, etc., evoke the Christian story and its sense of reality in our lives and therefore help illumine life and its circumstances. If one sees oneself as a Pilgrim of the People of God, or as an Heir to the Kingdom of God, then one envisions life as a journey, and the way entails all that needs to be done to build up the human community. This general stance toward life in the world is itself part of the contours of the Christian story.

By reading the Bible and by living in a Christian community, a person comes to see that there are certain states of the person and the community that are in fact desirable. This is what is meant by the term "value."[13] A fundamental Christian value is realizing a genuine community that acknowledges and responds to the love of God, a place where people can live and work together in mutual fulfillment. The Bible helps us feel our way into a standpoint where we can begin to grasp what "genuine fulfillment" and "community" might mean—a communion of love in Christ. The Bible widens our perspective and deepens our understanding. To attain this basic value there are a whole host of other values that have to be preserved, such as trust, friendship, a just social order, openness, honesty, and health, as well as the seven values considered in Chapter 2.

Rules and principles[14] governing human life arise when people try to realize certain values. The function of rules and principles is to promote or protect a value. For example, the value of a fulfilling community is promoted by the principle, "Love your neighbor." Jesus' life helps us see what it means to be a person and what genuine fulfillment might be like. Reading the New Testament and living in the Christian community help us feel our way into the standpoint of the persons we were created to be, persons with values reflected in the Gospel. Jesus provides not only the power and strength for these possibilities, but also the model for all humankind to follow in their return to the Father by their lives of loving service.

Once we understand that the Gospel and the Judeo-Christian tradition provide certain values, that is, states of the person or the community that are in fact the intentions of God for humankind, the challenge then moves to the task of formulating principles and rules to protect these values. In the area of business this proves to be an extremely demanding task that ultimately depends on the creativity and ingenuity of the Christian business person. There are no simple rules that will ensure that the values reflected in the Bible will be maintained in the business world. Intelligent business people must understand values shaped by the Gospels and discover ways to introduce them into the highly complex business world.

Reinhold Niebuhr referred to the challenge of appropriating the unmeasured love of Christ into the human community as the "impossible possibility." By this term Niebuhr points out the ever-present need to overcome the sinful tendency to take advantage of each other, and the reality that often a situation will only allow for a *relatively* good solution. In this world, institutional structures will not be modeled so much on the unmeasured love of Christ, as on the justice that flows from this love, and that takes into account the realities of the situation. For example, persons in business management positions come to know that every delinquent worker could not possibly be treated like the Prodigal Son. The biblical stories are not unalterable models for institutional structures. The goal is to work toward realizing the values reflected in these stories.[15]

RELATION BETWEEN SECULAR HUMAN VALUES AND BIBLE VALUES

Although, as stated above, basic values for a Christian are taken to be those affirmed in the Bible, this is not to say that many of these same values cannot be rationally inferred from any experience of people struggling to lead a human life in community. In fact, it is often the case that noble human values emerge in communities with no explicit religious profession. It may be helpful here to clarify the relation between secular human values and the principles and values known from the Bible.[16]

Jesus Christ is taken by Christians to be *the* experience of the presence and power of God. This is not to say that God's presence and power cannot be experienced in any other way, for Christians also affirm that God's will is revealed in his work, in the whole creation. The beauty of nature, the human being, and the fruit of human intelligence are all revelations of the Father. Yet Jesus gives us the most luminous revelation of God; with Jesus we are confronted with the mystery of God *par excellence,* more than we can ever grasp. The accounts of the New Testament can be understood as various writers' attempts to record the community's experience of the reality of God's power and presence in Jesus.

The early Christians seemed to allow their experience to be governed by the great images provided by Jesus and nurtured in the community, images such as Kingdom of God, Son of Man, the Cross, etc. The writers of Scripture, by recording this experience, enable Christian communities of the future to apply these same archetypical images to their own lives and situations.

Many in the Christian community hold that God's will is found in creation, although not with the compelling clarity that is present in the life and work of Jesus. God is understood as the designer of a world that itself exhibits his intentions. Thus whatever people find necessary using their God-given reasoning powers, and whatever they

find wholesome and pleasing through the exercise of their free will
are indeed the intentions of God implanted in creation. The values
and rules emerging in any human community, and judged humane in
the light of the Gospel, are God's will.[17] This follows from the assumption that God reveals himself in his work. Just as his work tells
us something about the artist, so creation tells us something of God.
The assumption, many Christians believe, comes into the Christian
community from the story of creation recorded in Genesis.

In the beginning God created the heavens and the earth. Now the earth
was a formless void, there was darkness over the deep, and God's spirit hov-
ered over the water.

God said, 'Let there be light', and there was light. God saw that light was
good, and God divided light from darkness. God called light 'day', and darkness he called 'night'. Evening came and morning came: the first day
(Genesis 1:1-5).

God said, 'Let us make man in our own image, in the likeness of ourselves,
and let them be masters of the fish of the sea, the birds of heaven, the cattle, all
the wild beasts and all the reptiles that crawl upon the earth'.

God created man in the image of himself, in the image of God he created
him, male and female he created them. God blessed them, saying to them, 'Be
fruitful, multiply, fill the earth and conquer it. Be masters of the fish of the
sea, the birds of heaven, and all living animals on the earth.' God said, 'See, I
give you all the seed-bearing plants that are upon the whole earth, and all the
trees with seed-bearing fruit; this shall be your food. To all wild beasts, all
birds of heaven and all living reptiles on the earth I give all the foliage of plants
for food.' And so it was. God saw all he had made, and indeed it was very
good. Evening came and morning came: the sixth day (Genesis 1:26-31).

In interpreting this story it is helpful to know that many scholars
affirm that the Israelites wrote it down after they had already come to
believe that God had done great things for them as a people. Unlike
most of their neighbors, the Israelites believed that God had absolute
power and that he created all things. Some other cultural epics of the
time portrayed creation as the result of a struggle between warring
gods. Hence no one god ever had absolute power. But the Israelites
believed that God had led them out of slavery in Egypt into the promised land, and was still guiding them. (The Book of Exodus of the

Bible tells this fascinating story.) Therefore they wrote this creation story in Genesis to affirm their faith that this same God was also the God of all nature and history.

The text tells us that a person is made in God's image. We take this to mean that the person is God's representative on earth and, as such, is charged with responsibility for all creation. The story also portrays the harmony that God intended among created things and people. Later stories go on to show how people thwarted God's intentions of peace and harmony—apparently by sin, a self-assertion that denied the power of the creator. This promised harmony is now awaited with the second coming of Christ, and it is anticipated by the actions of all who are Christians. The Christian is one who is aware of sin and evil but even more aware of the redemptive and healing quality of God's love. It is possible to live the values of Scripture, although it is not easy.

In the face of all kinds of adversity, the Christian may live in the world confident that God is at work in the universe and that it will be fully redeemed in God's good time. Meanwhile, Christians celebrate God's love by living their lives as God intended. Creation is not understood as having been completely finished by God; human beings are placed on the earth and commissioned to fashion the world into a more humane and Christian place. From the Genesis story of creation as it is told in the Christian community, Christians have confidence that creation is fundamentally good and that, in fact, values emerging in community are a revelation of God's will for humankind.

This has implications for the world of business, for as rules are formed by people of good will on the basis of their experience in the business world, there gradually emerges a code of business ethics.[18] This code of ethics is an attempt to formulate rules designed to protect values that reasonable people have discerned to be at stake in the business enterprise. Thus there are rules to protect such values as honesty, integrity, fairness, justice, and so forth.

The Bible does not necessarily contradict or supersede values that have emerged in the business community. Rather the Bible, taken as the revelation of the living God and his intentions for humankind, widens and deepens and helps us clarify our understanding of human values. The way of life encouraged by Judeo-Christian values might never negate a rule of business ethics, although it may invite the business person to do much more than is required by such a rule.

CONCLUSION

The opening remarks of Part I referred to a puzzling dilemma: "Decent" people who apparently are living their religious values at home and in their church community so often seem to check those same Christian values at the office door. How can the business world gain such a hold on persons? George de Mare, in a study of corporate lives, argues that in all too many cases the pull of the corporate world wins out and comes to dominate every waking moment of a person's life. He quotes an executive who typifies this response, a vice-president who lost two wives to the office: "The corporation, the job, has dominated my whole life. Everything else has been secondary."[19] While it may be true that many readers would not accept for themselves such a statement, most would recognize the tremendous hold that the business world can have on a person.

George de Mare suggests that to understand this powerful attraction, one ought to focus on two aspects of human life: personal identity and power. He means that the business world provides something to which to give oneself, something that is significant and worthy of total dedication. It also offers a legitimation of authority, standards of excellence, and rules for advancement that one can easily perceive.[20] Knowing what has to be done to find acceptance and win rewards brings security and a kind of peace. In our terms, the business world has a "story," a pattern of meaning. Chapter 3 will show how a business story and a Christian story might be woven together harmoniously. Chapter 2 will prepare for this discussion by focusing on the values that often seem to be in conflict for Christian persons in the business world.

Notes

1   For a good discussion of the role of profit in our economic systems see Peter F. Drucker, *The Practice of Management* (New York: Harper & Brothers, 1954) pp. 34-48.

2   Some would argue that the function of a corporation ought to be redefined to in-
    clude social goals, although at times this idea finds little acceptance in the business
    community. For example, see Donald E. Schwartz, "Corporate Responsibility in
    the Age of Aquarius," *The Business Lawyer* Vol. 26 (November 1970), pp. 510-20.
    Also, see Thomas A. Petit, *The Moral Crisis in Management* (New York: McGraw-
    Hill Book Co., 1967).

3   For an excellent scholarly discussion of the various meanings of "authority" of
    Scripture, see David H. Kelsey, *The Uses of Scripture in Recent Theology* (Phila-
    delphia, Pa.: Fortress Press, 1975). The approach in this book is influenced by Kel-
    sey's constructive proposals.

4   This approach is sometimes identified as a theology of character. While not a new
    idea (See Aristotle, *Ethics,* Bk. 10, Chap. 9, and *Politics,* Bk. 1, Chap. 13; and
    Thomas Aquinas, *Summa Theologica,* Part I-II, Q. 95, AI, ANS.), it has received
    new attention in some recent studies. For scholarly analysis, see Stanley Hauerwas,
    Character and the Christian Life: A Study in Theological Ethics (San Antonio,
    Tex.: Trinity University Press, 1975). For a comprehensive summary of the ap-
    proach, see Bruce Birch and Larry Rasmussen, *Bible and Ethics in the Christian
    Life* (Minneapolis: Augsburg Publishing House, 1976); James M. Gustafson, *Can
    Ethics Be Christian?* (Chicago: University of Chicago Press, 1975); and Charles
    Curran, "Dialogue with the Scriptures: The Role and Function of the Scriptures in
    Moral Theology," in *Catholic Moral Theology in Dialogue* (Notre Dame, Ind.:
    Fides, 1972), pp. 24-64.

5   This understanding of the decision-making process is based on the work of Bernard
    J. Lonergan. For a thorough and scholarly presentation of the process see his
    Method in Theology (New York: Herder and Herder, 1972). For a popular presen-
    tation see Louis M. Savary, *Integrating Values* (Dayton: Pflaum Press, 1974).

6   Although there are occasions in the New Testament where reward and punishment
    seem to be held out as an acceptable motive for an ethical life (the rich man and
    Lazarus in Luke 16:19-31), the overriding thrust of the New Testament message is
    to be good because God is good. See chapter 7 of Amos Wilder, *Eschatology and
    Ethics in the Teaching of Jesus* (New York: Harper & Brothers, 1939).

7   For an excellent, one-volume commentary on the Scriptures that incorporates
    the best of modern scholarship, see Raymond E. Brown, S.S., Joseph A. Fitz-
    myer, S.J., and Roland E. Murphy, O. Carm., eds., *The Jerome Biblical Commen-
    tary* (Englewood Cliffs, N.J.: Prentice-Hall, Inc., 1968). This book's interpretation
    often follows that volume.

8   To explore further the role of parables in the New Testament, see chapter 2 of Rob-
    ert W. Funk, *Language, Hermeneutic, and the Word of God* (New York: Harper
    & Row, 1966).

9   Flannery O'Connor, "The Turkey," in *The Complete Stories,* Robert Giroux, ed.
    (New York: Farrar, Straus, & Giroux, 1971), pp. 42-53.

10 *Ibid.*, p. 44.

11 *Ibid.*, p. 48.

12 The literature on story and religion is plentiful. For a very readable introduction, see Michael Novak, *Ascent of the Mountain, Flight of the Dove* (New York: Harper & Row, 1971). See also John S. Dunne, *Time and Myth* (New York: Doubleday, 1973); Stanley Hauerwas, *Vision and Virtue* (Notre Dame, Ind.: Fides, 1974); James Wm. McClendon, Jr., *Biography as Theology* (Nashville: Abingdon Press, 1974); and Sallie TeSelle, *Speaking in Parables: A Study in Metaphor and Theology* (Philadelphia, Pa.: Fortress Press, 1975). For a comprehensive survey of the literature, see George W. Stroup III, "A Bibliographical Critique," *Theology Today* Vol. 32, No. 2 (July 1975), pp. 129-143.

13 This understanding of "value" relies on the philosopher Max Scheler. An important theologian appropriating this perspective is Bernhard Haring. See his *Law of Christ* (Paramus, N.J.: Paulist Press, 1961). This section closely follows the discussion in Albert R. Jonsen, *Responsibility in Modern Religious Ethics* (Washington, D.C., Corpus, 1968), pp. 86-107 and 198-205.

14 A principle is taken to be a conception having to do with choice, which, when adopted by a moral agent, allows his or her action to be qualified by the moral predicate "right" and his person by the predicate "good." A rule is more detailed conception of action. For example, "Love your neighbor" is a principle, while "Do not lie" is a rule. See A. R. Jonsen, *Responsibility in Modern Religious Ethics* (Washington, D.C.: Corpus, 1968), p. 189.

15 For example, see Peter Smith, ed., *Love and Justice: Selections From the Shorter Writings of Reinhold Niebuhr* (Gloucester, Mass.: World Publishing Co., 1967). This approach reflects a more positive stance on the possibilities of living Christian values in the business world than Niebuhr seems to allow.

16 For an insightful summary of much of the current thinking in theology on this question, see Hans Küng, *On Being a Christian* (New York: Doubleday, 1976), especially pp. 554-602, "Being Christian as Being Radically Human."

17 The values referred to here are newly-emerged values such as the dignity of women, or sensitivity to racial issues. Regrettably, these values often emerged without benefit of the leadership of the Christian community, although they were *later* clarified and supported by that community. For instance, the position of the Roman Catholic Vatican II succinctly states the role of the Church: "For it is her (the Church's) task to uncover, cherish, and ennoble all that is true, good, and beautiful in the human community." W. M. Abbott, S.J., ed., "The Church Today," in *The Documents of Vatican II* (New York: Guild Press, 1966), p. 289.

18 Texts in business ethics include the following: Robert Bartels, ed., *Ethics in Business* (Columbus, Ohio: Ohio State University Press, 1963); Raymond Baumhart, *An Honest Profit: What Businessmen Say About Ethics in Business* (New York:

Holt, Rinehart and Winston, 1968); Gerald F. Cavanagh, *American Business Values in Transition* (Englewood Cliffs, N.J.: Prentice Hall, 1976); Thomas M. Garrett, *Business Ethics* (New York: Appleton-Century-Crofts, 1966); Sylvia K. Selekman and Benjamin M. Selekman, *Power and Morality in a Business Society* (New York: McGraw-Hill Book Co., 1956); Samuel Southard, *Ethics for Executives* (Nashville: Thomas Nelson, 1975); Christopher D. Stone, *Where the Law Ends: The Social Control of Corporate Behavior* (New York: Harper & Row, 1975); and Joseph W. *Towle, ed., Ethics and Standards in American Business* (Boston: Houghton Mifflin Co., 1964).

19 George de Mare, with Joanne Summerfield, *Corporate Lives* (New York: Van Nostrand Reinhold Co., 1976), p. 192.

20 *Ibid.*

Chapter Two
Values and the Christian Story

Chapter 1 discussed in general terms how one might be guided in life by the Bible. This chapter will suggest more specific ways that the Bible might shape the decision maker. The chapter will consider seven values that are formative of the Christian way of life. There is no claim that these values define *the* Christian character. The values discussed here portray a Christian vision and *illustrate* the kind of challenge that is involved in trying to be a Christian in the business world. The values are understood in the context of the Christian story and its images. In order to highlight the influence of these biblical values in a life story, a contrasting value is listed for each of the seven. For example, the biblical value of power as service is contrasted with the value of power understood as domination and control. These are at least two ways of understanding power in our world, and there are decisive differences in the sort of person one becomes, depending on which one is valued most. The same holds true for the other six values considered.

The term "value" includes one's vision, attitudes, and intentions; it refers to a mode of behaviour as well as a goal in life. Values not only shape the way a Christian sees the issues and determines what is significant in a business decision, but also can serve as standards that guide the decision. For example, consider the first value discussed here, power over individuals. A Christian has been formed by this value so that he or she spontaneously has regard for the uniqueness and potential of the individual. Yet the value could also be put in the form of the norm: "Be as concerned about others as you are about yourself." This rule promotes and protects the value of power as service and could serve directly as a standard in making a decision. The same dual role—as both character trait and standard for action—can be seen in each of the following values. Table 2.1 displays the values to be considered.

Table 2.1 Definition of Values.

Judeo-Christian Value[1]	Contrasting Value
1. Value of power over individuals as service to help others develop their unique gifts (Phil. 2:1-18; John 13: 1-14).	Value of power over individuals as domination and control of others.
2. Value of power over nature as a stewardship by persons over *God's* world. Persons are called to transform nature in harmony with the whole of creation (Gen. 1:26-31).	Value of power over nature as a mandate to produce a maximum of consumer goods and creature comforts.
3. Value of wealth and property as an opportunity for increased service for humankind, yet as a *possible* obstacle to salvation (Luke 16:19-31; Luke 12:13-21; Mark 12:41-44).	Value of wealth and property as the measure of a person's worth.
4. Value of happiness as achieved through following God's intentions for humankind (Mark 8:36).	Value of happiness as achieved through acquiring possessions.
5. Value of justice as the right of each person to the means of leading a human life (Acts 2:42-47; Lev. 25:1-55; Gal. 3:27-28).	Value of justice as the protection of property already possessed.
6. Value of deferring gratification of wants (John 12:23-26; Luke 14:27; Matt. 16:24; Matt. 10:39).	Value of immediate gratification of wants.
7. Value of time as reverence for God (Luke 12:22-32).	Value of time as money.

POWER AND INDIVIDUALS

Whether it be a high salary, the key to the executive washroom, or membership in an exclusive country club, symbols of status and power are ever-present in today's world of business. Large organizations depend on power and influence to move the various segments of the corporation toward its goals. Power often seems to degenerate into a goal in itself, and the degree of domination and control of others seems to become the measure of a person's self-worth. Techniques for manipulating people are taken to be a valid tool to advance the cause of the firm, the number one priority. Michael Maccoby, director of the Harvard Project on Technology, Work, and Character, in a penetrating study of 250 business managers from twelve United States companies, concludes that often the hierarchical corporate system screens out generous and compassionate people who might have much to contribute. Either you "fit in" and narrow your visions to suit limited goals and objectives, or you are one of the "weak" persons who never make it to the top.[2]

The Judeo-Christian tradition has a radically different conception of power—power as service. Here the influence and power enjoyed by people of position is to be employed in ways that help others realize their unique gifts and talents. As Paul says in his letter to the Philippians: "Always consider the other person to be better than yourself, so that nobody thinks of his own interests first but everybody thinks of other people's interests instead" (Phil. 2:3-4).

John tells us a story that tries to communicate the value of power as service.

It was before the festival of the Passover, and Jesus knew that the hour had come for him to pass from this world to the Father. He had always loved those who were his in the world, but now he showed how perfect his love was.

They were at supper, and the devil had already put it into the mind of Judas Iscariot son of Simon, to betray him. Jesus knew that the Father had put everything into his hands, and that he had come from God and was returning to God, and he got up from table, removed his outer garment and, taking a towel, wrapped it round his waist; he then poured water into a basin and began to wash the disciples' feet and to wipe them with the towel he was wearing.

He came to Simon Peter, who said to him, 'Lord, are you going to wash my feet?' Jesus answered, 'At the moment you do not know what I am doing, but later you will understand!' 'Never!' said Peter 'You shall never wash my feet.' Jesus replied, 'If I do not wash you, you can have nothing in common with me'. 'Then, Lord,' said Simon Peter 'not only my feet, but my hands and my head as well!' Jesus said, 'No one who has taken a bath needs washing, he is clean all over. You too are clean, though not all of you are.' . . .

When he had washed their feet and put on his clothes again he went back to the table. 'Do you understand,' he said, 'what I have done to you? You call me Master and Lord, and rightly; so I am. If I, then, the Lord and Master, have washed your feet, you should wash each other's feet. I have given you an example so that you may copy what I have done to you' (John 13:1-15).

Just as Jesus used his power in loving service of all persons— even to the point of reversing the roles of master and slave—so all Christians are called through their union with Christ to use their talents and power to help others realize their own unique vocation in this world. This might mean, for example, examining and refashioning systems to provide for a maximum humanization of work.

Once we have identified the value of power as service as a value for Judeo-Christians, then the challenge passes to the business person to develop rules and principles to protect this value in business life. Discovering creative ways to help others develop their humanity in the business world is often a formidable challenge for executives. Yet this may be one challenge of the Gospel. The person, understood as created for union and friendship with God, possesses a dignity that has its full flowering only in community. A person is constituted as a social being, and needs others simply to be a person. Without others, one has no chance of a fully human life.

The import of business decisions in the wider community is also of concern. Business decisions might better reflect Christian values if decision makers always considered the probable effect of the decision on the "common good," where "common good" refers to a community that enhances the prospects of individual self-fulfillment and includes such things as a healthy environment, political rights, and cultural advantages. It seems that many decision makers today work from a model of "interest group pressures," a model that envisions the challenge as balancing the interests of the various groups that are currently pressuring for attention. The presupposition of this model is that the common good is the sum of individual or group interests. Yet the Christian notion of human dignity demands respect for the intrinsic worth of all persons, whether they can compel accountability by the clout of their interest group or not. The executive is challenged to develop a vision and work from a model that seeks the common good as the probable outcome of his or her decisions.[3] Often those with the least political clout or organizational skill, for example, the elderly or the poor, get little attention from the powerful and have few, if any, opportunities to voice effectively their needs and concerns. Christians, conscious of the value of power as service, should be restless until these situations are given attention.

POWER AND NATURE

It is a fundamental Judeo-Christian doctrine that the world was made for people and that humankind is called to have dominion over all creation. "Be masters of the fish of the sea, the birds of heaven, and all living animals on the earth." Yet people often lose sight of the Judeo-Christian character of this dominion. Natural resources and the beauty of the land are often seen solely as raw material to be transformed into a plethora of consumer goods and creature comforts. The Bible tells us that humankind is steward or caretaker of God's world, and that although the resources of the universe are to be used, there is an obligation to maintain some sense of the harmony of creation.

The conviction of the Judeo-Christian community is that this is God's world, and it is therefore at root "good." Although God's intended harmony (Gen. 1:29-30) has been disrupted by sin (Gen. 9:2-4), humankind is called on to transform nature in harmony with the whole of creation, and thus close the rift between the human race and nature.

It is relatively simple to accept this value, yet the business executive faced with complex data on the environment often finds it exceedingly difficult to develop rules and principles that clearly embody the value. When the environment has become so laden with pollutants that people have difficulty breathing, it is evident that humankind has overstepped the boundaries of intended harmony. Regulating strip mining, developing oil and gas reserves, or preserving other natural resources present other difficult questions. Decisions on the uses and production of nuclear energy are even more complex. The matter is complicated and the state of the research is often inadequate for solutions acceptable to all legitimate claimants in this area. The Scriptures offer no facile solutions to the manifold issues, yet they do hold out a value to be protected and promoted.

WEALTH AND PROPERTY

The value of wealth and property is number one in the hierarchy of values for many people today. Self-worth is defined in terms of what a person *has* rather than what a person *is*, and the accumulation of possessions is a mark of "success" and status. Madison Avenue encourages this perspective on life in the world of advertising for the obvious reason that it sells more products. The popular TV ad for greeting cards, "When you care enough to send the very best," captures the equation of personal worth with financial outlay so prevalent in our culture today. One can gauge "care" by how much one spends.

A *New Yorker* cartoon captures the spirit of what seems to be a common understanding of wealth. A smartly dressed, obviously well-to-do woman is pictured on the veranda of her home, cocktail glass in hand, showing a visitor their expansive and beautiful acreage. The caption under the cartoon reads: "Ed's security blanket. Two hundred and twenty acres!"[4]

Against this focus on material possessions as *the* value to be sought is the biblical understanding of wealth as an obstacle to salvation. Luke's Gospel makes the point that a rewarding and fulfilling life in this world cannot be founded on an accumulation of material goods. This is expressed well in the parable of the rich fool.

A man in the crowd said to him, 'Master, tell my brother to give me a share of our inheritance'. 'My friend,' he replied 'who appointed me your judge, or the arbitrator of your claims?' Then he said to them, 'Watch, and be on your guard against avarice of any kind, for a man's life is not made secure by what he owns, even when he has more than he needs'.

Then he told them a parable: 'There was once a rich man who, having had a good harvest from his land, thought to himself, "What am I to do? I have not enough room to store my crops." Then he said, "This is what I will do: I will pull down my barns and build bigger ones, and store all my grain and my goods in them, and I will say to my soul: My soul, you have plenty of good things laid by for many years to come; take things easy, eat, drink, have a good time". But God said to him, "Fool! This very night the demand will be made for your soul; and this hoard of yours, whose will it be then?" So it is when a man stores up treasure for himself in place of making himself rich in the sight of God' (Luke 12:13-21).

In the story "The Rich Man and Lazarus" (Luke 16:19-31) wealth is portrayed as an obstacle to salvation. An abundance of material possessions obscures vision and dulls sensitivities so that a genuinely humane life is difficult, if not impossible. In this parable, sin is portrayed not as a commission (doing something you should not have done) but as an omission (not doing something you ought to have done). Sin is simply living in luxury while poverty is near. It is the indifference to the suffering and hunger of the poor, and the lack of any constructive action to remedy their situation. Consider the parable.

'There was a rich man who used to dress in purple and fine linen and feast magnificently every day. And at his gate there lay a poor man called Lazarus, covered with sores, who longed to fill himself with the scraps that fell from the rich man's table. Dogs even came and licked his sores. Now the poor man died and was carried away by the angels to the bosom of Abraham. The rich man also died and was buried.

In his torment in Hades he looked up and saw Abraham a long way off with Lazarus in his bosom. So he cried out, "Father Abraham, pity me and send Lazarus to dip the tip of his finger in water and cool my tongue, for I am in agony in these flames". "My son," Abraham replied "remember that during your life good things came your way, just as bad things came the way of Lazarus. Now he is being comforted here while you are in agony. But that is not all: between us and you a great gulf has been fixed, to stop anyone, if he wanted to, crossing from our side to yours, and to stop any crossing from your side to ours." 'The rich man replied, "Father, I beg you then to send Lazarus to my father's house, since I have five brothers, to give them warning so that they do not come to this place of torment too". "They have Moses and the prophets," said Abraham "let them listen to them." "Ah no, father Abraham," said the rich man "but if someone comes to them from the dead, they will repent." Then Abraham said to him, "If they will not listen either to Moses or to the prophets, they will not be convinced even if someone should rise from the dead".' (Luke 16:19-31).

In this parable Jesus was addressing those who were convinced that salvation could be won as a result of scrupulous observance of the law. Yet Jesus had the insight to see that their problem was that they "loved money" (Luke 16:14); although they might look good in people's sight, God knew the hardness of their hearts. Their material possessions insulated them from the realities of life, and they lacked compassion for the poor.

In many ways this parable may have much to say to the contemporary business person. Jesus was continually criticizing those persons who, although they might scrupulously follow their rules, often neglected to cultivate and internalize the values that the rules were designed to protect and promote. Jesus' point in this parable is that no matter how many rules and observances the rich man may have followed, lack of compassion for the destitute inhibits any relationship with God. What is important is promoting and protecting the biblical value, not following rules.[5] The business person has this same challenge.

The Jewish people in fact had a rich tradition reflecting the value of compassion for the poor. Every landowner according to the Book of Leviticus was God's tenant: "for the land belongs to me, and to me you are only strangers and guests" (Lev. 25:23). The poor were considered God's representatives on earth and thus they were *owed* "taxes" in the form of alms by the landowners (Isa. 58:7). The rich man in the parable seemed totally oblivious to the needs of others and the value at stake. Luxury and wealth often insulate people from genuine human concern and the conversion (the adopting of new values) that Jesus preached by his words and deeds.

HAPPINESS

"Bubble up with 7-Up" captures what for many is a guiding value for life—everything can be purchased, including happiness. Happiness is attained by material comfort and possessions. A pill, a double martini, an "escape" cruise, a big car, a fine home—these are the things that bring the good life.

Jesus, while certainly not denying the value of happiness flowing from the enjoyment of the good things of this world, widens and deepens our understanding of happiness and fulfillment.

He called the people and his disciples to him and said, 'If anyone wants to be a follower of mine, let him renounce himself and take up his cross and follow me. For anyone who wants to save his life will lose it; but anyone who loses his life for my sake, and for the sake of the gospel, will save it. What gain, then, is it for a man to win the whole world and ruin his life?' (Mark 8:34-36).

There is more to life than the period from birth to death. Even in this world there is something more worthwhile than the happiness that comes with quantitative increases in material goods. A dimension of the person resonates with the Gospel message of love and selfless giving, and the happiness that this sort of life brings is promised to be only a foretaste of what is to come. The contemporary emphasis on "quality of life" issues (contrasted with the "quantity of life") is a reminder that "man does not live by bread alone."

Drawing by Weber; ©1973 The New Yorker Magazine, Inc.

A business executive may find it difficult to carry this value into the corporate office. So much of the advertising world operates on the assumption that whatever sells products is good advertising, and a superficial and sensuous appeal to the less noble features of the human person often makes good sales. Discerning the right place to draw the line to protect this understanding of happiness is one task of the Christian business person.

Often companies require executives to move to various branches of the firm in all parts of the land in order to advance quickly in the corporate hierarchy. The assumption sometimes seems to be that any and all values (family stability, for example) ought to give way to enable a rapid increase in salary and prestige. The Bible reminds us that an increase in money brings little happiness in itself. The cartoon pictured above graphically portrays the utter frustration and illusion that accompanies a single-minded quest for money.

JUSTICE

The cry for "justice" is heard across the globe by a host of constituencies, but on closer examination it appears that there is no common agreement on precisely what the term means. The objective of this volume is to explore the biblical value of justice underlying the Judeo-Christian convictional community and to compare it with the more narrowly focused understanding of justice that often seems to prevail in the business world.

Justice in the business world is often equated with the protection of property already possessed. The call for "law and order" arises from a legitimate concern to preserve the peace and harmony of the community. Yet peace without justice is of little value to the Christian, and justice demands that all have the means to lead a human life. Today this would include material goods as well as services.[6]

While not belittling the obvious benefits to a society that preserves good order by laws and adequate protection, it is important to note that the Christian ideal of justice is much more generous. The Christian is obliged to strive for much more than this narrowly understood notion of justice. Peace without Christian justice cannot be accepted. The Book of Leviticus in the Old Testament portrays a vision for the ideal society based on a profoundly religious concept of justice. Leviticus 25:1-55 speaks of the sabbatical and the jubilee years, times in which land was to be surrendered and slaves freed in celebration that the Lord was the sole proprietor of all of creation. The sabbatical year (one out of every seven years) and the jubilee year (one out of every fifty years) were occasions to remind all loyal Jews that the land belongs to the Lord and that the Israelites were only stewards for the Lord by virtue of their covenant. All people were equal in the Lord's sight, and all had the right to the fruits of the land.

During the sabbatical or seventh year all cultivation of the fields and vineyards was suspended (Lev. 25:2-7). The land was given a rest, not only to ensure its future vitality, but also, and more importantly for the Jews, to celebrate God's dominion over all creation. The jubilee year was a grand sabbatical and the Book of Leviticus provides general rules outlining its observance (Lev. 25:23-55). Similar to the sabbatical year, jubilee prescriptions included land return, debt resolution, and slave liberation. Although scholars agree that it is highly unlikely that these ideals were ever fully implemented in Israelite society, it is important to note that this appears to be a vision of what life ought to be.

The New Testament develops this notion of the Lord's justice. Consider the parable of the vineyard laborers.

'Now the kingdom of heaven is like a landowner going out at daybreak to hire workers for his vineyard. He made an agreement with the workers for one denarius a day, and sent them to his vineyard. Going out at about the third hour he saw others standing idle in the marketplace and said to them, "You go to my vineyard too and I will give you a fair wage". So they went. At about the sixth hour and again at about the ninth hour, he went out and did the same. Then at about the eleventh hour he went out and found more men standing round, and he said to them, "Why have you been standing here idle all day?" "Because no one has hired us" they answered. He said to them, "You go into my vineyard too". In the evening, the owner of the vineyard said to his bailiff, "Call the workers and pay them their wages, starting with the last arrivals and ending with the first". So those who were hired at about the eleventh hour came forward and received one denarius each. When the first came, they expected to get more, but they too received one denarius each. They took it, but grumbled at the landowner. "The men who came last" they said "have done only one hour, and you have treated them the same as us, though we have done a heavy day's work in all the heat." He answered one of them and said, "My friend, I am not being unjust to you; did we not agree on one denarius? Take your earnings and go. I choose to pay the last-comer as much as I pay you. Have I no right to do what I like with my own? Why be envious because I am generous?" Thus the last will be first, and the first, last.' (Matt. 20:1-16)

This parable seems to suggest that Christians ought not be displeased with the generosity of their Lord. God's gracious good will toward the latecomers takes nothing away from those who have labored all day. God insists on his right to bestow his generosity where he will. The parable was perhaps told to make the point that the Gentiles who converted late to Christianity were on an equal footing with the Jews who were the original disciples. So, too, the later disciples had an equal standing with the original disciples. All Christians had full participation in the reign of God regardless of when they joined the community. (It should be clear that the parable of the vineyard laborers is *not* suggested as a model for the institutional arrangements between employer and employee in business life!)

Paul in his letter to the Church in Galatia sums up the full flowering of this notion of the equality of all people before the Lord. "All baptized in Christ, you have all clothed yourselves in Christ, and there are no more distinctions between Jew and Greek, slave and free, male and female, but all of you are one in Christ Jesus" (Gal. 3:27-28). Some scholars understood Paul to mean that if we adopt the moral dispositions and outlook of Christ ("clothed yourselves in Christ"), all distinctions vanish. In virtue of a common Father all are entitled to a share in the good things of creation.

Incorporating this biblical perspective on justice in the business world may not mean a wholesale disregard for the rules of fair play that undergird the enterprise. The biblical perspective on the value of justice demands a creative generosity on the part of the manager, a sensitivity to the occasions that require a departure from or change of the "rule" in order to promote the common good. The Christian is guided by a profound respect for the personhood of another and is sensitive to seek out those who are neglected in society and assist them.

There are some signs that this biblical value is finding some acceptance in a few quarters. For example, some corporations allow their executives time to provide free consulting to minority businesses. Some firms recognize the responsibility to remain in the downtown area of cities rather than fleeing to the suburbs. Some companies actively seek contracts with minority-managed firms. For example, Honeywell, Inc. purchased more than $28 million in goods and services from minority-managed firms from 1972 to 1977. A report issued in February 1978 by a subcommittee of the U.S. House of Representatives surveyed eight hundred of the largest business firms and asked them about their plans to remain in or locate in the inner city. The report indicated that the situation is far from ideal, but that there were some outstanding examples of socially responsible leadership in the business community. For example, Control Data Corporation of Minneapolis has aggressively sought out central city settings and focused their training programs on the persons most in need of jobs. A representative of the company stated that Control Data "felt it could help solve a major societal problem by taking meaningful job and career opportunities to inner-city residents."[7]

GRATIFICATION OF WANTS

There is a curious paradox in the fact that the nation's businesses project in their advertising a vision of life that encourages immediate gratification of wants, ("You only go around once . . ."). On the other hand, "to make it big," to do well and advance in the business world takes an enormous amount of deferred gratification, (i.e. long hours in the office, much time away from family and loved ones, weekend work, and openness to being transferred to locations around the world without much advance notice). This deferred gratification is motivated by a desire to serve the company well and therefore advance up the corporate ladder as quickly as possible. For some, there may even be an immediate gratification in this strenuous, spartan routine.

The Bible, too, holds out a model of deferred gratification as the secret of success, yet it projects a much more comprehensive understanding of human fulfillment than rising to the top in the world of business.[8] The Bible asserts that living life "to the hilt," and pampering oneself in a life of selfishness, will not bring fulfillment. Rather it will end in the loss of the true self. The grain of wheat only bears fruit when it has died and is buried, and the same paradox is present in human life. Life comes through death; self-sacrifice yields a richer and more rewarding life. This is the mystery of Christ's atoning death and a key that may help all Christians make sense of their lives.

> Now the hour has come
> for the Son of Man to be glorified.
> I tell you, most solemnly,
> unless a wheat grain falls on the ground and dies,
> it remains only a single grain;
> but if it dies,
> it yields a rich harvest.
> Anyone who loves his life loses it;
> anyone who hates his life in this world
> will keep it for the eternal life.
> If a man serves me, he must follow me,
> wherever I am, my servant will be there too.
> If anyone serves me, my Father will honour him (John 12:23-26).

This value may put the life of the business executive in a new perspective. It forces the issue of what one wants out of life. Accepting this value creates a wider and deeper vision of the "good life," a new kind of care for others, and a more comprehensive range of considerations in making decisions. The danger lies not in enjoying life, but in living it as if "that's all there is!" A cartoon that captures the spirit of this view of life pictures two well-dressed men obviously in affluent surroundings, with drinks in hand, surveying a luxurious beach. The caption has one gentleman saying to the other: "I try like hell to be honest, Arthur, but who can be honest these days and *live*?"[9] The Bible has quite a different message about what *living* is.

TIME

"Time is money" sums up the way time is understood in many quarters of contemporary society. Underlying this value is the viewpoint that most problems can be solved by the calculative, human intelligence. Designing methods, techniques, seem to have captured the imagination of many today. Every waking moment ought to be used productively—either solving problems with new techniques or improving personal talents to prepare for the competitive world. The name of the game is "survival of the fittest," and efficiency is a crucial value. Often the method of getting the job done seems almost more important than the job itself. We are fascinated by techniques and captivated by achievement. They have almost become our gods. Jacques Ellul, a French lay theologian, has written well on this point and sounded a warning lest we uncritically accept technology as a new god in our society.[10]

The Bible portrays quite another understanding of time. If one has trust in God then there is time for leisure, for play, and for worship. Our times need to hear the biblical call to trust the Lord; there are things simply beyond our control. Harvey Cox, in *Feast of Fools*, calls us to realize that our culture's great stress on goal-oriented activity may eclipse the great value of enjoying the moment.[11] Consider how Luke recounts Jesus' teaching on the matter.

> Then he said to his disciples, 'That is why I am telling you not to worry about your life and what you are to eat, nor about your body and how you are to clothe it. For life means more than food, and the body more than clothing. Think of the ravens. They do not sow or reap; they have no storehouses and no barns; yet God feeds them. And how much more are you worth than the birds! Can any of you, for all his worrying, add a single cubit to his span of life? If the smallest things, therefore, are outside your control, why worry about the rest? Think of the flowers; they never have to spin or weave; yet, I assure you, not even Solomon in all his regalia was robed like one of these. Now if that is how God clothes the grass in the field which is there today and thrown into the furnace tomorrow, how much more will he look after you, you men of little faith! But you, you must not set your hearts on things to eat and things to drink; nor must you worry. It is the pagans of this world who set their hearts on all these things. Your Father well knows you need them. No; set your hearts on his kingdom, and these other things will be given you as well.
>
> 'There is no need to be afraid, little flock, for it has pleased your Father to give you the kingdom' (Luke 12:22-32).

Life is not a problem to be solved but a mystery to be lived. Although the Bible would certainly not mandate a wholesale condemnation of our technological society with all the gains it has made in humanizing the world, it refuses to make technique an absolute.

There is more to life than that which can be predicted and controlled. The Bible frequently portrays time as the opportunity for reverence to God by word and deed. Time is for worship of God, and the development as well as the enjoyment of creation. The notion of "the Lord's Day" and the Sabbath rest is a traditional way of highlighting this value. New breakthroughs in science and technology are progress only to the extent that they enhance the prospects for a more humane world. Technique without purpose and intelligence without wisdom often follow when time for leisure, prayer, and enjoyment are neglected.

The business person is ever tempted to think and live as if all that really counts is domination, control, and achievement. Recognizing that a full life includes celebration, leisure, and trust in the Father may provide an expansive new horizon for business decisions.

THE HORNS OF THE DILEMMA: CYNICISM OR DESPAIR

Given the values we have cited from the Judeo-Christian Scriptures, the committed Christian is thrust into a painful tension. He or she is living in a world shot through with social injustice, and yet the Christian values call for a radical change in such a world. There are at least two ways of dissolving this tension: (1) making an accommodation with the *status quo* and arguing that social injustice is inevitable (the cynic), or (2) giving up after having exhausted oneself struggling to realize the Kingdom of God here on earth (the idealist turned to despair).

One reading of the Gospel takes us between the horns of this dilemma. There is neither a lowering of the demands nor a flight from reality, but a prudent perseverance in the struggle to bring the values of the Kingdom of God into this world, a struggle nurtured and animated by the inner presence in each Christian of the spirit of love. Paul reminds us of the source of our strength and confidence.

Everyone moved by the Spirit is a son of God. The spirit you received is not the spirit of slaves bringing fear into your lives again; it is the spirit of sons, and it makes us cry out, 'Abba, Father!' (Rom. 8:14-15).

Mark tells us that Jesus began his ministry by announcing the coming of the Kingdom of God.

After John had been arrested, Jesus went into Galilee. There he proclaimed the Good News from God. 'The time has come' he said 'and the kingdom of God is close at hand. Repent, and believe the Good News' (Mark 1:
14-15).

The Kingdom or Reign of God, which includes the Christian values we have discussed is initiated by the words and deeds of Jesus. But
the New Testament is careful to note time and time again that the
Kingdom is not yet fully realized and will only be realized at the end
of time.[12] The words and deeds of Jesus are taken to reveal God's intentions for humankind and all of creation. The New Testament
writers themselves infer from the experience of Jesus certain values
that ought to inform the Christian community's way of life.

For example, consider how Paul in his letter to the Corinthians
infers certain values necessary for the well-being of the community.
Paul tells them that although there are many gifts given to persons in
the community, there is but one giver, and that these gifts have one
purpose, the common good of the community. Paul, although conscious of human weakness and the relativities of existence, does not
compromise the absolute demand of the words and deeds of Jesus.

There is a variety of gifts but always the same Spirit; there are all sorts of
service to be done, but always to the same Lord; working in all sorts of different ways in different people, it is the same God who is working in all of them.
The particular way in which the Spirit is given to each person is for a good purpose. One may have the gift of preaching with wisdom given him by the Spirit;
another may have the gift of preaching instruction given him by the same Spirit; and another the gift of faith given by the same Spirit; another again the gift of
healing, through this one Spirit; one, the power of miracles; another, proph-
ecy; another the gift of recognizing spirits; another the gift of tongues and another the ability to interpret them. All these are the work of one and the same
Spirit, who distributes different gifts to different people just as he chooses.

Just as a human body, though it is made up of many parts, is a single unit
because all these parts, though many, make one body, so it is with Christ. In
the one Spirit we were all baptized, Jews as well as Greeks, slaves as well as
citizens, and one Spirit was given to us all to drink (1 Cor. 12:4-13).

Paul is writing to people in Corinth addressing their particular
concerns, yet his reflections must be read in the light of his experience

and from the community accounts of Jesus. Paul is saying that certain obligations follow from a commitment to this way of life. Since Jesus' life and work reveals God's intentions for the fulfillment of persons and community, the Christian community has these intentions as basic values. It could be that when Paul was writing to the Corinthians he was reflecting on the way of life that Jesus set out in his Sermon on the Mount. Here Jesus provides some values that reflect the intentions of God for all humankind. It is important to note that the values encouraged here are in conflict with many of the conventional values of both the Jewish and the Hellenistic-Roman world of the time. Wealth, status, and anything that requires self-assertion and strife for its defense are played down in importance. The Sermon on the Mount offers a new vision, indeed a moral revolution, that was clearly not a present reality in the community. Consider the text.

Seeing the crowds, he went up the hill. There he sat down and was joined by his disciples. Then he began to speak. This is what he taught them:

'How happy are the poor in spirit; theirs is the kingdom of heaven. Happy *the gentle: they shall have the earth for their heritage.* Happy those who mourn: they shall be comforted. Happy those who hunger and thirst for what is right: they shall be satisfied. Happy the merciful: they shall have mercy shown them. Happy the pure in heart: they shall see God. Happy the peacemakers: they shall be called sons of God. Happy those who are persecuted in the cause of right: theirs is the kingdom of heaven. Happy are you when people abuse you and persecute you and speak all kinds of calumny against you on my account. Rejoice and be glad, for your reward will be great in heaven; this is how they persecuted the prophets before you' (Matt. 5:1-12).

Paul in writing to Corinth may have presupposed this new set of values and built on them.[13] The Christian community has continued to affirm these Sermon on the Mount values, because they have been found to be true in the living of the life. Indeed by trying to live creatively the life that Jesus held out as a real possibility, the Christian community has grown in confidence that the intentions of God for humankind and all creation are in fact manifested in the words and deeds of Jesus.

Jesus offers a story with a different logic than that of most of the world, yet that logic curiously enough seems to yield its own verification in the living of the life. For example, to be merciful or to work for the rights of the poor seems to be fulfilling and rewarding. Thinking of others before oneself is the new ideal, and the leaders of the Christian community must continually spell out through the centuries what this might mean for their times. The challenge is to speak to the community of believers fully aware of its limitations without adjusting or leveling the ideals of the message of Jesus.

Consider how St. Paul meets this challenge. In writing to the people of Corinth (and elsewhere), Paul had a clear perspective on the values advocated by Jesus. He offers a summary of these values throughout his writings. For example, he writes to the Romans:

> All the commandments: *You shall not commit adultery, you shall not kill, you shall not steal, you shall not covet,* and so on, are summed up in this single command: *You must love your neighbor as yourself.* (Rom. 13:9).

On the one hand, salvation has already been won and we can be confident that the values of God's kingdom will eventually triumph at the end of time.

> But God loved us with so much love that he was generous with his mercy: when we were dead through our sins, he brought us to life with Christ—it is through grace that you have been saved—and raised us up with him and gave us a place with him in heaven, in Christ Jesus (Eph. 2:4-6).

On the other hand, evil remains a part of the world and the task of the Christian is to overcome evil with good. In fact, all will be judged on the basis of their responses to God's intentions for creation.

> For all the truth about us will be brought out in the law court of Christ, and each of us will get what he deserves for the things he did ..., good or bad (2 Cor. 5:10).

THE KINGDOM OF GOD AND TEMPORAL PROGRESS

Theologians have long debated just how best to understand the relationship between the world and the Kingdom of God, temporal activity and salvation, human wisdom and the Gospel message. On the one hand, few theologians today identify the Kingdom of God with temporal progress, as if somehow we could create heaven on earth. This tendency would collapse the Kingdom of God into the world, and the eternal into the here and now. This position is sometimes known as naturalism or secularism. On the other hand, most theologians want to avoid the sharp dualism between the progress of the world and eternal values. This dualistic position holds that cultural advances count nothing in the Kingdom of God and that developing the temporal order and making life more humane have little bearing on a person's supernatural destiny. Here one would shun this world and prepare for the next by withdrawing from "earthly" causes.

The position taken in this book is that the world and the Kingdom of God are not identical. They are mutually interconnected, do affect one another, and yet are distinguishable. The Kingdom of God is already present here in the world although in a preliminary way; the redemptive process is only to be completed at the end of this world.[14]

The Christian business person today has the uniquely difficult challenge of trying to realize Christian values in a highly complex world. Now that we have explored some central Christian values, the task that remains is to develop skills that help realize this vision in business life. In the face of what sometimes may seem to be overwhelming odds against success, the Christian business person may harken back to the words of St. Paul.

Never try to suppress the Spirit . . .; think before you do anything—hold on to what is good and avoid *every* form of *evil.* (1 Thes. 5:19-22).

Pope John XXIII interpreted the apostle's message in his encyclical letter, *Mater et Magistra.*

The teachings in regard to social matters for the most part are put into effect in the following three states: first, the actual situation is examined; then, the situation is evaluated carefully in relation to these teachings; then only is it decided what can and should be done and in order that the traditional norms may be adapted to circumstances of time and place. These three steps are at times expressed by the three words: *observe, judge, act.*[15]

Part II of this book provides exercises in observing, judging, and acting in situations likely to confront a contemporary business person.

CHRISTIAN VALUES AND CORPORATE LIFE

This chapter has outlined the vision and some of the values of the Christian "story," and the sort of person one must become as a follower of Christ. We may have perhaps given the impression that all that is necessary is for *individuals* to begin living Christian values in the business world. Of course, this in itself would be an enormous gain. There is much that an individual can do on the strength of his or her influence in business life. Yet the Christian commitment of individuals is only part of the challenge. For large-scale organizations have lives of their own, and, unless the business is very small, the policy process itself may preclude the hearing and the airing of certain concerns.

For example, a corporation may be deciding whether to move the home office from Cleveland to Dallas. The board of directors has this matter on its agenda as one of twenty items to be decided. After a heavy morning of briefings and a working lunch, they reassemble to discuss the move. They are provided with a mass of financial data indicating that profits will definitely increase and costs will decrease if they approve the move. The proposal to move receives a unanimous vote. All the persons on the board, as individuals, may espouse Christian values, and they may all feel that they have done no wrong in this decision. Granted, this example is simplistic. Yet, the lingering question for a Christian in this type of situation is: Is the corporate policy process itself Christian? When this corporate action is evaluated by the standards of Christian values, does it meet the test? That is to say, should not a corporate policy process involve more factors than corporate self-interest narrowly measured by the profit yardstick?

Does not a corporate entity have multiple responsibilities—the community, employees, the elderly, etc.? Are corporations only accountable to those groups that can compel accountability? Should not corporations develop a social vision and take an active part in making the world more humane through their policies?

The values of the Gospel serve to evaluate not only the actions of individuals but also the operations of organizations. Significantly, the values of a corporation are not simply the sum of the values of individuals in the corporation. Sociology has helped us understand how social structures come to embody a distinctive character with dominant images and a hierarchy of values.[16] For example, consider the contrast between the United States Postal Service and the United States Marine Corps. Each of these organizations has its own characteristic flavor, which shapes and forms all who join.

Some contemporary biblical scholarship has focused attention on the fact that sin can be social as well as personal. We are accustomed to think of sin in exclusively personal terms—an *individual* turning away from God and his will. Conversion is seen as the individual accepting Jesus Christ and thus a new way of life and its values. Scholarship has helped us see that John and Paul use the word "sin" to refer to a state or condition of the person and not so much to personal acts.[17] Social structures can often support and encourage a state or condition embodying a whole set of values antithetical to the Christian way of life. For example, the governments of some nations seem to foster a way of life that systemically denies full human rights to certain groups. Think, for example, of South Africa and the sad lack of equality for the black majority. The mandate to struggle against sin (Mark 1:15) is a call to overcome *both* personal and social sin.

If concern for structural social injustice does not follow personal conversion, there seems to be cause to wonder about the depth of the conversion. The question for the business executive is whether the policy process or systems in the corporation are not at times agents of social injustice. Part II of the book will consider some cases where this appears to be an issue.

CONCLUSION

In his classic work, *Moral Man and Immoral Society*, Reinhold Niebuhr reminds us that while the injustice of individuals might be overcome through good will and human reason, social injustice is generally overcome only through the judicious use of power.[18] The Christian business person is called not only to change his or her own vision, but also to seek changes in the *policy process* so that a wider array of concerns might be incorporated in decision-making. Of course, we live in a pluralistic world, and it would be naive to assume that all hold Christian convictions and values. One task of the Christian, then, is to find the common ground where the core values can be advanced and thus make a collaborative effort to move toward a more humane world. Democratic capitalism has within it the resources to push beyond a notion of self-interest narrowly measured by the profit column on the balance sheet. While human frailty and weakness cannot be denied the magnitude of our challenges today calls for an enlightened self-interest that sees that only in advancing the common good can any of us be assured of the good life.

Notes

1   Use of the term "Judeo-Christian" value is meant to indicate what is assumed throughout the volume: that Jesus appropriated much of the code of daily living of the Jewish tradition in his revelation of the spiritual presence of God. The challenge of this volume is to begin to formulate a pattern of daily living for the Christian business person in the twentieth century. For a good discussion of the import of the "Jewishness" of Jesus for pastoral ministry, see Don S. Browning, *The Moral Context of Pastoral Care* (Philadelphia, Pa.: Westminster Press, 1976).

2   Cf. *The Gamesman* (New York: Simon & Schuster, 1976). Maccoby is especially critical of the motivational theory of Abraham Maslow. Maslow is famous for the development of a "hierarchy of needs," i.e., from the primitive needs like food, shelter, and security to the higher needs like self-actualization and self-realization. See his *Motivation and Personality* (New York: Harper & Row, 1954). In *The Gamesman*, Maccoby comments (p. 233): "Despite his conscious attempt to develop a modern humanistic psychology, Maslow ends by supporting, even celebrating, some values—hierarchy, mechanistic thought, idealization of success, careerism—that block the development of the heart."

3   Socrates, speaking in Plato's *Republic*, develops a notion of the common good. Locke's *Toleration* and Hobbes' *Leviathan* lay the basis for determining the common good from private interests rather than the dignity of the human person. Jacques Maritain's work is an attempt to return to a fuller notion of community: cf. *The Person and the Common Good*, trans. John J. Fitzgerald (New York: Charles Scribner's Sons, 1947).

4   *The New Yorker* Vol. 51, No. 21 (July 14, 1975), p. 38.

5   Reginald Fuller presents a lucid exposition of the Bible's position on wealth: "if affluence is understood genuinely as charisma, a gift to the faithful believers in the Gospel of the crucified and risen Lord who justifies the ungodly, then it becomes a charisma, a gift of grace, and is used as such. It is used in the service of the community." Reginald H. Fuller and Brian K. Rice, *Christianity and the Affluent Society* (Grand Rapids, Mich.: Eerdmans, 1966), p. 59.

6 For one account of how to spell out the concept of distributive justice, see John Rawls, *A Theory of Justice* (Cambridge, Mass.: Harvard University Press, 1971). Here justice is "fairness," meaning that society ought to provide for the weak who have less ability or social status. For some excellent church statements on what justice means for Christians today, see the official report of the Fifth Assembly of the World Council of Churches: David M. Patton, ed., *Breaking Barriers: Nairobi: 1975* (Grand Rapids, Mich.: Eerdmans, 1976). Also see Joseph B. Gremillion, *The Gospel of Peace and Justice: Catholic Social Teaching Since Pope John* (Maryknoll, N.Y.: Orbis Books, 1976).

7 United States, 95th Congress, second session, 1978. House Document: Large Corporations and Urban Employment, p. 109.

8 For a very scholarly analysis of the indispensable role of Christian freedom for an adequate understanding of political and psychological freedom, see Peter C. Hodgson, *New Birth of Freedom* (Philadelphia, Pa.: Fortress Press, 1976).

9 *The New Yorker* Vol. 52, No. 27 (August 23, 1976), p. 42.

10 Jacques Ellul, *The Technological Society*. Translated from the French by John Wilkinson. (New York: Knopf, 1964).

11 Harvey Cox, *The Feast of Fools: A Theological Essay on Festivity and Fantasy* (New York: Harper & Row, 1969).

12 See Mark 12:34; 14:25; 15:43.

13 Biblical scholars point out that there is a difference in the ethical teachings of the Epistles and the Gospels. The instructions in the Epistles were to be applied, as written, to the daily conduct of the individual and community, while Jesus' teachings are not meant to be applied directly to conduct. C. H. Dodd notes that the teaching of Jesus, for example, The Sermon on the Mount, indicate the *quality* and *direction* of action. The teaching of Jesus provides "spurs to action" and a "certain outlook on life." See C. H. Dodd, *Gospel and Law* (New York: Columbia University Press, 1951), pp. 46-83.

14 After considerable debate and with the consultation of some of the best theologians, the assembled Roman Catholic Bishops at the Second Vatican Council adopted this stance. Consider several key sentences in the decree, "The Church Today": "On this earth that Kingdom is already present in mystery. When the Lord returns, it will be brought into full flower." (par. 39). "That the earthly and the heavenly city penetrate each other is a fact accessible to faith alone. It remains a mystery of human history, which sin will keep in great disarray until the splendor of God's sons is fully revealed." (par. 40). In Walter M. Abbott, S.J., ed., *The Documents of Vatican II* (New York: Guild Press, 1966), pp. 237-239. For an excellent discussion of this question see: Carl E. Braaten, *Eschatology and Ethics: Essays on*

the *Theology and Ethics of the Kingdom of God* (Minneapolis, Minn.: Augsburg Publishing House, 1974).

15 W. Gibbons, S.J., trans., *Mater et Magistra* (Washington, D.C.: National Catholic Welfare Conference, 1961), p. 66.

16 Peter Berger is perhaps the most influential sociologist who has written about the interplay between social structures and persons. Although a human product, institutions and systems have a crucial formative influence on persons in their purview. See Peter Berger and Thomas Luckmann, *The Social Construction of Reality: A Treatise in the Sociology of Knowledge* (New York: Doubleday, 1966).

17 For a comprehensive discussion of sin, see Piet J. Schoonenberg, *Man and Sin: A Theological View* (Notre Dame, Ind.: University of Notre Dame Press, 1965).

18 Reinhold Niebuhr, *Moral Man and Immoral Society* (New York: Scribner's, 1932). For a more developed position on the dialectical relationship between man and society, see his *The Nature and Destiny of Man*, 2 vols. (New York: Scribner's, 1941).

Chapter Three
Images That Guide Life Stories

Many would characterize the challenge of living a Christian story in the business world as similar to "the man who jumped astride two horses and rode off in different directions." Before we can reject the skeptic's challenge, we will have to lay bare the underlying issues with considerable care. First it is essential that we agree about the issue implied in the challenge: riding two horses going in different directions. The skeptic is saying that the "horse" of religion with its dominant images and values must inevitably veer away from the "horse" of business with its images and values. Mark Twain expressed this position well when he said, "An ethical man is a Christian holding four aces." Fundamentally, the argument is one of incompatibility, which further rejects any possible reconciliation of the two commitments. Rebuffing this argument will take careful thought. It is a difficult issue, because it asks the fundamental question: Is it possible to live the Christian story with a master image from the Bible in the world of business?

This chapter will present a way of answering that question. It will first show why the focus on the role of images is justified. Then there is a brief discussion of three dominant images from the Bible that many today might find appealing. Following this, there is a description of the central images that seem most prevalent in the contemporary business world. The chapter concludes by showing how the two sets of images might be harmoniously blended to guide the story of a Christian business person.

ROLE OF IMAGES

A number of theologians today find it helpful to speak of conversion to Christian faith in terms of a change in story; where a story is understood as a series of images. Just as Jesus apparently trained his disciples by telling them stories and providing a new language for them to "live into," so too, conversion to Christian faith involves a "living into" the Christian language with all the changes in habits and behavior that such a move entails. The Church communicates the faith through the stories of the Gospel and the liturgy or worship. The values of the Christian story come fully alive in the person of Christ. One task is to appropriate biblical images and the Christian way of life in such a way that a total life takes on these new values. Christianity is not just for church and home; it entails the conversion of the whole person, and it must permeate all that person's activities and social structures. This is a crucial challenge to people in the business or other professional or vocational worlds today.

The concern for the integration of thought and action, theory and practice, is common to all educational endeavors, particularly professional schools—law, medicine, business, and divinity. Many of the problems of legal education are similar to those of theological education.[1] Professor Harold Berman[2] of the Harvard Law School, when addressing a group of professors of religion expressed it well when he noted how in law the "restatements" or abstract principles never quite state the real situation; the restatements themselves are not sufficient to analyze a new legal situation.[3] A book of the principles of law is worthless without the actual cases that inspired the principles. To have the ability to apply principles well to new situations, one must know how those principles evolved from the original cases. Because of this conviction Harvard Law School uses the case method extensively.

An insight similar to Professor Berman's has led many theologians to use biography in teaching theology. By reading a biography or autobiography and becoming involved in the life of a Christian—"passing over" to his or her standpoint—one can learn something about doctrine and biblical images that escapes abstract formulation. If we find that another is grappling with the same problems we are, this "passing over"[4] gives added insight into the question. By examining another standpoint we gain added clarity on just what story we are in and what we might have to do to be in another story. The story enables the statements of theology to come to life. Only in the context of the story do the traditional expressions of faith have the concreteness, the imagery, that is so essential for understanding. In examining and "trying on" a story, the significant things to look for are the great biblical images that are applied to a life and its circumstances and hence govern the experience of an individual.

This is saying more than that we need an example or two to ensure that everyone understands a point. Rather a story through its narration and imagery sets the context or widens the horizon so that an insight is actually available to a person. Speaking in the province of the moral life, one Christian ethicist has said it well: "Moral life is not simply a matter of decisions governed by publicly defensible principles and rules; we can only act in the world we see, a seeing partially determined by the kind of beings we have become through the stories we have learned and embodied in our life plan."[5]

It is not possible to abstract the meaning from the stories and to present an abstraction to participants as if it were the essence, all that really counts. If principles are to be put into action, then the stories are necessary in order to see the general orientation and shape of the situation. Even more importantly, principles, whether they be in business or theology, might be explored more sensitively with contemporary stories that embody the principle. To understand better what it means to become a Christian business person, one must "try on" some stories and get a feel for the process.

Often we assume an obvious separation between thought and action. Reflection provides the thought, and the learner can then apply it. Yet if what has been said up till this point is true, there is an intimate connection between thought and action; beliefs about ourselves, others, and the world have a direct bearing on our actions. More precisely, actions simply reveal embodied beliefs. Our words and deeds speak the beliefs that we have derived from the stories and images that are held sacred.

In the Christian community we seek to pass on not only the stories of faith from the past, but also some hints on how a story of faith is shaped today. A life takes its shape from the models that are guiding the story. Striving to become a certain sort of person entails having models to follow, and knowing the models that are guiding a story often tells more about a person than knowing the principles that he or she holds dear. Understanding behavior in decision-making is not simply a matter of discerning what rules are being followed. For example, the principle "Be honest" might be understood and embodied in one way by an executive who is focused single-mindedly on increasing profits, and in quite another fashion by a colleague who has a broader vision of the responsibilities of business. "Being honest," then, would dictate different behavior patterns in similar situations for these two persons. They are acting out different stories with different dominant images. Hence they follow different hierarchies of values.

Each of us has a number of self-images, sometimes clashing ones, that provide meaning to our experience. Consciously—and often unconsciously—we select images (or pictures) of the sort of person we would like to become, and these images motivate and guide us toward life goals. We remember doing this quite openly as children, whether our master image was a favorite uncle (Uncle Bob), or a character from a novel (Tom Sawyer), or even a sports hero (Mickey Mantle). As adults we shy away from doing this as openly, but we still do it: Master Craftsman, King of the Business Mountain, Heir to the Kingdom of God, or Respected Leader of the Community. Sooner or later, we settle on a master image, that is, we accept one image as the dominant one to guide our life story. Once a person has a dominant image, a self-image that feels right, then his or her life begins to have some direction. Although the dominant image may change in the various stages of a life, it continues to bring order and coherence to a life. The self-image helps to shape emotions, actions, and intentions. Its guidance highlights certain character traits and mutes others.

IMAGES AND DOCTRINE

A Christian is one who guides his or her life by a central biblical *image*. Yet many Christians have persistently been taught that to be religious it was necessary to follow church *doctrine*. What is the connection between doctrine and images? The assumption in the discussion of images throughout the book is that the only way a doctrine can permeate and become the center of a life is through the "images" of that doctrine, that is, through images whose point is the same as the point of the doctrine.[6] For example, consider the doctrine of the atonement as it is stated in the Epistle to the Hebrews.

> ... he has made his appearance once and for all, now at the end of the last age, to do away with sin by sacrificing himself. Since men only die once, and after that comes judgment, so Christ, too, offers himself only once *to take the faults of many on himself,* and when he appears a second time, it will not be to deal with sin but to reward with salvation those who are waiting for him (Heb. 9:26-28).

The doctrine of the atonement as interpreted here has four key elements:

1. God and humankind are estranged, and this sin frustrates all genuine relationships among people.

2. Alienation is overcome and openness is restored.

3. The work of atonement is costly (Christ appears, "to do away with sin by sacrificing himself").

4. There is activity on the part of God, Christ, and us in the work of atonement.

The doctrine tells about a once-and-for-all event in history, but what does it mean to say it is *believed* by Christians today? James W. McClendon, Jr., in a very insightful analysis of the life stories of Martin Luther King, Jr., and Dag Hammarskjold, shows that although these men had no interest in presenting a formal statement of the doctrine, their vision was formed by images whose point is the point of the doctrine.

Martin Luther King, Jr. was a well-educated black pastor who first led the fight to end racial discrimination on public buses in Montgomery, Alabama, in 1955. In 1957 he moved to Atlanta and there became the first president of the Southern Christian Leadership Conference, and in that position he struggled to free blacks from racial injustice in major cities in the south as well as the north. In April 1968, he was killed by an assassin in Memphis, Tennessee. A Ph.D. in philosophical theology, King understood that although God is acting in history, that is all the more reason for humankind to take up the challenge of making this a more humane world. King interpreted life and circumstances in terms of the Bible. His master image seemed to center on the Exodus story in which Moses led the oppressed Hebrews out of Egypt where they were in bondage to the Pharaohs. He saw himself as another Moses, never to enter the promised land, but to have a glimpse of the freedom that would some day be commonplace to all his black brothers and sisters. The master image also entailed the story of Jesus (the New Moses), his sacrifice, and the cross, as he struggled to bring unity and harmony to the races despite personal costs.

Dag Hammarskjold was born to a distinguished Swedish family in 1905 and had the benefit of fine culture and an excellent education culminating in a Ph.D. in economics. He had a top post in the civil service in Sweden and served in the rebuilding effort of the European economy after World War II. In 1953 he was appointed Secretary-General of the United Nations and became a strong active leader for peace in the world. He took firm stands for peace in the Suez, Lebanon, and Cambodia early in his tenure. On September 18, 1961, while on a United Nations mission to the Congo, he was killed in a plane crash in Northern Rhodesia. Shortly after his death, his diary, later published as *Markings*,[7] came to light. In his diary he often interpreted the events of his life with a key image from the Bible. Experiencing untold personal suffering, Hammarskjold saw this as bound up with the suffering of Christ, and as a part of his mission to bring some measure of reconciliation to the world. His master image seems to have been the Cross, and he interpreted his experience with this image as he struggled for peace in the world.[8]

The *images* that guided these lives, for example, the Cross, Sacrifice, Servant of the Lord, etc., are only understood in light of the doctrine of the atonement and its work of restoration of unity among all peoples. Both King and Hammarskjold experienced great suffering in their struggles to realize some measure of unity among the races and the nations. The biblical images fleshed out the doctrine of the atonement so that it could provide the vision and the very lifeblood of their struggle for unity. Jesus tells us that as much as we participate in his life and death, we will also share in his resurrection. The image of the Cross, then, provided the vision that enables this sort of participation by King and Hammarskjold, and in turn this image enables them to be examples for us. We can be "moved" from one story of life to another story (perhaps the Christian one), by the powerful example of a rich and rewarding life.

SOME MAJOR BIBLICAL IMAGES

The Bible reveals to us the sort of person we are called to become and provides images of Jesus to guide our life story. In the words of the Second Letter of Paul to the Church at Corinth, we "grow brighter and brighter as we are turned into the image that we reflect" (2 Cor. 3:18). While it would be a major project to review even the central images in the Bible, it may be helpful to consider three images that articulate the self-understanding of Christians today.[9] Of course, readers may know of many other fruitful images in the Bible, and these are presented only by way of example.

A Pilgrim of the People of God

As a Pilgrim numbered among the people of God, you would see yourself on a journey, sometimes filled with joy, sometimes with sorrow, but always led on by faith. Harkening back to the ancient journey out of bondage in Egypt into the freedom of the Promised Land, this image taps deep forces welling up within us, forces that give intimations that life was meant to be more than what is presently experienced. The New Testament authors give us Moses as a model of faith (Heb. 11:23-29). From his story we know that there will be wilderness and hardship before reaching the Promised Land, but that the community will survive by the power of God's grace. For as Moses has promised, a new prophet has come to care for his people (Acts 3:22). By the life, death, and resurrection of Jesus, the Pilgrim is given renewed hope and love for the voyage (John 3:13-16). The vocation of the Pilgrim of the People of God is spelled out in 1 Peter 2:9-9: "to sing the praises of God who called you out of the darkness into his wonderful light." The challenge for the Pilgrim is to find ways, by the words and deeds of a life, to thank the Lord for his great gifts. Concern for the brethren, building up the community, using your talents to make the world more humane—these might be the agenda for the Pilgrim today. He or she is marked by idealism, generosity, and a restlessness that yearns for a world of peace through justice.

An Heir to the Kingdom of God

As an heir, you have a responsibility to continue the good name of the family, and to preserve the values and way of life that have nurtured you. In the case of an Heir to the Kingdom of God, your hallmark is stated well by Paul in his Letter to the Romans: the Kingdom of God "means righteousness and peace and joy brought by the Holy Spirit" (Rom. 14:17). (See also Gal. 5:21 and 1 Cor. 6:9-10).

In trying to portray the impact of Jesus' words and deeds on the community, the New Testament writers looked for images in their Hebrew heritage. They often used the imagery of Genesis to describe the Kingdom of God inaugurated by the words and deeds of Jesus. Just as Genesis told of the beginning of the universe, so the New Testament writers spoke of another fresh start, a transvaluation of values that came with the person of Jesus Christ.

Understanding yourself as an Heir to the Kingdom of God accents the fact that you are prepared to defend this vision and way of life, even in the face of the possible adverse consequences. Although realizing that God's Kingdom is not finally present on this earth, and that it will come only in God's good time, the vision and the values of the Bible render the "Heir" more sensitive to injustices, and spurs him or her on to risk personal position to advance the Master's way of life. Matthew's Sermon on the Mount makes the challenge abundantly clear: speaking out against social injustice, standing for the rights of the poor and elderly, etc. (See Matt. 5:3-10).

Servant of the Lord

Understanding yourself as a Servant of the Lord might mean that you see yourself as a person like all others, thrust into the hopes and cares of this world, and yet with a vocation to realize God's love and justice on this earth. The Gospel stories portray a vivid picture of the Christian community's belief in the ultimate significance of the suffering, death, and resurrection of Jesus. The paradox is that although Jesus claimed great authority, a fact denoted by the Messianic title Son of Man, he shaped his Messianic role in a new way. He was to be the suffering Servant of God. "For the Son of Man himself did not come to be served but to serve . . ." (Mark 10:45).

Jesus assumed the form of a servant, and gave his life so that others might live. To describe his mission of service, Jesus quotes Isaiah 61:1-2: "He has sent me to bring the good news to the poor, to proclaim liberty to captives and to the blind new sight, to set the downtrodden free . . ." (Luke 4:18). He was "the man for others" (Mark 2:15-17). As a result of his openness to God's will, even unto death, (Mark 8:31) a new community was formed to follow after him, sharing his way of life and celebrating his presence. This community has a future phase (Matt. 13:41), but the lives of its members on this earth stand as a witness to his sustaining presence.

The New Testament exhorts the followers of Christ to follow the Master's way of service to others (Mark 10:41-44). The Second Letter to the Corinthians outlines some of the character traits that are evoked and encouraged by the image of Servant. "We prove we are God's servants by our purity, knowledge, patience and kindness; by a spirit of holiness, by a love free from affectation; by the word of truth . . ., by being armed with the weapons of righteousness . . ." (2 Cor. 6:6-7).

TAKING ON A MASTER IMAGE FROM THE BIBLE

To live as a Christian means, among other things, that some of the great biblical images are used to interpret experience and guide the progress of a life, images such as Pilgrim of the People of God, Heir to the Kingdom of God, Servant of the Lord, etc. A life and its circumstances are interpreted, and actions guided, by these core images.

How is it that we come to take on a master image from the Bible? Jesus used stories to communicate his way of life. Consider the parable of the Prodigal Son spoken of in Chapter 1. As the words of the parable are read to us we are allowed to enter into the story. All kinds of experiences may be evoked: the joy the young man must have had when his father gave him the inheritance, the great sights he must have seen in his travels, the remorse he felt when the money ran out, and finally, the pain of hunger he experienced when things really got tough. Then the story goes on to say that the young man decides to return home, realizing that at home even his father's servants eat better than he does. The parable tells of the son's being sighted in the distance by the father. We see the young man returning home; we experience his reluctance, and perhaps even fear at facing his father. Now, at this point, we think we know how the story will end. From our past, we have an image of "father" as someone who is fair but also just, so we assume that the father will take the son back, but will require that he make amends for his carousing. Yet it is precisely here that the parable makes its point, it gives us *a new standpoint, a new master image to govern our experience.* It does this by depicting the father in quite unexpected terms: celebrating, unconditionally forgiving, and rejoicing over the return of the fallen heir. If we accept the father in this new way, then we may have to change our own self-images, for we too would then want to be compassionate and generous.

It may be helpful to consider briefly a way of understanding how images give expression to all that we "see." When we listen to the parable of the Prodigal Son our experience is already shaped by the story we are living out and the set of images that go to make up that story. As we hear the parable, *before the ending comes,* we might have the kind of process going that is portrayed in the upper level of Table 3.1. Here the reader's self-image of being just and fair colors the way the reader projects the father's behavior in the story. So the image of a just and fair father governs the response to the son: the father is relieved that the son is home, but angry that he has been such a scoundrel. The father will exact a punishment for the son's irresponsible revelry, and we take it that this is the way we should always act as well.

At the end of the parable, however, we are given a new image, the unconditionally loving father. Now the parable, with this new image governing the experience, might start the sort of process portrayed in the lower level of Table 3.1 (below the double line). The experience of the father is one of joy and delight, and the son will be the beneficiary of gifts beyond his wildest imaginings. The point of the parable is that God the Father loves us much more than we could ever deserve, and we ought to respond to his love with lives of care and compassion for his people. Thus the reader is given a new self-image, a master image to guide a life story. For example, in this instance the new master image might be Heir to the Kingdom of God.

Table 3.1. The Controlling Role of Images.

Experience →	Image →	Insight →	Concept or Formulation of Insight →	Guide for Life
1) Feelings of fear, hunger, and remorse on the part of the Son.	Picture of a caring but *fair* Father, a *just* man.	Insight into the course of action open to the just and fair Father.	The Son will work for the Father to pay back the debt. He will live with the hired hands.	I will be *just* and *fair* in all my dealings with others, just as God the Father is with me.
2) Sighting of the Son by the Father.				
3) Feelings of *relief* and *anger* on the part of the Father.				
1) Feelings of fear, hunger, and remorse on the part of the Son.	Picture of a Father who lavishes love on his children without regard for merit.	Insight into the course of action open for an extraordinarily loving Father.	The Son will receive incalculable unmerited gifts upon his return home.	I will be *caring* and *compassionate* imitating in a small way the love the Father showers on all his people. I now understand myself as an "Heir to the Kingdom of God."
2) Sighting of the Son by the Father.				
3) Feelings of great joy that the "lost is found" and the "dead is alive" on the part of the Father.				

The strength of the parable is that it draws the hearer into a new world, provides a new story and set of images to govern experience. In effect, it says, "Try on this new way of looking at things, use these new images to interpret your experience, and see if life does not ring true." The parable draws one into a new world and offers intimations that it might be the true world, but only in the living of the life is this ascertained. The movement toward belief occurs when we get the feeling that the loving and compassionate father is the right way to be, when we adopt this image as our master image. Only when we start becoming caring and compassionate can we say we are "becoming a Christian." The parable is a particularly appropriate vehicle to convey the message of Jesus, because it moves us from the familiar (a young man sowing his wild oats, a hard-working brother, a farm scene, etc.) to the unfamiliar (the Kingdom of God and its values, e.g., unmerited love). A key point here is that this movement takes place through a story and a set of images; we instinctively feel comfortable listening to a good story because we are all living a story, that is, human experience has a basic narrative quality.

A story tells about movement from here to there and all the ups and downs, sidetracks, and dead ends that are involved in a life. Believing is not a once-and-for-all thing; it has moments of darkness as well as of insight. There are set-backs as well as discoveries. Believing is a story. We Christians are each writing stories of faith as we struggle to find light in our experience as perceived through the images of the Scriptures.

SOME IMAGES GUIDING LIFE IN THE BUSINESS WORLD

Business organizations come to have a life of their own, that is, they have traditions, history, and standard operating procedures. There are goals, and assumed standards for what constitutes good performance as well as bad. The organization comes to have a sphere of influence, which has been carved out through past practice. All of these factors go into what we are calling a story. One of the ways to gain insight into the business story is to ask about the images that seem to be guiding life in the business world. The key images of a corporation—not the images of the public relations department, but the ones that actually motivate lives and systems—reveal to a newcomer what is actually considered worthwhile in that organization. Similar to the situation in churches, universities, and most other institutions, the images that actually motivate persons in business may not be the ones that are publicly proclaimed.

By knowing the images that seem to be shaping the lives of persons in an organization, we can gain further insight into their goals, motivation, values, and dominant character traits. Knowing a significant image in a life story helps us see what holds that life together. Based on work with people in business and the biographies and autobiographies of business executives, there seem to be six types of dominant images. Seldom is any one person perfectly matched with an ideal type; most persons guide their business lives with two or more of the images. While "typing" a person can be hazardous, in that the uniqueness of persons resists neat categorization, it is at least a beginning in the attempt to understand the very complex phenomenon of the business world.

Too much of what we "know" about business motivation stems from literary and artistic sources, i.e., novelists, playwrights, and filmmakers, who are sometimes biased against anything commercial or industrial. While we recognize the importance of an *adversary* culture to the business world, artistic license seldom provides the most accurate analysis. For example, Budd Schulberg, an important writer in the 1940s and 1950s, published his opinions of the business world in a book called *What Makes Sammy Run?*[10] It is a bitterly satiric novel about a hard-driving, upwardly mobile, and self-centered person, who easily forgets friends and readily steps on the weak as he reaches for the next rung on the career ladder. For many who reject business values, Sammy represents the qualities essential for business success: "Wealth and power are everything, even if the cost is ethics, loyalty, love, a sense of good taste . . . anything!" While it is true that *some* people in business are "Sammies," the extreme characterization of Sammy is unacceptable as a norm, partly because it demonstrably does not describe the motivations and tactics of most business people, and partly because such an image is counterproductive. Sammy is so distasteful that no one would suggest, let alone attempt, to integrate biblical images or values with that kind of person. The Sammy image implies that business and its managers are irredeemable, a conclusion that is contrary to this book's purpose.

Not all intellectuals have been as critical of business people as Schulberg. It is interesting to note that in *The Communist Manifesto* of Marx and Engels, business people are characterized as having "created more massive and more colossal productive forces than have all preceding generations together."[11] Also, they have "accomplished wonders far surpassing Egyptian pyramids, Roman aqueducts, and Gothic cathedrals."[12] This declaration is more generous, more lavish in praise, than we might expect from business people themselves. Of course we have to remember that Marx and Engels go on in the *Manifesto* to forecast the early demise of the profession. Business people would probably reply: "With friends like that, who needs enemies!"

But to return to the question: What images predominate in the lives of business people? Six images have been observed in the business lives studied here. Table 3.2 summarizes those observations. The names of the six types, while not always original, are an attempt to depict the sort of person referred to in each case.[13] It should be clear that the images are *descriptive* at this point. There is no intent to say that any of the images are incompatible with a master image from the Bible. In fact, the next section will show how most of these images might be compatible with a controlling biblical image.

A theological premise of the presentation of the six types of images is that all persons are inclined to an excessive self-regard. As Reinhold Niebuhr said, "The doctrine of original sin is the only empirically verifiable doctrine of the Christian faith."[14] The images attempt to capture the ambiguity in life, the relative goodness and relative evil that may be present. They are presented as exaggerations to draw out the implications that may be latent in the guiding images of most persons. Few would recognize themselves in *one* of the six images, but many might see their own self-images in some subtle combination of those presented. Finally, there is no intention to say that persons in the business profession are the only ones inclined to sinful self-interest. A similar analysis could be offered for lawyers, doctors, politicians, clerics, professors, and any other profession devised by humankind.

The Millionaire

With this self-image guiding one's life in the business world, the primary objective of one's activities would be to accrue wealth, "making a million" as the image tells us. Higher salaries and greater stock dividends can buy the good things of life—vacations, fine homes, yachts, luxury cars, servants, etc. These are what many call the "perks" of financial success.

It seems that this image probably guided the stories of the persons of the "Horatio Alger" type. Alger's novels generally focus on a poor boy who reaches financial success through persistent effort and tireless attention to the job.[15] Men like Thomas Mellon, John Jacob Astor, and John D. Rockefeller are classic examples of how perseverance and ingenuity can transform a life-style from rags to riches. Although this sort of person often makes large donations to charity, the style of their organizations and personal life often displays little concern for the more humanistic character traits such as compassion and idealism.

The strength of this self-image is that it provides an enormous amount of psychic energy, which is translated into motivation to develop the business community and increase profits. The enterprising spirit unlocked with this motivation has opened up new markets, created untold number of jobs, and offered the possibility of a more humane life to countless millions. The weakness of this sort of person is that the "quality of life" issues often become overshadowed in the relentless quest for economic growth. This sort of person may never stop and consider what is really worthwhile in life.

Although most people today want to enjoy the good things of life, few are single-mindedly focused on accumulating wealth and living in luxury. On the contrary, some top executives live a relatively spartan existence and display little interest in enjoying the luxuries that their wealth might provide.

King of the Mountain

King of the Mountain is a popular children's game where the object is to get to the top of a hill and remain there alone, fending off all competitors by physical force. If one is not on top in power over the contenders, then one is subordinate to whichever of the others is on top—so the logic of the game goes. Using this image to articulate one's self-understanding would reinforce a set of character traits centered on being tough, competent, and demanding. Maccoby uses the term "jungle fighter" to discuss a type similar to the King of the

Table 3.2. Master Images in the Business World.

Image	Millionaire	King of the Mountain	Craftsperson	Company Person	Gamesman	Captain on the Bridge
Goal in the Business World	To accumulate capital and live in luxury.	To wield power over others.	To see the job well done.	To help people develop, and to protect company interests.	To be a winner at whatever one does.	To maintain control by appeasing interest groups.
Most Developed Character Traits	Persistence and ingenuity	Toughness and cleverness	Fidelity to standards	Loyalty	Coolness under stress and ability to solve problems.	Flexibility
Least Developed Character Traits	Sensitivity to the needs of others and justice.	Compassion	Flexibility	Independence from company and creativity.	Intimacy and generosity	Idealism

Mountain. He notes that there are few of these types in high positions today, although their kind often were the ones that built our industrial complex.

However it does seem that the drive to be on top is still present, although in subtle form. We see it in a need for recognition by peers and associates: "He made it to the top, so he must be good." We all know people like this, whether they be university professors, surgeons, politicians, or business people. This recognition is a psychic reward that money cannot buy. Others might see the drive as a need to have power and influence over people and resources.

The strength of this type of person is that in the quest to make it to the top the person does not hesitate to practice the self-discipline involved with being a leader and developing skills and competence. Most persons recognize that their best efforts are elicited only when there is a vision and an objective, and this sort of individual may set that kind of tone in an office. The weakness of this type is that "getting to the top" seems to be an end in itself, and the dignity and value of other people may be overshadowed in the rush for "success." Compassion and care for others may be neglected.

The Master Craftsperson

A craftsperson is one who understands him- or herself in terms of doing a task or work of art well. This sort of person takes pleasure in performing according to high standards. The craftsperson is creative and tends to have a full and rich family life, but often finds corporate "politics" distasteful. This person more than likely would be viewed as a loner in the business world. Chemists, physicists, mathematicians, and accountants are perhaps the most obvious examples.

The strength of this type is that there is emphasis on the quality of performance, and that work is not drudgery but actually a delight. The sort of person would probably be happy as a farmer, small business person, or a skilled worker in one of the trades. However, the craftsperson may find participating in corporate life frustrating, since this type is not easily drawn into team efforts. He or she would probably have little interest in acquiring the political skills that are prerequisite to forming the coalitions that may be needed to reshape corporate life. Without these skills the influence of the craftsperson in humanizing the corporate world is not likely to be significant.

The Company Person

Understanding yourself as the custodian of the long-term interests of the company, and as a humanizing agent in the firm, means that your self-image is the Company Person. Frequently found in the middle management level, this sort of person comes to identify almost completely with the company, learns the rules of the game well, and generously assists fellow workers in the firm.

Joseph Schumpeter, the historian of economic analyses, points out that the "prizes and penalties" of the business class are relatively simple to understand: "Going up and going down means making and losing money."[16] And any number can play the game according to the rules, as long as the players have something that potential customers may want. This is the commercial calculus of sellers and buyers.

To the adherents of this view, motivation stems from participating in a game with rules that are sensible and rational in practical, everyday affairs. The term "rationality" refers to the whole process of monetary accounting: rational cost-profit calculations, balance sheet and operating statement, etc. Here business people have a highly effective tool to measure "how well" the enterprise is doing. Unlike the Church, the State, and the University, business has a "bottom line" that is a sensible, tangible, universally accepted (within the business fraternity) index of success or failure. Business people stake out a claim to a discrete segment of human affairs, i.e., buying and selling of relatively measurable goods and services. In this view, business leaves to other institutions such as the Church, the State, and the University the more comprehensive questions about human affairs. In return, the business community expects a minimum of interference.

The Company Person's strength is that he or she is loyal to people and to the institution.[17] The traits often underdeveloped, however, are independence and creativity. This sort of person would be unlikely to challenge the status quo, since the institution seems to provide the security so essential in a human life.

The Gamesman

A more recent characterization of a business person is that of the flamboyant Gamesman who relishes "calculated risks" and is fasci-

nated by new techniques and methods. This business person is unlike
earlier types, who might say: "I made it; I can spend it"—often on
stately mansions in Newport, but just as often on municipal libraries
(Carnegie) or colleges and universities (Stanfords and Rockefellers).
This type is also unlike a post-World War II business person who saw
efficiency and organizations through the micrometer and the stolid
engineering worldview. The gamesman is excited by the business
contest (Johnny Unitas or Bart Starr?).

> Unlike other business types, he is energized to compete not because he
> wants to build an empire, not for riches, but rather for fame, glory, the exhil-
> aration of running his team and of gaining victories.[18]

Peeling away the athletic hoopla, these gamesmen, similar to the
real Unitas or Bart Starr, are deadly serious about their "work-
play." They pride themselves on their competence, hard work, and
challenges.

The reader will find some of the traits of the gamesman in the story
of Robert C. Wilson, the head of the Memorex Corporation. The
author of the article, Eleanor Johnson Tracey, uses a title, "The
Loneliness of the Master Turnaround Man,"[19] that suggests both the
drive and the pathos of a person so motivated. Wilson prides "himself
on being able to manage anything," but he is "in a quest that never
ends." He is driven by his own conception of what a superior business
person and manager ought to be.

That restless philosophy impels him to prove himself over and
over again as he moves from industry to industry, job to job, in a continuing test of his abilities. He has no time to savor success. His sense
of accomplishment comes from leaving each business better than he
found it, moving up and moving on. But there is often a price to pay
for this obsessive nomadic life and its unceasing quest.[20] For Wilson
and many like him the price may be few "real" friends, no home with
roots, and, for some, the loss of their marriages and families.

Maccoby's work documents that the Gamesman is the type at the
top of many of the most influential businesses at the present time.
Seeking new ways to expand this image to include more of the human
values (generosity, compassion) is one of the challenges of this book.

The Captain on the Bridge

Finally, there is the image of the patient, long-suffering business person who is besieged on all sides by powerful interest groups: customers, consumer groups, employees, and unions; stockholders, bankers, dealers, and suppliers; competitors, regulatory agencies, public opinion, and critics. This sort of person survives by appeasing each one of these groups to a certain extent, as much as he or she has to, in order to keep peace and ensure that the firm can continue to operate. Like the parent on a hot day with four restless children and three ice cream bars, this executive has some social power to decide "who gets what," but it is often a thankless task.

The strength of this type of person is that he or she knows how to "give and take." If a powerful lobby for the elderly presents some demands to the company, for example, the Captain on the Bridge will know how to meet their concerns. The weakness of this type is that he or she may never form convictions and act on them. It seems that there are some things that are right and good to do whether any interest group can compel accountability or not. For example, a company should strive to avoid what it believes to be harmful pollution, even if local laws will tolerate the practice, and no interest group is protesting.

One of the functions of the New Testament is to provide a vision that builds ideals that motivate action and sensitize persons to the ever-present injustices of an organization. With a Christian vision, the Captain on the Bridge will be continually nurtured by lofty ideals, and will be motivated to use his or her power to realize Christian values in the business world.

HOW MASTER IMAGES SHAPE A LIFE

After listing the strengths and weaknesses of each of the six dominant images guiding life stories in the business world, the challenge then becomes to show a way to accent their strengths and mute their weaknesses. It is to that task that we now turn in the sections which follow.

It may be helpful at this point to consider some examples of how master images play a key role in shaping life stories. John Ehrlichman, one of Richard Nixon's chief staff officers, is an example of a person who, although having immense power, never consciously appropriated a story. Reflecting on his fall from power, in an interview with *New York* magazine, Ehrlichman made the startling statement:

> I'm more and more realizing that I lived 50 years of my life without ever really coming to grips with the very basic question of what is and is not important to me, what is and is not right and wrong, what is and is not valuable and worthwhile . . . I've begun a process that my own kids began almost from the beginning . . . developing my own sense of values. I'm a beginner . . .[21]

Here is a fifty-year-old man, recently dismissed from one of the most powerful positions in the White House, saying that he had never taken time out to reflect on what was really of value in this life. The significant point here is that just because Ehrlichman never conciously reflected on the thrust and direction of his life—his "story" —does not mean he was not living out a story. He had a set of images that got his juices flowing, and this imaginative context set the stage for all his deliberations and his enormous expenditure of energy in the service of the presidential administration.

What Ehrlichman is telling us is that he never consciously appropriated his story, but just "bought into" the prevailing understanding of what is real, appropriate, worthwhile, and what constitutes good and bad performance. He was conditioned into this standpoint, this set of images. To discern with certainty the dominant images that controlled John Ehrlichman's life story, we would need an autobiography and a careful analysis. Yet it is possible, on the basis of his public statements, to project that the images that may very likely have controlled his story were a combination of King of the Mountain and Captain on the Bridge. Any course of action that would "get the job done" without adverse press or bad public relations would be acceptable. If it "worked well," it was acceptable, and there was no need to ask "Is it true, or moral, or wrong?" Keeping in power was the name of the game. That standpoint ultimately ended in failure for John Ehrlichman, and, quite courageously, he tells us that he is now searching for some more suitable values to guide his life. In our terms, he is looking for a story that is richer and fuller than his professional story. He needs a place to stand to assess that professional story.

For purposes of contrast, consider a hypothetical example. Imagine a successful business executive, Mr. S, who candidly says that he may still have a long way to travel on his journey of becoming a Christian. Yet the images that set the context for all his deliberations and guide his life are consciously Christian. He understands himself as an Heir to the Kingdom of God. This is his master image. He speaks of his task of preaching the Kingdom of God by his deeds in the corporate world, and of the focal role the parable of the talents plays in his life.[22] Consider this simple example of how images can govern experience and serve as a guide for life. Compare Mr. S's course of action to another top executive, Mr. A, who has an image of the business world as a place where only the fittest survive and where the name of the game is increasing company profits at any expense. (Mr. A is above the double line in Table 3.3, while Mr. S is below.)

Mr. S's sense of reality is governed by an image of a gracious God who expects his children to return his love by their lives of generous service. This image influences the way he perceives the incompetent manager—with frustration yet compassion. The vision governed by the image sets the context for the way he finally resolves the problem.

Mr. A, with the master image, King of the Mountain, has a sense of reality that says that the only issue at stake in the corporate world is: "Can an employee enhance company profits?" A weak link in the organization must be replaced. There is no room in this perspective for certain "human" factors—feelings are selectively screened out and hard-headedness and efficiency reign supreme. Again, the image controls the way Mr. A perceives the manager—with anger and intolerance—and it influences the final resolution—firing the incompetent and replacing him with a hard taskmaster. The images of the story set the vision and determine what is seen and valued in analyzing a situation.

Consider another example of how master images shape life stories. The cover of *The New Yorker* magazine of September 6, 1976, captured the dilemma of the contemporary business person. It pic-

Table 3.3. A Contrast of Controlling Images.

Experience	→	Controlling Image	→	Insight	→	Formulation of Insight
A plant in the corporation is losing money because of an incompetent manager. Feelings of anger and intolerance towards the manager on the part of the president.		Picture of a company president as "King of the Mountain." Staying on top is the name of the game. The profit and loss sheet is in control. Mr. A is to become a successful company president. (Master image is King of the Mountain)		Insight into the course of action open to a shrewd business person trying to maximize profits.		Fire the incompetent manager and hire a tough, no-nonsense man who understands profit and loss.
A plant in the corporation is losing money because of an incompetent manager. Feelings of frustration and compassion for the manager on the part of the president.		Picture of a God who has given Mr. S many talents and who challenges him to make the world more humane in his role as company president. Mr. S is to become an Heir to the Kingdom of God (master image).		Insight into the course of action open to a Son of God gifted with power and talent.		Offer the manager a less responsible position, and hire a competent manager who can run the plant at a profit and yet deal with the workers while respecting their human dignity.

tured a bewildered man standing in the center of the cover surrounded by sixteen arrows which represented some of the interest groups and concerns vying for his attention. Included were such things as: "solar energy," "the work ethic," "sound fiscal policy," "market reports," "Judeo-Christian tradition," "miles per gallon," "offshore oil," and "corporate responsibility." The cover seemed to be telling us that business persons today are bombarded by a host of interest groups and significant concerns, all of which claim to have a say in decisions.

If the gentleman looked befuddled as he peered out at us from *The New Yorker* cover, did he not have the right to be? Our first response might be to wonder how he even survives under such intense pressure. Because he is open to a whole host of influences beyond the mere concern for the profit and loss columns on the balance sheet, he has a more difficult task than his narrowly focused colleagues. Yet on further reflection, we can find ways for our harassed executive to be both competent and humane.

A decision maker today has to attend to a great number of factors in a very complex business world. Yet if our business person is consciously living a story, then he or she has the skills to order and give proper expression to most of the claims made. If there is no center or focus to the life of the business executive, no master image that brings unity to the array of other images guiding a life, then indeed there will be befuddlement at the very least. He or she will be making decisions simply on the basis of what will work best without sufficient reference to standards or values or the sort of person he or she is becoming.

It may be helpful to elaborate how a master image might function in the lives of our troubled executives. If they are like most of us, they have a number of images of themselves, pictures of the sort of person they would like to become, and these images serve to guide and motivate them toward their goals. By now in their lives, our executives have probably settled on a constellation of images that they judge will lead toward fulfillment. These images will shape their stories. The key problem is to have a master image that orders and brings together all the other images from the various stories that comprise a life, and for a Christian the master image will be a central biblical image.

To illustrate the way a master image might be operative in a harassed executive's life story, let us assume that the female executive, in this case, has three core stories: The business story, the wife story, and the Christian story. Assume that for each story our executive has an image of the sort of person she is (or would like to be): In the business story, she is a Company Person; in the wife story, she is a Wife and Mother; and in the Christian story, she is an Heir to the Kingdom of God. She takes the Christian story to be her central story and the image, an Heir to the Kingdom of God, to be her master image.

Her master image puts limits on the way she lives out the other two images; it provides a standpoint from which to see values that are to inform the business story and the family story. For example, consider how the input "the work ethic" could find its way into the business story. Let us assume that the work ethic is a particularly strong feature in our executive's company. The work ethic is characterized by thrift, hard work, and stoic perseverance on the job which is rewarded by high salary and success. Since our executive is striving to be a Company Person, one who embodies all that the company stands for and who is ever vigilant for the long-range welfare of the firm, the work ethic could easily take over her life. She could find herself a prisoner of her role, her *primary* identification of herself being the Company Person.

Yet with a master image, an Heir to the Kingdom of God, there would be constraints on the influence of the image the Company Person. The Christian story would provide the images to confront the reality of the corporate world with its monetary reward system and its appeal to some of the less noble character traits of humankind. Our executive could still be exceedingly competent and successful; she could be paid well and enjoy the good things of life, but she would have an expanded vision of what her life is all about, and she would have the freedom to take a stand against some of the expectations of her corporate role. She would not be trapped in this corporate role. Again, consider the influence the inputs of "sound fiscal policy," "market reports," "miles per gallon," "offshore oil," and "corporate responsibility" might have on the decision-making process of our executive striving to be a Company Person. If she were striving to be simply a Company Person, she would very likely be concerned about how all these terms translate into financial data relating to profits for her company. Yet if the image Company Person is influenced by the master image an Heir to the Kingdom of God, the concerns would be expanded in at least two ways:

1. The Christian story would be a stimulus to develop a social vision, an ordering of social priorities leading to a more humane world, and the executive would see her firm as instrumental in advancing this vision.

2. The Christian story would enable our executive to see herself as accountable to all groups affected by corporate decisions, not just to those groups that can muster the clout to compel accountability. She would thus ascertain who would be affected by corporate decisions, and initiate dialogue with them in order to adjudicate legitimate competing claims.[23]

Thus the master image, an Heir to the Kingdom of God, would have enabled our executive to expand her understanding of corporate self-interest to include consideration of the long-range goals of society, and accountability to all groups affected by corporate policy. We are not unaware that implementing these two new factors into a policy process is fraught with difficulty. Yet a Christian sees that this is the agenda. It will, to be sure, entail much more discussion. No doubt, more sophisticated means for providing data on the social impact of corporate decisions must be developed. The next ten chapters present cases of actual situations that portray the ambiguity and the magnitude of the challenge.

Notes

1 It should be clear that we are not claiming that legal education poses precisely the same challenge as theological education. Theological education hopes to call forth a change in the whole person and to provide a constellation of images that determines the coherence and integrity of that person. Legal education has much more modest goals. For a succinct discussion, see James Moody Gustafson, "Theological Education as Professional Education," *Theological Education* Vol. 5 (Spring 1969), pp. 243-61.

2 See Harold J. Berman, *The Interaction of Law and Religion* (Nashville, Tenn.: Abingdon, 1974).

3 Berman was a lecturer at the 1975 Case Study Institute Summer Workshop spon-
    sored by the Association of Theological Schools and the Boston Theological
    Institute.

4 The term "passing over" was first used by Gandhi, although John Dunne has giv-
    en it fuller meaning in his work on autobiography and theology. See John Dunne,
    A Search for God in Time and Memory (New York: Macmillan, 1969).

5 Stanley Hauerwas, "The Self as Story," *Vision and Virtue* (Notre Dame, Ind.:
    Fides, 1974), p. 69.

6 This discussion follows James Wm. McClendon, Jr., *Biography as Theology*,
    (Nashville, Tenn.: Abingdon, 1974). See pp. 99-108.

7 Translated by Leif Sjoberg and W. H. Auden (New York: Knopf, 1965).

8 Chris Argyris, Professor of Education and Organizational Behavior at Harvard
    University, has shown quite persuasively that most people do not in fact act accord-
    ing to their espoused principles. Argyris discusses the problem in terms of the "dis-
    crepancy between the espoused theory and theory-in-use." Use of the term "master
    image guiding a life story" is intended to raise consciousness on what is actually
    giving shape to the actions of a life. For example, in Hammarskjold's case, know-
    ing his master image was the Cross helps understand why he did what he did.
    For Argyris' presentation, see Donald A. Schon and Chris Argyris, *Theory in Prac-
    tice* (San Francisco: Jossey-Bass, 1974); and Chris Argyris, *Increasing Leadership
    Effectiveness* (New York: John Wiley & Sons, 1976).

9 For a description of ninety-six images of the Church, see Paul S. Minear, *Images of
    the Church in the New Testament* (Philadelphia, Pa.: Westminster Press, 1960).
    This book follows his discussion in its presentation of the three images.

10 Budd Schulberg, *What Makes Sammy Run?* (New York: Random House, 1941).

11 *Essential Works of Marxism,* ed. Arthur P. Mendel, (New York: Bantam Books,
    1971), p. 17.

12 *Ibid.,* p. 16.

13 We are particularly indebted to Michael Maccoby's work, *The Gamesman: The
    New Corporate Leaders* (New York: Simon & Schuster, 1976). Maccoby's typol-
    ogy includes four character types: (1) The Jungle Fighter, one who will do most
    anything to look good; (2) The Craftsman, one who takes pride in the work; (3) The
    Gamesman, one who thrives on a fast-paced, competitive game; and (4) The Com-
    pany Man, one who is concerned about the long-range value of the institution.

14 Reinhold Niebuhr, *Man's Nature and His Communities* (New York: Scribner,
    1965), p. 24.

15 Horatio Alger, *Struggling Upward, and Other Works* (New York: Crown Pub-
    lishers, 1945). This volume is a collection of most of Horatio Alger's writings, in-

cluding *Ragged Dick* and *Street Life In New York.*

16 Joseph A. Schumpeter, *Capitalism, Socialism, and Democracy* (New York: Harper & Brothers, 1950), p. 73.

17 The classic work on the company person is William H. Whyte, Jr., *The Organization Man* (New York: Simon & Schuster, 1956).

18 Michael Maccoby, *The Gamesman: The New Corporate Leaders* (New York: Simon & Schuster, 1976), p. 100.

19 Eleanor Johnson Tracey, "The Loneliness of the Master Turnaround Man," *Fortune,* Vol. XCIII, No. 2 (February, 1976), p. 118.

20 *Ibid.*

21 Quoted in Richard Reeves, "What Ehrlichman Really Thought of Nixon," *New York* Vol. 9, No. 19 (May 10, 1976), p. 42.

22 Theologians will note that the stress on defining a Christian as "a person who has a master image from the Bible shaping his or her story" allows for the case of a *Christian* who has not yet realized an appropriate external expression for his or her faith. This is an improvement on a type of liberation theology that, in its great stress on social involvement, seems completely to neglect the interior life of faith. For a discussion of some of these issues, see John C. Haughey, ed., *The Faith That Does Justice: Examining The Christian Sources For Social Change* (New York: Paulist Press, 1977). This volume has excellent essays by John R. Donahue, a professor of New Testament at Vanderbilt University; Avery Dulles, a professor at Catholic University, and others.

23 There are some business firms providing outstanding leadership in this area, for example, Cummins Engine Company of Columbus, Indiana. A number of knowledgeable scholars in business are advocating the sort of change we have outlined. Leonard Silk, a fellow of the National Association of Business Economists and a member of the editorial board of *The New York Times* sums up the case: "In the past the essence of American business power has been ideological—that is, it has provided the value conceptions and set the limits upon what the nation is doing or trying to do. Those conceptions must now be made more humane and sensitive to the needs and aspirations of all people, but especially to those at the bottom of society." In "Business Power Today and Tomorrow," *Daedalus* Wol. 98 (Winter 1969), p. 188. This entire issue of *Daedalus* is devoted to exploring whether business can and should assume new roles to meet the social crises of our age. See also Leonard Silk and David Vogel, *Ethics and Profit* (New York: Simon & Schuster, 1976); Robert Heilbroner, *The Limits of American Capitalism* (New York: Norton, 1966), and *Business Civilization and Decline* (New York: Norton, 1976). For another survey of the problem, see *The Future of the Corporation,* ed. Herman Kahn (New York: Mason & Lipscomb, 1974). This volume includes essays by Peter Drucker, Daniel Bell, Herman Kahn, and others.

Part II

Exercises
for the
Christian Business Person

"You're always wearing your jumpsuit, but you never jump."

Just as a good athlete would never dream of going out on the playing field without first going through a rigorous training period, so the Christian business person needs some challenging exercises to develop the skill and the discipline required to be faithful to the Christian values. The ancient Greeks stressed that the virtuous life is acquired by developing character, that is, it is an art cultivated over time through training. These exercises are provided to assist in that training.

A Christian is one who is trying to live a Christian story, and this story informs all the other stories appropriated by a person—business, husband, wife, Republican, Democrat, etc. Biblical images inform all the other images that are guiding a life, that is, Heir to the Kingdom of God informs the Company Person, for example.

THE USE OF CASES

The next ten chapters consist of ten cases that call for decisions both about how one is to understand some data, and about how one is to act in a given situation. The cases portray actual situations that have happened to real people, although individuals and situations are often disguised to protect the privacy of persons involved. The cases have been written by trained case writers.[1] The aim is to have the reader decide the point at issue in the case and, more importantly, see how the values in question in the case might apply to his or her own personal life and circumstances.

After each case there is a section titled "Reflections on the Story."

These "Reflections" include four parts: some key issues for discussion, an analysis of the case, an application of biblical images, and suggested readings. Readers should analyze the case on their own *before* reading the reflections provided in the book.

One of the best ways to do these exercises is in a group with a leader who has had some experience with the case method approach. However, the exercises can be done profitably by individual readers working on their own. The first step is to read the case carefully, perhaps two or three times. Make an outline of the central figures in the case, their dominant character traits, and the images controlling their stories. List the values that each person seems to be defending. Mull over the case, read some of the suggested readings should you want to pursue the question in more depth, and then list the significant broader issues in question. Now, if you are part of a group using the book, you will want to engage in a vigorous discussion of the case where you can pool insights and try out hunches. In the very process of articulating a position, sometimes we learn about our own most treasured values. The case discussion affords readers the opportunity to try on new self-images, and to interact with others who see things quite differently. Finally, each person should bring closure to the question and decide. After deciding, it is helpful to ask yourself explicitly, "What does this case say about me, my lifestyle, and my life story?"

Each "Reflections on the Story" includes some suggested topics for discussion and an analysis of each case. There may be times when readers will disagree with this presentation, and perhaps devise a more complete and comprehensive reflection. The material presented in the book is not necessarily designed to be the only correct answer. The analyses provided here are simply one way of focusing the material; they offer a *process* for developing a correct answer for any case a person might encounter. If the reader takes an analysis in another direction and comes to another conclusion, he or she should be prepared to offer the evidence and rationale for such a move. What do you see as the relevant data? Why? How do you interpret the data? What are the values at issue, and what values are likely to be preserved with each of the possible alternatives? Finally, what should be done in the case, and what would *you* do, were you a principal character?

Our format for presenting the case analysis follows the decision-making model presented in Chapter 1.

1. Ascertain the data.
2. Interpret and clarify the data.
3. Discern the values in conflict in the case.
4. Consider the alternatives and make a decision.

THE CASE TEACHER

Although the cases that follow can be done by individual readers working on their own, a more effective way to use cases is in a discussion group guided by a case teacher. They can be used in a college or graduate class, an adult education program, or in a workshop or retreat setting. A teacher might sometimes have an image of him or herself as an information source, an encyclopedialike resource that supplies data to apprentices in the field. In case teaching, the teacher serves in quite a different fashion. Robert and Alice Evans, and Louis and Carolyn Weeks[2] propose three very insightful images for the case teacher: catalyst, probe, and referee.

A Catalyst

The case teacher is a catalyst in that he or she calls forth new growth in the participants, evoking new insights into the material and broadening their concerns and understanding. The teacher might do this in any number of ways. Most teachers come to the case well versed in the facts and analysis of the material, and they open the discussion by a simple question. For example, "What is the key issue in the case?" or "How would you vote, were you Senator Berg, and why?" One task of the teacher is to keep some direction to the discussion, and elicit the best from the participants.

A Probe

The art of asking the incisive question is the mark of a good case teacher. Probing the position of a participant ensures that all see the underlying insight and perhaps offers an opportunity to move to the issues in a broader context. One of the goals of the case approach is to gain experience in the method of coming to truth by a self-corrective process. People put forth their proposals and their rationales, and then others have a chance to criticize or build on those proposals with new evidence or another perspective. A participant comes to have confidence in his or her position when it can be defended in the face of objections and when no objections (new evidence, another interpretation) seem overwhelming.

Referee

The third image of the case teacher points us to the task of mediation. The instructor is required to elicit the basis for differences of opinion, and to engage persons as directly as possible. Often role playing helps draw out the issues. Two or more disputants who seem to hold convictions similar to characters in the case might act out a particular episode in the case and strive to reach some understanding of why they say what they say.

The teacher is also charged with keeping the discussion on a coherent track. This might mean reminding some participants about time limits and the need to keep to the point. While it is generally not helpful to call on everyone present, an instructor should be sensitive enough to encourage participation by all who are interested in contributing.

Concluding the Case

The instructor is also charged with concluding the discussion. This is a particularly important skill for case teachers. A conclusion should outline the various alternative solutions, highlighting the values at stake and the probable results of each. Also, there should be some mention of what the members of the group have learned from each other. The teacher may want to comment on the "Reflections on the Story" for the case, and perhaps sketch why the group either agrees or disagrees with the authors.

Participants may sometimes expect the instructor to give his or her own analysis of the case at some point in the discussion. The teacher should beware lest everyone wait until *the* answer is presented. Emphasis on the *reasons* for a position gives the other participants freedom to develop alternate positions based on what they hold to be more compelling reasons and arguments.

CONCLUSION

Each of the next ten chapters begins immediately with a case. There are no introductions or set of instructions other than those provided here. It is hoped that the cases will provide exciting and challenging exercises, and that the collaborative effort of readers will be a small step in the task of making our world more humane and more Christian.

Notes

1   Most of the authors of the cases used in this book have been trained at the Case Study Institute. The Case Study Institute was founded in 1971 as a result of a grant to the Association of Theological Schools from the Sealantic Fund. With the assistance of professors in Harvard Business and Law Schools, the Institute has trained almost 200 theological educators in the case study method. Cases developed by Fellows of the Institute are presently listed in annotated bibliographies published by Intercollegiate Case Clearing House, Harvard University, in Boston, Massachusetts, 02163. All cases in this book are taken from that source.

2   Robert Evans, Alice Evans, Louis Weeks, and Carolyn Weeks, *A Casebook for Christian Living* (Atlanta, Ga.: John Knox Press, 1977), pp. 34-40.

Chapter Four
The Story of Harold Geneen's ITT

Professor Kean leaned back in his chair and carefully weighed his words. "Phil, at ITT the monetary rewards are high but the demands are heavy. People are free to make their decisions whether they want to come into that environment. There is nothing hidden or devious about Harold Geneen's approach. People know exactly what is expected and demanded from them. They know that they either perform or they are out. It is a highly professional company from the standpoint of management techniques so people do learn a lot while working for International Telephone and Telegraph."

Philip Baxter, a bright and personable M.B.A. student, stood there waiting for Professor Kean to say more. He had been offered a very good salary for a middle-management position at ITT, and he sought advice from one of his profs.

Professor Kean remained silent, and stared pensively out his office window into the blinding Indiana snow. This past semester he had taught Philip in a course on values in the business world, and he knew him to be a sensitive and idealistic young man. The professor reflected on all that he had heard about Hal Geneen's ITT in the fifteen years he had been preparing students for the business world.

HAROLD S. GENEEN

"HAROLD GENEEN HAS NO TIME TO BE NICE," read the title of a feature story on the Chairman of ITT in *Life* magazine. "I think he'd like to devote a certain number of minutes per day to being nice," said a colleague, "but usually more pressing problems intervene." At age 49, in 1959, Hal Geneen moved into the number one spot at International Telephone and Telegraph when the corporation was worth $800 million in annual sales. Less than 12 years later, and after merging with 172 companies in 80 countries, ITT reported an annual revenue of $8 billion.

A veteran executive of ITT who knew Geneen for a number of years expressed his opinion: "Geneen wanted to become the highest paid management executive on earth. He wanted to run the biggest operation on earth. He wanted the most power. He cannot stand the presence of anyone else who wants power. Money he will give them. Power, no."*

EDUCATION AND EARLY TRAINING

Geneen's early life was marked by hardship and a meager family life. He was the son of an American father and a British mother. Although born in England, he was brought to New York by his parents before he was a year old. Hal's father, who was a manager of concert performers, separated from his mother, Aida, before Hal was five years old. His mother sent the young Geneen to a Suffield, Connecticut, boarding school, and the remaining years of childhood were all spent in boarding schools and summer camps.

Writing about his childhood years, Geneen said: "I spent the entire time either boarding at the school or again at camps, except for the occasional holiday vacations when I got home. Even a number of the lesser ones of these, i.e., Thanksgiving or Easter, being short, and for family reasons, I spent at school . . . I left there in 1926, to go to work."

To work it was at age 16 for young Geneen. As a Wall Street page boy, he also studied accounting at New York University night school. Making ends meet was no easy matter, and Geneen recalled getting along for a whole week on bread and taffy. "They had one-cent sales on taffy, two pounds for nine cents, and bread filled me up." In 1934, he graduated from NYU and worked as an accountant for eight years before moving to corporate finance jobs. A colleague characterizes

---

*Harold S. Geneen was chief executive officer of ITT from 1959 to December 1977, when he stepped down and assumed the less active post of board chairman.

the Hal Geneen of the 1940's as "a bloodhound on the trail of a wasted dollar."

CORPORATE LIFE

In 1956, Geneen joined Raytheon Co. as executive vice president and was given one task: "Make Money." Till then, all policy had been in the hands of Boston "Brahmin" Charles Adams, the president. One management expert described Adams as "kindhearted, human, and ethical, but not cost-conscious and inclined to walk away from hard decisions." Under the new vice president, earnings increased four-fold in three years while Raytheon stock soared from 15 to 70 dollars.

Geneen wanted a bigger share in policy-making than Adams would allow. At the same time, a committee from ITT was searching for someone to take the helm of their loose-knit confederation of companies. Hal Geneen signed on with ITT in 1959. His publicly stated goal when he took over the company was to double profits every five years, and the record shows a remarkable accomplishment. From 1959 to 1967, earnings increased from $29 million to $122 million. Geneen is quite candid about what he takes to be the single purpose of corporate life: profits. David Lush, a former vice president of ITT-Europe, declared: "Geneen has a lot of complexes about European managers. He was worried that a lot of them didn't have profits as their first aim in life." The company profits climbed as indicated by the growth shown in Table 4.1.

Table 4.1. ITT's Growth (in millions of $'s).

Data from *Fortune:* July 1959, p. 126;
July 15, 1968, p. 188, and May 1977, p. 366.

	Sales	Assets	Net Income	*Fortune's* 500 Largest Companies — Ranking
1958	687	869	26	49
1967	2,760	2,961	122	21
1976	11,764	11,070	494	11

THE QUESTION OF STYLE

"Cents per share are the only thing that interests Harold Geneen," is the favorite self-characterization of the head of the giant conglomerate known as ITT. When Geneen took over ITT at the age of 49, he was already proficient in finance and accounting.

Geneen contrasted his style with Colonel Behm, the former head of ITT: "People around here, like Colonel Behm, used to be great gourmets, and loved wine, and spoke all kinds of languages. The world has changed. Now no one gives a damn if you give him a ham sandwich, and you don't have to worry about wines. They're interested in facts. The Colonel had the training for his time. I have it for mine."

In a memo to all his executives, entitled "Facts," Geneen set out his perspective. "Whole trains of events and decisions for an entire management can be put in motion in the wrong direction with the inevitable loss of money, time, and morale—by one 'unfactual fact,' 'accepted by,' or 'submitted by'—YOU—however unintentional. The highest art of professional management requires the literal ability to 'smell' a real fact from all the others—and moreover to have the temerity, intellectual curiosity, guts, and/or plain impoliteness, if necessary, to be sure that what you do have, is indeed what we call an unshakable fact."

The key forum for review and analysis of these "facts" is the monthly General Managers' Meeting where the forty top ITT managers from around the world report on their companies. Held on the second Wednesday of every month, the GMM runs for two to three days and nights. According to his colleagues, Geneen takes a prosecuting attorney style and is known for his harsh attacks on fellow executives. He masters mounds of material and expects others to do the same. "He demands no more from anyone else than he demands of himself, which is limitless," says a former colleague. He has no patience with those who cannot deliver, and openly dresses them down. "Many of us have frankly left the organization for having been spit upon publicly," said a former unit manager.

M. Richard Mitchell, Geneen's general counsel, has another perspective. "Geneen is excellent at cutting clean, at head-chopping neatly. He does not indulge in the avoidance of issues. There is not that false quality present. There are no whited sepulchres here."

A man of incredible drive and stamina, Geneen has kept tabs on his whole operation with what he calls "multilayered management." "I delegate but I don't abdicate," says Hal Geneen. The intensity of life has its financial rewards. Salary and bonuses for Geneen amount to over $800,000 a year and he is reported to be worth $9 million in stock. In business circles, ITT has a well-known reputation. Executives who are ambitious and who will give their all to making profits for the company find Geneen's ITT a welcome challenge.

"If you are bright and aggressively ambitious, and you can block out the feeling that it all might be madness, it could be for you," reported one middle-aged manager. "I, for one, wonder if it is worth it all."

WHAT TO SAY?

Professor Kean glanced back at Philip Baxter and wondered what more to say to this ambitious but sensitive young man.

This case was prepared by Professor Oliver F. Williams, C.S.C, of the University of Notre Dame as a basis for class discussion, rather than to illustrate either effective or ineffective handling of an administrative situation. It is based on the following sources: Stanley Brown, "Harold Geneen Has No Time to Be Nice," *Life* 72 (May 19, 1972), pp. 79-80; William Rodgers, "How to Succeed in Business by Really Trying," *Ramparts* 11 (March 1973), pp. 30-34, 55-58; "ITT: The View from Inside," *Business Week* (November 3, 1973), pp. 43-48; Walter Guzzardi, Jr., "ITT Gets the Message," *Fortune* 63 (February 1961), pp. 112-118; "Double the Profits, Double the Pride," *Time* 90 (September 8, 1967), pp. 86-93.

Williams is Assistant Professor in the Theology Department of the University of Notre Dame. He did both graduate and undergraduate work at the University of Notre Dame and received his Ph.D. from Vanderbilt University. He is a Fellow of the Case Study Institute, president of the Association for Professional Education for Ministry, and a Fellow of the Society for Values in Higher Education. He is a contributor to *Christian Theology: A Case Method Approach,* eds. Robert A. Evans, Thomas D. Parker (New York: Harper & Row, 1976). He is an ordained Roman Catholic Priest, of the Congregation of Holy Cross (C.S.C.).

Reflections on the Story

Discussion of the case might begin by asking what story Geneen seems to be living out. Groups often seem to profit by focusing on the relation between the shape of a personal story and the values of the corporation. This case presents an opportunity to examine how a corporation tends to mold the character and shape the life stories of its executives. Further discussion might explore alternate ways to organize corporate life so that other values might be highlighted.

I. ISSUES FOR DISCUSSION

A. *The Corporation and Character Formation.* One of the major themes of this book is that organizations play an important role in shaping the sort of person one is becoming. Different organizations stimulate different character traits and capacities depending on the embodied values and goals in the organizational process. Although early family life has a major influence on attitudes, it also appears true that most persons are relatively malleable and continue to be formed by the significant organizations in their lives. To live as a Christian it is necessary to become actively involved in the Christian community where character is molded so that one comes to embody spontaneously the values nurtured by the community in the name of Christ.

Many groups find it helpful to reflect on the character traits that would most likely be reinforced in the corporate life described in the case. To begin, consider the following list of personal characteristics and select those that would be likely to receive support in Harold Geneen's ITT. (Readers may have other traits to add to this list.)

competence	generosity	persistence
compassion	hardheadedness	rationality
creativity	honesty	self-control
fairness	idealism	spontaneity
flexibility	justice	tolerance
friendliness	loyalty to colleagues	

What personal characteristics are likely to be underdeveloped in the corporation as described in the case? Would you advise a friend, or a son or a daughter, to accept a position in this type of firm? Why?

B. *Alternate Styles of Corporate Life.* If the corporation is single-mindedly focused on profit maximization and efficiency, then care for people, generosity, justice, concern for pollution, etc., would seem to count little and would be given minimal reinforcement in the organization. Traits so valued by Christians will be muted in anyone aspiring to the executive suite. However, is it possible for a corporation to have a social vision that places profit maximization in a wider context that stresses human development as the overall goal of life on this earth? Systems might be assessed not simply with economic criteria, but also with social criteria. Would this put a new question for geniuses like Hal Geneen, that is, "Will the human values be promoted with this product, or system, etc.?"

Is it possible to explore an expansion of the rules of the game to include a broader vision, a vision that takes into account that people are not just interested in goods but also in Good? Democratic capitalism has frequently presupposed a humane ethical business community as its cornerstone. Without some level of trust and care for each other, without minimal justice, would trade and commerce have flourished? Perhaps the world of business has arrived at the time to reflect explicitly on values and find new ways to incorporate them into economic life. It appears that corporate values have too long been narrowly focused on self-interest in economic terms and neglected the common interest of a humane community where one might more truly enjoy the fruits of our system. In any event, all these questions provide much material for vigorous discussion and proposed action.

II. AN ANALYSIS

To assist Philip Baxter in making his decision, we might use the following process: ascertaining the situation, clarifying and interpreting it, determining the values in conflict, and finally, making a decision after considering the various alternatives. How do you react to this presentation?

A. *Ascertaining the Data.* For Baxter's concerns, the significant data seem to be:
1. Trained in finance and accountancy, Geneen advanced rapidly through the executive ranks by applying his skills relentlessly.
2. Geneen has shaped company policy with a principle he has stated repeatedly: the single goal of corporate life is the maximization of profit and growth.

B. *Interpreting and Clarifying the Data.*
1. Geneen understands the role of the corporation in terms of the classical doctrine of the free enterprise system. Thus, while remaining within the bounds of the law, his role is to maximize profit and growth. This ensures that people have jobs and that the government has tax income. With this money, individuals and government have the freedom to address social issues, should they be so inclined.
2. Geneen has developed the art of effective management to the point where prediction and control are realizable possibilities for the huge conglomerate.
3. The profit and loss statement is the principal index of success or failure.
4. As a manager, Geneen has adapted himself to corporate needs and has developed the traits of his personality that are required to make it to the top: competence, self-control under stress, demanding, etc. He has other traits that, at least in his corporate life, appear underdeveloped: idealism, generosity, compassion, concern for others, etc.

C. *Values in Conflict.* The following are some of the values at issue:
1. Maximization of profit and growth. This requires functional rationality, hardheadedness, and a singleminded stress on productivity or performance.
2. Social values of generosity, compassion, justice, respect for persons, and sensitivity to the common good.

D. *Alternatives and Decision.* Philip Baxter could accept the position with ITT, but if he wanted to live Christian values in that context, he would have to be very determined and exceptional. He would have to raise some fundamental questions about the system, i.e., what it might be doing to him and others in its purview. Baxter could also decide to try for a position with another firm that has an articulated social vision.

III. IMAGES OF FAITHFULNESS

Assume that Philip Baxter understands himself a Pilgrim of the People of God as that image has been explained in Chapter 3. As a "Pilgrim" Baxter would see himself as on a journey illuminated by the revelation of God. The guidance he might find in the Bible and his Church, however, is more like the assistance that is provided by the needle of a compass than that provided by a detailed road map. That is, as a Christian, he is given some basic values and a way of life, but he has to make the concrete decisions that govern how he incarnates the Christian message in his life and circumstances.

Appropriating the values and way of life of the Bible means that Baxter comes to see the world, including the business world, with a broadened perspective. Baxter might see that he is called to employ his talents in ways that advance the prospects for a more humane world. For example, he would want to use his power and influence as instruments of service to help others lead a fulfilling life. As a Pilgrim, issues of social justice would be an ever-present part of his agenda.

How might Philip Baxter view Harold Geneen's ITT? From reading the accounts of the life of Harold Geneen, Baxter might come to see him as someone who has been primarily shaped by the values of his corporation. ITT has the goal of maximizing profit and growth, and its organization tends to reinforce all those traits and capacities that advance its aims. Geneen is known as highly competent, tough, and demanding, but fair. Although he seems to need to be in control, he is cool under stress and displays little emotion. He is said to have a contempt for weakness and to humiliate people publicly when executive performance is less than expected. Yet he acknowledges a job well done with financial rewards. Measured by the yardstick of profits, Hal Geneen is an outstanding success. An advertisement in the December 1977, *Wall Street Journal* proudly proclaimed in large, bold print: "ITT Shareholders Will Receive an Increased Dividend for the 14th Year in a Row." From one perspective, profitability says it all. The man has abilities that are remarkable.

Yet Philip Baxter might ask just what story does Hal Geneen understand himself to be living out. What holds his life together? By looking at what he does over a period of time, Baxter is then prepared to ask just what view of the world, of himself, and of others might be necessary to make that pattern of activity attractive to Hal Geneen. What experiences are counted as significant, and what perceptions are blocked out of his life? What images and metaphors play a controlling role in Geneen's story? Evidence in the case seems to indicate that the dominant images that have guided his story are a combination of King of the Mountain and Company Person. The thrill of power, "climbing to the top," and unyielding loyalty to the firm seem to have spurred him on to the heights of corporate life and have kept him there.

The lingering question remains for Baxter: "Is it possible to be a serious Christian in the business world of Hal Geneen's ITT?" With the master image Pilgrim of the People of God, Baxter might come to see that what Geneen demands of his executives is a reshaping of their attention and a redirecting of their energies so that the *real* world is exclusively the *practical* world. Biblical images that elicit such values as generosity and compassion seem to have no role in these executives' lives—at least in the part spent in the office. Using "reason" and the disciplined structures of the company, the total effort is geared toward prediction, power, and control. The business story taken as the model here is the one that speaks of growth and profits and the one that brings wealth and power. Experience, perceptions, and images are all selectively screened so only what can be counted and analyzed is taken as significant. One is schooled to attend only to facts, and a "real" fact is countable. It enhances prediction and control and thus leads to power. This sense of reality comes to dominate one's whole life, or one does not survive. If one has a personal vision and a set of values that differ from this particular business story, it had better be checked at the corporate door each morning.

Of course, with his master image Baxter would acknowledge that the world of science and technology that underpins this business story has had an exemplary effect on our human world. Only when the practical and countable is taken to be *the* measure of reality does the world become less human. Taken in a limited and instrumental sense, scientific reason obviously has much to commend it.

What would Philip Baxter make of Hal Geneen? One way to look at his life is to say that he is simply following the logic of the free enterprise system to its natural conclusion. That is, if the primary aim of corporate life is profit maximization, then Harold Geneen is clearly a winner. Yet does not the free enterprise system presuppose some human (and Christian) values, if it is to function over the long run? From this perspective could Geneen's style be considered ultimately self-defeating? With a master image of Pilgrim of the People of God, Philip Baxter might wonder how the sort of person held up as a model in ITT would function as a husband or as a citizen. That is, would the underdeveloped traits—generosity, idealism, concern for others— hinder a fully human life at home or in the community.

Should Philip Baxter take the position with ITT? Only he can answer that question.

IV. SUGGESTED READINGS

Neil Chamberlain, *The Place of Business in America's Future: A Study in Social Values* (New York: Basic Books, Inc., 1973). The author provides an analysis of the changing values in today's social environment, and offers three possible scenarios for the values that will be dominant in the business life of the future.

Alex Groner (and the editors of *American Heritage* and *Business Week*), *The American Heritage History of American Business and Industry* (New York: American Heritage Pub. Co., 1972). This is a positive discussion of the crucial role of American business in the development of the nation. It includes biographical sketches of a number of important leaders.

Michael Maccoby, *The Gamesman: The New Corporate Leaders* (New York: Simon & Schuster, 1976). This book is particularly helpful in studying how systems of management influence character.

The following are biographies of business leaders:

Carl Ackerman, *George Eastman* (Boston: Houghton Mifflin, 1973).

Bernard M. Baruch, *Baruch: My Own Story* (New York: Holt, 1957).

Alfred D. Chandler, Jr. and Stephen Salsbury, *Pierre S. DuPont and the Making of the Modern Corporation* (New York: Harper & Row, 1971).

J. Paul Getty, *My Life and Fortunes* (New York: Duell, Sloan & Pearce, 1963).

Peter J. Grace, *W. R. Grace and the Enterprise He Created* (New York: Newcomen Society in North America, 1953).

Theodore Gregory, *Ernest Oppenheimer* (Cape Town: Oxford University Press, 1962).

Patrick O'Higgins, *Madame* (New York: Viking Press, 1971). (Helena Rubinstein).

Alfred P. Sloan, *My Years with General Motors* (Garden City, N.Y.: Doubleday, 1964).

Chapter Five
Walnut Avenue Church

Harry Tillotson, Moderator of the Walnut Avenue Church, was uncertain about what he should do next to help resolve a problem that had deeply divided his congregation. The difficulty, which began when lightning severely damaged the church's historic steeple in September, had by the following January come to involve in Mr. Tillotson's mind some fundamental questions concerning how and for what purpose the church was to govern its affairs. The following several pages include first a description of Walnut Avenue Church and second a summary of the events surrounding the steeple episode.

WALNUT AVENUE CHURCH

Walnut Avenue Church was Congregational in polity and tradition and located in the downtown section of a middle-sized industrial city on the outskirts of Philadelphia. The church, dating back to colonial times, had a membership of 900 of whom approximately 400 were active members. As is typical of most churches in this sociological situation, its membership had gradually been declining over the past several decades as people moved to surrounding suburban areas. Walnut Avenue Church had remained, however, feeling it had a ministry to the city and its people and was highly regarded in church and lay circles as a responsible and dedicated institution.

The congregation was highly diverse in age and interests. About half the church family were older people, many having children who had grown and left the city. There were only a few families in the 30 to 50 age bracket with growing children. Slightly less than half the congregation were younger people, both single and married, in college and working, many of them related to the universities located nearby. The youth education program was modest in size.

Between annual meetings, the church was governed by the Prudential Committee, composed of the chairman of standing committees, the entire Board of Deacons, the Treasurer, Secretary, two members elected at large, and the Moderator, who acted as chairman. Members of all committees including designated chairmen were placed for election by the Nominating Committee before the congregation at the annual meeting. The elections were not contested and there had rarely been a dissenting vote. Mr. Tillotson, in his six years as Moderator, had confined his role to assembling the agenda and chairing meetings of the congregation and the Prudential Committee.

The Prudential Committee approved the budget before it was submitted to the congregation for final ratification. In recent years the church had had to strain to maintain its level of activities though it was fortunate to have a small endowment to ease the impact of fluctuations in pledging. The fundraising and investment management functions were handled by the Finance and Property Committee, which also had responsibility for the church building. Over time this committee had come to view itself as responsible for the "secular affairs" of the church—those matters involving money and physical assets.

During the past several years, the Mission and Community Committee had expanded its activities beyond making contributions to traditional charitable and denominational agencies and participated in social action programs of various kinds, sometimes involving modest expenditures of funds. On one occasion the committee asked for and received approval from a special meeting of the congregation of a resolution expressing support and concern for the Black community during disturbances in a nearby ghetto area. The resolution was sent to the mayor and referred to in the press. The committee, and especially its chairman, had subsequently drawn strong criticism from some in the parish who felt the use of the resolution to be "quasi-political" and hence inappropriate.

THE CHURCH STEEPLE

On a Friday night in September lightning struck the steeple igniting a fire which caused severe structural damage.

The following morning the Finance and Property Committee met in emergency session. They concluded that an architect should be engaged immediately to ascertain the extent of the damage and the probable cost of repairs. Three days later the architect reported that emergency measures were necessary to ensure that the steeple would not collapse on the next windy day. He also informed the committee that these measures, costing about $1,000, were not sufficient, and that either the steeple should be taken down or completely rebuilt at a cost he thought would run about $40,000. After some discussion, the committee told the architect to proceed with the emergency work and that Fred Thornton, chairman of the committee, would contact him about further steps to be taken. After the architect left, the committee, without dissent, agreed that the steeple ought to be rebuilt and a special gift campaign should be organized to raise money to cover the cost.

At a special meeting of the Prudential Committee the following week, Fred Thornton traced what had happened and presented its recommendation to rebuild the steeple. The response was immediate.

"In a time like this, with all the poverty and problems in the city, and world refugees and war and all, how can we justify this much money on a steeple which has no function even for us?" asked Danny Cranston, chairman of the Mission and Community Committee.

"Because," replied Fred Thornton, "if we don't fix it, it will fall down, and if we take it down, who will know this is a church?"

An elderly gentleman, Richard Gilroy, a loyal churchman and substantial giver, then offered to contribute a neon lighted cross, to go atop the repaired steeple so that the whole neighborhood would see the church identified by this radiant symbol.

Though there were no immediate remarks expressing negative feelings about the cross, several scowls from members implied to Mr. Tillotson a two-fold problem. How could one stand out against the cross without hurting Mr. Gilroy, and if his gift were refused, would it jeopardize his sizable pledge, which was almost 10% of the entire budget? However, Henrietta Gibson, a deacon, came to his support, saying, "This church is the church of my childhood, and I want the steeple to stay on. I know there are many others who feel the same way about it. The Finance and Property Committee voted unanimously to fix the steeple and if Mr. Gilroy wants to put a cross up there, we ought to go along."

Carlotta Carlyle, another deacon, who said she had joined the church because she thought it could work to bring changes in society, was aghast at this, and literally shouted to the meeting, "This world is going to pot, and we sit here discussing spending money on a steeple. It seems to me we have our priorities turned upside down. Jesus sent the church out to minister to mankind, not to make monuments out of our buildings."

The moderator, by now ill at ease, suggested a subsequent meeting because it was now already 11:00 p.m. Mr. Thornton indicated that he felt his committee ought to secure a detailed estimate of the cost of rebuilding. Wallace Berry, Chairman of the Music and Arts Committee, then said that since the bells were a part of the music program, his committee ought to be represented. After some discussion, this latter suggestion was put aside on the ground that the matter could best be handled by Finance and Property at this stage. Mr. Berry was encouraged, however, to secure the views of his committee before the next Prudential Committee meeting.

During the ensuing month, Reverend Anderson, who had kept his opinions on the matter to himself, preached on the virtues of compassion, forgiveness, acceptance and brotherly love and reconciliation. He also began to visit the Messrs. Tillotson and Thornton to try to reach an accommodation that would not split the church. Mr. Thornton had urged him to pave the way for conciliation in his preaching. He had also been heard to say, "These ministers don't know anything about money and bricks and real estate values; they ought to stick to spiritual matters." He further implied that as a friend of Richard Gilroy, he thought that if the steeple didn't get fixed, and the cross was refused, Gilroy might very well withdraw his membership and pledge.

By the end of October, when a second meeting of the Prudential Committee was called, the Finance and Property Committee had secured estimates from three builders and after much consultation settled on one for $50,000. Although the estimates were roughly comparable in price (the others were $46,400 and $53,000), the choice was complicated by the great many factors to be considered—design, finish, etc. The recommendation was put in a motion to the Prudential Committee including the neon cross at an additional cost of $3,500.

Exhibit 1. WALNUT AVENUE CHURCH Organization Chart.

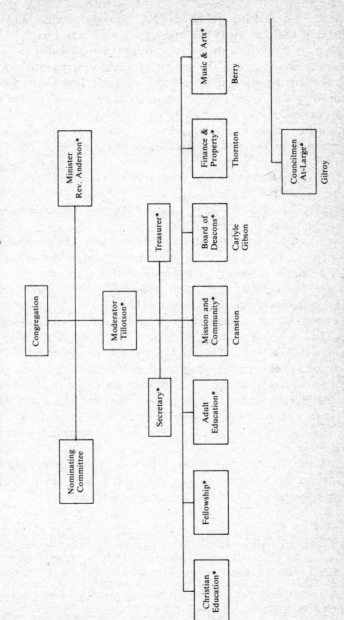

*Members of Prudential Committee. Including nine deacons and Reverend Anderson, there were 21 people on the committee.

In the following debate, Wallace Berry noted that while his committee, in a 3-2 vote (with two members absent), was in favor of retaining the steeple and the bells, he personally opposed it and was uncertain how to vote on the motion. One deacon responded by saying, "I think this whole thing is getting out hand. Let's let those who want to have the steeple replaced raise the money among themselves and leave the rest of us out of it."

Another member answered, "But that is no way for a Christian community to behave—we must learn to work and worship together!"

Eventually the motion was brought to a vote. It lost 11 to 9 with Reverend Anderson abstaining. A resolution was then passed respectfully declining Mr. Gilroy's gift but thanking him for his generosity and thoughtfulness.

Through Christmas the atmosphere was tense. The Finance and Property Committee refused to do anything at all in the way of arranging for the removal of the steeple. Reverend Anderson, bearing the brunt of well-intentioned but often harsh criticism from some parishioners, began to feel isolated and alone.

Finally, in mid-January, Mr. Tillotson was informed that a meeting of the congregation was being called by a group of parishioners including several on the Finance and Property Committee to consider a motion having the effect of reversing the Prudential Committee vote. Should this motion carry, a second one was to be made requesting that the Moderator appoint a committee on governance to consider changes in the by-laws that would have the effect of involving the congregation more directly in the decision-making process in the church.

It was in this situation that Mr. Tillotson pondered over the nature of the church's purpose and what, if anything, he could do to help resolve Walnut Avenue Church's current dilemma.

Names and places have been disguised. This case was prepared by Robert W. Ackerman as a basis for class discussion rather than to illustrate either effective or ineffective handling of an administrative situation.

Ackerman is vice-president for finance and administration, PRECO Incorporated, a pulp and paper manufacturer. He was an undergraduate student at Yale, and has an M.B.A. and a Ph.D. in business adminstration from Harvard. As well as writing a number of cases about corporate social responsibility, he is the author of *The Social*

Challenge to Business, (Cambridge, Mass.: Harvard Univ. Press, 1975), and coauthor of *Strategy and Organization* with Hugo Uyterhoeven and John W. Rosenblum (Homewood, Ill.: R.D. Irwin, 1973), and *Corporate Social Responsiveness* with Raymond A. Bauer (Reston, Va.: Reston Publishing Co., 1976). He is a member of the United Church of Christ.

Reflections on the Story

The Walnut Avenue Church appears to be deeply divided over what to do about restoring the steeple. The good that some of the members of the congregation hoped to achieve by serving the inner city seems jeopardized as the divided congregation polarizes around differing views about how a church is supposed to serve its membership, the neighborhood, the wider community, and the world. This dispute about the steeple may reflect a debate going back centuries in the history of the church.

I. ISSUES FOR DISCUSSION

Various ways of viewing the church are reflected in the statements of the disputants: Fred Thornton, Danny Cranston, Richard Gilroy, Deaconess Henrietta Gibson, Deaconess Carlotta Carlyle, and Wallace Berry. Each one of these involved leaders of the congregation, in living out his or her personal story, has dominant images that provide direction and meaning to his or her life. It may be helpful to probe the roles assigned to the Walnut Avenue Church by these people. As each of the characters of the case gives expression to the expectations he or she has of the church, we might ask ourselves: What biblical images, if any, inform a commitment to a particular policy position? Another major issue in the case concerns a basic question: Why have steeples on churches? What is it about Christian communities that would warrant such things as steeples?

A. *Operational and Adoptive Values.* Clarence C. Walton, in his book *Ethos and the Executive,* makes a helpful distinction between *operational* and *adoptive* values.[1] He refers to the fact that some values are internalized and actually influence behavior (operational values), while other values, although outwardly professed, are not wholeheartedly accepted and have little bearing on actual behavior (adoptive values). This book has pointed to that same reality, that is, that practice often belies stated doctrine, by referring to the master image that actually guides a life story. It has suggested that a person's behavior pattern, speech *and* action, reveals what that person's master image really is.

To integrate a set of values and a master image into the fabric of a life pattern is a process that takes time. Often by discerning the master images and values of others, and the ease of their self-deception, we can learn something about our own. In this case, a role play may be instructive. The discussion group might begin by portraying the membership of the Prudential Committee. At this imaginary meeting of the committee, the role-players could extend the arguments of each person in the case. Participants might select the person in the case with whom they most agree.

Of course, Mr. Tillotson should chair the meeting. As the meeting progresses each participant may be challenged as to why he or she said what was said, and how each one perceived the story that was being acted out. If we listen carefully, perhaps we may hear through the medium of these disputants the voices of real people around us arguing similar questions about the role of the church in their personal stories. After the role play the group might spend some time discussing the master images and values involved with each character.

B. *Why A Steeple?* The first three chapters developed the idea that the Bible could be viewed as the Christian story, that is, the Christian account of what life is all about. Through its images the Bible tries to communicate not only to our intellects but also to our feelings and emotions. The vivid images of the Bible address the whole person and call us not only to see things in a new way but also to live life in a new way.

Because of the life, death, and resurrection of Jesus, Christians have new insights about how life might be lived; they also have fears and hopes, joys and sorrows. Christians express this constellation of responses with their images or symbols. One such symbol is a church steeple. Can you think of others?

Chapter 3 pointed out that the skill for Christians is learning how to have a master image from the Bible that controls other images from home and business. Thus if one is becoming a Company Person, that image would be constrained by a master image from the Bible, for example, Heir to the Kingdom of God. If the business image is in no way constrained, it might just happen that the corporation becomes "the shrine and place of worship," and the firm's best economic interests the "religion." Are some peoples' "steeples" in the corporate office?

The following are some questions that may help discussion:

1. If the business person's work is so important and rewarding, how can he or she give any time to the church and its needs?

2. Realistically, can any church, as a place, a building, a liturgy, a faith, creed, or a community, compete with business "faith"?

3. What does one owe to the church in order to maintain counter-veiling attraction to business work and career?

4. When he or she participates in the various committees of the church, what values and techniques of measurement should he or she bring to the work?

5. Can a church be measured by the standards of the business world?

II. ANALYSIS

What should the members of the Walnut Avenue Church do? Consider one way of displaying the process of deciding that.

A. *Ascertaining the Data.*
   1. Danny Cranston: "with all the poverty . . ., how can we justify this much money on a steeple that has no function even for us?"
   2. Fred Thornton: "if we take it down, who will know this is a church?"
   3. Richard Gilroy: He volunteered to "contribute a neon lighted cross, to go atop the repaired steeple so that the

whole neighborhood would see the church identified by this radiant symbol."

4. Henrietta Gibson: "This church is the church of my childhood, and I want the steeple to stay on."

5. Carlotta Carlyle: "The world is going to pot, and we sit here discussing spending money on a steeple. It seems to me we have our priorities turned upside down."

6. Wallace Berry: "Let's let those who want to have the steeple replaced, raise the money among themselves and leave the rest of us out of it."

7. Reverend Anderson: "bearing the brunt of well-intentioned but often harsh criticism from some parishioners, (he) began to feel isolated and alone."

B. *Interpreting and Clarifying the Data.* The responses of the characters indicate that the Church serves a number of functions: cultural, philosophic, and religious. However, there is no unanimity on the precise nature of the Church. Why was it founded, and why has it survived till now?

C. *Values in Conflict.* The following are some of the values in conflict:

1. The value of service to others.
2. The value of symbols, like a steeple, stained glass windows, etc., to further our perceptions of religious truths.
3. The value of commonly shared viewpoints, activities, and traditions to promote community in the Church.
4. The value of individualism.
5. The value of pluralism.
6. The value of equity.
7. The value of the love of God.

D. *Alternatives and Decision.* The Church might call its people together for a day of prayer and reflection. Perhaps each could be asked to focus on his or her master image from the Bible. While, in itself, a master image from the Bible will not avoid conflict, it may provide a core of commonly accepted values, which could enhance genuine dialogue on the problem.

III. IMAGES OF FAITHFULNESS

Paul Minear discusses ninety-six images of the Church found in the New Testament.[2] He suggests that these images "cure[d] the blindness" of early Christian churches whenever they lost their authentic identity. While no particular image is recommended for Walnut Avenue Church, the congregation should employ creative imagination to cure their blindness and return to the New Testament images.

A reader might question the appropriateness of locating a case about a struggling church so prominently in a casebook on business and Christianity.

A modern business person is, to be sure, an activist looking for challenges and finding practical solutions to problems. This business person is frequently responsible for large amounts of resources and people, and he or she operates in the dynamic context of changes in customer requirements, competitor responses, and legal and social environments. Is it reasonable to expect this person, committed to the high-pressure world of business, to find anything of value in the problems of the Walnut Avenue Church?

The authors suggest that the reader consider this proposition: congregations or parishes, like Walnut Avenue Church with all its faults, are the special places where religiously based images and truth claims are found and recognized, and where believers in Jesus Christ gather together in mutual support to respond, often inadequately, to these images and claims. Walnut Avenue Church, like its counterparts in thousands of congregations and parishes, is quite simply the physical place and human collective that accepts certain statements of religious faith found in Scripture. It is the locus of support Christians need in order to grow in faith and to respond effectively to the profound reality of Scripture. Without the likes of the Walnut Avenue Church, the religious tradition would probably wither away, and there would be little chance to challenge the modern business story to integrate its images and values with those of Scripture. For it is in the congregation and parish that the business decision maker can realistically hope to be informed *and sustained* in his or her commitment to Christ and his way of life.

IV. SUGGESTED READINGS

John C. Bennett, *The Radical Imperative: From Theology to Social Ethics* (Philadelphia, Pa.: Westminster Press, 1975). Written by one of America's most influential churchmen, this book is especially helpful in understanding the role of social action in the churches. (See Chapter IV, The Conflict in American Churches Over Social Ethics).

Andrew M. Greeley, *The New Agenda* (Garden City, New York: Doubleday & Co., 1973). Chapter 6, "From Ecclesiastical Structure to Community of the Faithful," is an insightful sociological analysis of the role of the Church as a support community.

Hans Küng, *The Church* (New York: Sheed & Ward, 1968). The book presents a very scholarly yet lucid discussion of the theology of the Church. Although written by a Roman Catholic theologian, the book has been acclaimed as an ecumenical landmark.

"The Boston Affirmation" *Andover Newton Quarterly* Vol. 16, No. 4 (March 1976), pp. 239-245. One of the drafters of this statement states that the *Affirmation's* goal was "to articulate an understanding of the faith in a contemporary situation where . . . much of the contemporary piety ignores the social dimensions of the gospel."

"The Hartford Declaration" *Christianity & Crisis* Vol. 25, No. 12 (July 21, 1975), pp. 168-169. This is a joint statement by theologians representing the many sects of the Christian Church, and has been interpreted by some observers as arguing for a *limited* role for social action by churches. The drafters of the Declaration would dispute this judgment, claiming that the intent of the statement is to call for a grounding of social action in prayer and communion with God.

Notes

1   Clarence C. Walton, *Ethos and the Executive* (Englewood Cliffs, N.J.: Prentice-Hall, Inc., 1969), pp. 33ff.

2   Paul S. Minear, *Images of the Church in the New Testament* (Philadelphia, Pa.: Westminster Press, 1960).

Chapter Six
Agenbite of Inwit

A class of teen-age boys in the Church School at St. Stephen's Church, Glencoe, Illinois, spent the fall term discussing the Ten Commandments. On the ninth Sunday they came to the commandment, "Thou shalt not bear false witness against thy neighbor," and they listened politely while their leader, Mr. James P. Landis, spoke to them about the evils of lying. Bearing false witness, he said, was a sin because it had been expressly forbidden by God. It was also intrinsically wrong, since it used speech, an avenue of communication, to thwart communication, and to convey an idea contrary to what was in the mind of the speaker. Finally, telling lies is dumb, because people learn not to trust the liar. He said that millions of dollars are exchanged every day over the telephone, because business people had learned that trusting each other was good business. The lesson sounded convincing to the boys, because of its logic and because Mr. Landis was known by everyone to be a man of unquestionable integrity, whose word was as good as a bond, who not only preached honesty but practiced it as well.

James Landis was a trust officer in Central National Bank, Chicago. He travelled a good deal, calling on actual and potential clients. His home was in the suburb of Glencoe, but he was normally there only on weekends, and so he had little time to enjoy the company of his wife and his two children. His son, James Jr., and his daughter, Lisa, regarded him with a certain amiable detachment, since he appeared to them as a friendly visitor who was not around long enough to be very helpful. However, James Landis was well thought of by his two publics, the La Salle Street banking world and the Glencoe community. There were signs that he was rising in the bank's hierarchy, and he had been elected Junior Warden at St. Stephen's, besides teaching his teen-age Church School class.

But Mr. Landis had begun secretly to question his own integrity. He had become increasingly uneasy about the discrepancy between the ethics which were preached and taken for granted at St. Stephen's, and some of the practices which were accepted in the world of banking. The self-sacrificing love which was so important to the Christian profession looked naively idealistic when compared with the kind of clever self-interest which seemed to pay off on La Salle Street. His inner distress came to a focus when he thought of how he had manipulated his expense account after he had returned from a recent business trip. He had padded the account. He had been doing this for years, as he was sure his colleagues were also, and he had thought very little about it, regarding it as the way in which this game was played, and giving him a very small compensation for the sacrifices he had been forced to make for Central Bank. But of late an odd phrase had kept coming back to him—Agenbite of Inwit. He had heard of it in an English Lit. course in college, and the instructor had said it was the title of a fourteenth-century book written by an English monk about "the again-biting of conscience." James Joyce had used it as a sort of refrain in *Ulysses*.

Fortunately they were not really bad bites, but only nibbles, though persistent enough to be irritating. Jim recalled that when he had left O'Hare airport on his last trip he had $300 in his wallet, and when he had come back to Chicago three days later he had $27 left. The trip had cost him $273. But when he sat down to prepare his expense account, he found that he could account for only $204. Not only had the trip been unprofitable from the bank's point of view, but it looked as though he himself was going to be out of pocket $69.

He had two options: he could quietly absorb the cost himself, chiding himself for not keeping a better expense account; or he could doctor the account to make up the difference. The bank would never feel it. He felt no great warmth towards his employer. Central Bank had treated him fairly, but in a cold, impersonal way. Only last week he had been on a business trip in Pennsylvania. Through excessive zeal he had worked late at a client's home and had driven home around midnight in a heavy rain storm. Anxious to get back to the motel and into bed, he exceeded the speed limit and was arrested by a police officer who happened to be trailing him. The affair cost him $45. When he explained the matter to his department chief, he was told that the expense should certainly be borne by Central Bank. But neither he nor his chief reckoned on Joel Miller, the young man newly appointed in the cost accounting department, who was anxious to gain a reputation as a watchdog of the company's expenses. Jim received the following memo from Joel Miller:

> TO: James Landis
> FROM: Joel Miller
> SUBJECT: Illegitimate expense item
>
> 1.   In your expense account for the trip Oct. 2-3, 1976, you have included a $45 traffic fine paid by you.
>
> 2.   According to Central Bank Directive, November, 1975, Expense Account Limitations 39-4 (b), any fines incurred by bank officials will be considered personal expenses for which the bank is not responsible.
>
> 3.   The $45 item is therefore denied.
>
> > Joel Miller
> > Cost Accountant

Jim was still smarting from this injustice. He felt Central Bank owed him far more than it had ever acknowledged for the sacrifices he had been asked to make. While other bank employees—Joel Miller, for example—worked an eight-hour day, officials who were on the road really worked a twenty-four-hour day. The incessant travel had begun to take its toll on his health. Irregular meals, the strain of travel on planes, sleepless nights in motels decorated like Algerian brothels, and nervous tension had aged him as they had aged Willie Loman in *Death of A Salesman*. As Willie's wife had said, "Attention must be paid." Boredom in strange cities had led to sizeable bar bills, and there had been temptations to sexual adventures unknown to clerks who rode the "L" home at 5:00 P.M. with the *Daily News* under their arms. He had been absent too long from his growing children and from his wife. Joel Miller should have a taste of what life was like in

Toledo with nothing but local TV to keep him from suicide! Central Bank had a debt to him which it had not acknowledged. In time it might cast him aside as casually as Willie Loman's boss had done.

The corporation would never settle its proper account, but it was rich enough to stand a little excusable diddling. Generations of salesmen had worked out conventions of expense account padding, and all of it was done with the knowledge of the higher officials, most of whom had come up through the works and were well aware of the customary practices. A salesman might miss a breakfast at home, but no salesman ever missed a breakfast on the road. At home he might eat one piece of toast and a cup of coffee, but on the road he ate like Balzac. Breakfast on the road might be eggs Benedict, listed at $4.50, and the tip and tax would drive the tab up to $5.50. Entertaining had fallen off at home, but on the road everyone was filled with hospitality, wining and dining anyone who represented a potential client. No salesman walked if taxicabs were around. A great many miscellaneous expenses were slightly less than $25, in tribute to the bank's policy of requiring vouchers for amounts above that amount. The sales force was very conscious of consistency, trying very hard to make their expenses check not only with cost records turned in by other men on similar errands, but with their own expenses on previous trips.

Jim felt a twinge of conscience when he thought about the movies and plays he had seen on the bank's money. The regulations Joel Miller administered specified that entertainment of any sort not related to the business of Central Bank must not be charged to the company. But the bank should not really expect him to sit isolated in a hotel room night after night, and any fair-minded person could see that if his morale stayed high he would make a more attractive representative for the bank on the following day. In a real sense his going to the theater was the bank's business, and so the cost of the tickets entered into his richly contrived reckoning.

Much the same could be said for his method of keeping his suits cleaned and pressed. Any laundering and cleaning at home were of course his own expense, even if his clothes had been soiled and rumpled on the bank's business. Therefore, he always set out with rumpled suits and as soon as he had checked into a hotel sent them out with a valet for speedy cleaning. The bank had a right to expect him to appear before a client without looking as though he had slept in his suit, and the bank should expect to pay for this necessity.

Consequently, when Jim discovered that he was $69 out of the pocket after his recent trip, he was not in the least disconcerted. He need only forget that he had been a guest at two lunches, which could then be charged to Central Bank. Several hypothetical taxi rides brought a new bill of $25. A few imaginary phone calls cost $5. The $69 deficit did not really tax his imaginative powers, and Jim accounted for it quickly, without charging the bank one more penny than he spent.

But there remained the difficulty of inwardly reconciling his belief in honesty with his business practice, and he would not dream of trying to explain the whole matter to his Church School class. The truth is that he had begun suffering of late from what his instructor had called "Agenbite of Inwit."

This case was prepared by Professor Paul Elmen of Seabury-Western Theological Seminary as a basis for classroom discussion and not to illustrate either effective or ineffective handling of a situation.

Elmen is Professor of Moral Theology at Seabury-Western Theological Seminary, Evanston, Illinois, and is also President of the Chicago Theological Institute. Harvard awarded him a Ph.D. degree. His most recent book is *Wheat Flour Messiah: Eric Jansson of Bishop Hill* (Carbondale: Southern Illinois University Press, 1976). He is an Episcopalian.

Reflections on the Story

There is a slightly gnawing discomfort being experienced by James P. Landis, and like most irritants, the critical question is what to do about it. One option is to confront the issues and take some time to examine his life and work. Another possibility is to find a bromide to ease the slight pain and to move on to the acceptable routine of the day: commuting to work, joking with coworkers at the bank, taking business calls, planning the weekend chores, and so forth. The discomfort will be lost in the rush of activities. "Keep busy, and don't look back," is often a pattern followed by people like Jim Landis. The question of what to do about this expense account problem can be safely tucked away in pushing a deadline while negotiating with a customer over the phone and eyeing the clock about the start of a scheduled meeting. Anyway, the family car needs winterizing and next Sunday School class must be prepared. If all this sounds familiar to the reader, then he or she is recognizing a commonplace technique of coping when the Agenbite of Inwit starts gnawing.

I. ISSUES FOR DISCUSSION

A. *Conflict in Roles and Values.* Jim Landis is living out at least three, sometimes overlapping, stories: business person, family man, and Christian. The challenge for Jim Landis is to put these three stories together in a fashion that does justice to all of them. It is appropriate to ask if Jim is doing justice to each one of his stories. What is entailed in Jim Landis' role as husband and father? As effective company person? As Christian and Sunday School Teacher? How might Jim integrate these stories more effectively?

B. *Professional and Family Goals.* Chapter 3 discussed how a master image guides a life story, reinforces some values and character traits, and focuses goals. What might be the master image in the Jim Landis story?

II. AN ANALYSIS

Jim Landis appears to be a person struggling to make some sense out of the three stories he is living: Christian, family, and business.

A. *Ascertaining the Data.*
  1. Jim Landis is normally home only on weekends.
  2. He is beginning to question his own integrity at the bank.
  3. He is experiencing inner distress.

B. *Interpreting and Clarifying the Data.* Jim Landis interprets his inner distress as "the again-biting of conscience." He is having serious doubts about the quality of his life.

C. *Values in Conflict.* The following are some of the values at issue:

1. The value of being an adequate parent to one's children.
2. The value of being able to tell the truth, which raises questions about company practices and procedures.
3. The value of integrity, that is, following the principles that one professes and teaches in Sunday School.
4. The value of trust in God, that is, placing one's life, career, and well-being in God's Hands.

D. *Alternatives and Decisions.* What should Jim Landis do, either about the expense account, or about his life? He may want to discuss his problem at length with his wife, a close friend, or a pastor. Perhaps a vacation with his family will afford him the opportunity of sorting things out, reorganizing his guiding images, and finding renewed inner direction for his life.

III. IMAGES OF FAITHFULNESS

Chapter 1 suggested that the temptation to check religious values at the corporate door is a continuing problem for persons in the business world. Chapter 3 focused on how one could be both a successful business person and, at the same time, a Christian. The key to meeting this challenge was said to be ordering business images under a master image from the Bible. It appears that Jim Landis needs to reintegrate the images that are guiding his life story.

First and foremost, as his children grow older and their needs change, he is finding that he has lost any meaningful relationship with them. His dominant image seems to be the Company Person, and his drive to "do all for Central National Bank" has reduced him to a breadwinner and a "boarder" at their Glencoe home.

His business image is on a collision course with his religious image. As he teaches Sunday School, he discovers the depth of the imagery from Scripture. The values taught there are warring with the values of going along with the formal and informal practices of the bank.

He, like all of us, is introduced to new possibilities as he moves through life and learns from experience how the dominant image he has appropriated works—what kind of person it makes him, how he perceives the world around him, and how he responds to that world. Is there any doubt that he must shift the image that dominates his story? But from Company Person to what?

It may well be that the gnawing inner distress that Jim Landis reports stems primarily from a growing realization that the *dominant* image of Company Person is insufficient to guide a rich and full life. While he may have successfully lost himself in the firm for a while, his self seems to be calling out for a story that will set some limits to the company role, provide space for the husband and father role, and give him the skills to discern where evil might be in his life.

Let us assume that Jim Landis comes to understand himself primarily as an Heir to the Kingdom of God as that master image has been explained in Chapter 3. This biblical image would then set the context for the images guiding his story in the business world. While he would perhaps continue to have an abiding sense of loyalty to the bank, he would be ever mindful of the wider context of that loyalty. His primary loyalty would be to the values and way of life set out in the Bible. Justice, power, happiness, and time would take on a new and compelling meaning.

The "new" Jim Landis would have the courage to speak out against company policy when he thought it was unjust. Losing notches in his career and even friends would not deter him from speaking his convictions. He might begin by seeking creative solutions to the common executive problems that he is experiencing. For example, perhaps wives should be encouraged to accompany executives on some business trips. Eliminating the need for employees routinely working evenings and only getting home on weekends, might be another important agenda item for Landis.

Finally, the expense account dilemma might well be the least of Jim's problems. It seems that some conversations with company executives are in order to regularize legitimate expense account practices.

IV. SUGGESTED READINGS

Bruce C. Birch and Larry L. Rasmussen, *Bible and Ethics in the Christian Life* (Minneapolis, Minn.: Augsburg Publishing House, 1976). This book is particularly helpful in understanding how character is formed in Christian life.

James T. Burtchaell, C.S.C., and Others, *Marriage Among Chris-*

tians: A Curious Tradition (Notre Dame, Indiana: Ave Maria Press, 1977). This book is a series of nine essays discussing the various aspects of Christian marriage. Eight married men and women speak from the lived experience of their married life together, and one priest-theologian probes the Christian tradition for some basic insights to guide married life today.

Thomas M. Garrett, *Ethics in Business* (New York: Sheed & Ward, 1963). This book discusses some of the standard issues in business ethics. Chapter six explores the ethical issues involved with expense accounts.

Robert K. Greenleaf, *Servant Leadership: A Journey into the Nature of Legitimate Power and Greatness* (New York: Paulist Press, 1977). The author points to a new perspective about leadership and power; they are to be considered as service to others and the common good.

Richard M. Huber, *The American Idea of Success* (New York: McGraw-Hill Book Co., 1971). A critique about the role that success, understood as accruing capital, has played in forming the American character.

Harry Levinson, *The Exceptional Executive* (Cambridge, Mass: Harvard University Press, 1968). A psychologist examines the pressures on the modern business executive and suggests more humane role expectations for people in large organizations.

Gail Sheehy, *Passages: Predictable Crises of Adult Life* (New York: Dutton, 1976). This book is helpful in understanding the inevitable personality and sexual changes that occur in our twenties, thirties, forties, and beyond.

Chapter Seven
Caribbean Corporate Strategy

Pastor Dave Hopkins stepped off the elevator and through the carved mahogany door into the quiet elegance of the Chicago Men's Club. He was struck by the contrast between this environment and the recent images of the Kingston slums which prompted his request for this luncheon meeting. After giving his name to the club's host, Dave was courteously informed that he was several minutes early; he was welcome to wait in the bar until Mr. Palmer and the rest of his party arrived.

Dave Hopkins' mind sifted through the events of the past four weeks as he considered how he would share his Jamaican experience with Frank Palmer and George Delaney, executives in multinational corporations with interests in the Caribbean as well as members of his affluent North Shore congregation, and Harold Shein, a management consultant to the travel industry and a good friend of George's. The previous month while Dave and his wife, Carol, were vacationing in Jamaica, they unexpectedly ran into Anthony Robinson, a Jamaican pastor who had done his seminary "field education" in the U.S. under Dave's direction. When Dave and Carol saw Tony for the first time in four years, he was playing the piano in their hotel cocktail lounge. They spoke briefly during Tony's break; he invited them to come with him the following morning to his new "parish."

After serving as a pastor—in Tony's terms "unsuccessfully"—in a large Jamaican congregation, Tony had requested and been granted by his conference an unsalaried, three-year leave from regular pastoral duties to work in the slums of Kingston. Tony worked primarily with a boys' club during the day and supported himself and his ministry by playing the piano at night in the lounge of a fashionable tourist hotel.

Dave remembered vividly the events of the next morning as they drove through Kingston in the Hopkins' rented car. At the time Dave expressed his astonishment at the contrast between the plush "tourist" zone and the homes of affluent Jamaican business and government leaders compared to the incredible poverty of the great mass of people in Kingston. In Tony's "parish" Dave and Carol saw hundreds of crude palm shanties, many with seven and eight occupants. There were no plumbing facilities and the only available water, as much as half a mile away from some huts, came from one faucet put in by city officials. Tony explained that most of the adult population was uneducated with little or no hope for employment in an increasingly urban-oriented nation.

In his words Tony was convinced that "the very presence of the concentrated wealth—the fruits of an economy largely based on the tourist industry—where those fruits are not shared with the nation although they are primarily the products of the natural tropical setting of our island—is essentially destructive and explosive." Tony continued, "The young people with whom I work, have virtually no public education available. They see the contrast between the haves and have-nots and are understandably bitter and frustrated. My boys turn to drugs and stealing out of desperation and a lack of self-worth. The human tragedy in this slum is a crime against God's good creation and the Christian gospel of love. This is not only my parish, but as a Christian it is also yours. When Jesus said 'for in as much as you have done this to the least of these my brothers . . .' applies here or no place."

In his spare time while still in the parish, and now full time, Tony worked with a gang of young boys. He used his gifts as a musician to teach the boys to play the few instruments he could gather. They had slowly formed a band. Now Tony felt there was real competition among the boys to belong to the band. "For most of these boys playing an instrument gives them the first feeling of accomplishment they have ever experienced. It is only with a concept of pride and self-worth that these young men can even begin to hope for a different life."

Tony's plea to Dave Hopkins still rang in his ears. "Reverend Hopkins, I've got 100 boys and 12 instruments. My church is struggling in Jamaica; it simply has no funds for work in the slums and most of the church members place no priority on this ministry. Through your congregation and your contacts in the U.S. can you get support for my club? I know from my time in your congregation that you have influential and powerful businessmen who could help us. The most striking example is the U.S.-based tourist industry which I feel has corrupted our culture by its presence, producing assembly line handicrafts, and phony festivals. Yet the industry annually grosses millions of dollars through the exploitation of our beaches and the cheap labor of our people. Don't they have some real responsibility for these brothers and sisters of Christ in Jamaica?"

Dave Hopkins snapped back to the present as Frank Palmer put his hand on Dave's shoulder and said, "Welcome to the club again. Our table is waiting." After the men had ordered lunch, Dave sketched the essence of his morning in Kingston and put Anthony Robinson's questions to his friends.

Frank Palmer, now 66, recently retired from the vice-presidency of Consolidated International Beverage Company, turned to Dave with a grin. "When the church gave you and Carol that vacation as a 25th wedding anniversary gift, I should have known you two couldn't just go and escape for two weeks! Well, to deal with the issues Tony put to us, we may first need to sort out why we have any responsibility. I personally believe that I *am* my brother's keeper. As a Christian I find it impossible to observe conditions such as you describe and not seek a responsible way to help. Revolting conditions of hunger and health address not only company executives but board directors and stockholders. There is a minimal but increasing sense of corporate responsibility. Tony is right. We get a profit—we must give in return. The issue then goes from rationale to strategy."

At this point George Delaney cut in, "Frank, as corporations we do give already in terms of salaries for individuals, opportunities for small local businesses, and taxes to the government which provide funds that country had no access to prior to our arrival. As you know, I am in the hotel business and Tony has got to face some realities. He speaks of U.S. companies grossing millions in the Caribbean which is true, but his is only a superficial view of gross operating profit. The return on investment is frequently very poor. After a hotel takes the initial risk, increased by political instability and danger of eventual expropriation of property, and the tremendous expense of building in a developing country, the management then has to continue to import at great expense the luxuries our customers expect. Most tourists really want to feel at home with familiar cuisine, in the air-conditioned comfort of their hotel which provides a secure base for a controlled exposure to an alien culture in the streets and markets. To provide that U.S.-like retreat center in another culture is expensive. In fact the percentage of operating profit in the Caribbean is the lowest of any major overseas operation as reflected in the studies for Worldwide Hotel Operations which I brought along for your reference. In addition Horwath and Horwath's statistics show the Caribbean to have some of the highest employee salaries and benefits. We return a tremendous amount of income to those people. Look, Frank, for me to say I'm against helping the less fortunate is like saying I'm against motherhood. But as you have said, in the past, you don't sell a moral attitude on its own merits. You've got to convince a company that it's in their own self-interest to create a good working environment in order for their business to prosper. Frank, I agree with you. Regardless of the reason, a controlled, careful strategy for corporate involvement in international issues that takes into account the long-term view of profitability and stability is the cruial question."

"But George," Dave Hopkins responded, "aren't we called as Christians to 'serve the world' and not to attempt first to maximize our own benefits? I've seen you personally take a strong stand in the community on issues you felt were morally correct, even when this might jeopardize your image or result in a personal loss in the view of some people. Why must the assuming of social responsibility for a corporation always be based on self-interest in contrast to the individual's responsibility?"

Harold Shein, 38, who headed one of the largest consultant firms in the midwest, had been silent up to this point. Harold now spoke clearly and firmly. "Self-interest or not, I frankly don't think there is *any* premise for a business to become involved in the social concerns of a host country. A corporation is not an individual. A business has one responsibility—to create customers. If it does this well, there's profit which benefits host and guest; if not, both are out of business.

An individual can afford to act responsibly in relation to his or her moral commitments. There is no corporate moral commitment in a business. Corporations do not have the luxury of being responsible in the same way. I may personally give money or time to some world social agency, but I'm not about to counsel my client to do the same thing. My client's primary responsibility is to his or her stockholders who have invested in a business, not in a philanthropic organization."

Frank Palmer slowly turned to Harold. "I used to operate with a similar logic in executive decisions, although I don't think I was ever asked to articulate it. Now, I am less persuaded. That logic appears, so my children argue, to divide one's life into neat compartments that don't correlate with one another. Why should a company be released from moral responsibility simply because it's a corporate institution? A business has several levels of obligation, only one of which is to its stockholders. True, you can't sell being a 'do-gooder,' but I am accountable for those in need *because* they are in need. Somehow I must assume responsibility for my influence in my private and corporate life. This is at the heart of any sense of stewardship for the natural and human resources of the world. I'm not thinking simply about myself; I'm worried about the world my grandchildren and my Jamaican employees' grandchildren will be living in."

As the lunch arrived, Dave Hopkins joked that, judging by the intensity of the conversation, he certainly didn't need to encourage his friends to express their opinions. Dave indicated that he was struck by the genuine ambiguity and complexity of the problem and needed to focus the concern he felt. "If we all agree that *some* moral responsibility exists—be that personal or corporate—how, for example, could an influential individual or a hotel chain in the Caribbean go about affecting change for those in need? How can we respond, if at all, to Tony's request for help?"

"I've learned from experience," responded George Delaney, "that it is a mistake to sidestep the established channels. Governments, even of developing nations, tend to thrive on the status quo. We must convince them that economic stability depends on a solid middle class. It's in both our best interests to establish technical training programs. We should also seek to support, through supervised grants, which use the resources of our money and our people, not only health and education but also indigenous crafts and music. This helps maintain the original culture; it also protects the reasons the tourists go to places like Jamaica. Mutual self-interest is the key."

Harold Shein retorted, "But how do you justify any immediate return to your stockholders? The hotels I advise pay fair wages by local standards; income for people who wouldn't otherwise have jobs. These people appear content with their lives. You're making paternalistic assumptions that they *want* to become a copy of our society. My hotels pay high taxes. It's the government's responsibility to channel the taxes into social programs *if* they see fit. It's none of my client's business. Personally, however, I would be willing to give Dave, here, money to be sent to Tony's boys' club."

"Now here's where I have to back off," interposed George. "Tony is not working through channels. It is my understanding that he had left the church after a dispute with his conference over priorities. I remember Tony as a responsible young man, but to give him money without some form of control is another matter. To ask a hotel to sponsor such a project could jeopardize their relationship to the established middle classes, and possibly to the government. If these boys reach a point of 'self-realization' in which they put on pressure to evict my hotels, or worse, expropriate the investment, a project without supervision would be self-destructive. We must face the realization that our businesses are parasites on another culture. We need to work for the most symbiotic relationship possible between a parasite and its host. We don't seek the death of the host or the extermination of the parasite. Both organisms can survive and flourish through negotiated mutual interest and respect."

Frank Palmer shook his head. "Our lives, our corporations are involved every day in risks. We must respond in a way which is not demeaning. We can't offer assistance to Tony and then show him we have no confidence in his vision for his own people. A semipaternalistic attitude is perhaps inevitable but the overpaternalistic style of the 'company mill' will corrupt our humanity and theirs. We need more than bigger mission gifts—strings or no strings attached. The request from Tony, our former pastor and student, is for a strategy for human development based on Christian concern. It ought to touch business, government, and church interests in Kingston and Chicago. Our church never touched me in this area, or perhaps I never listened. I feel called—I just don't know where."

George Delaney responded, "Frank, this is the vision of a retired corporation executive who has leisure and security. I wish you luck. Project-oriented, mutual-interest programs are what Tony really needs and if my competition will concur, we could make some headway here. A low-profit region like the Caribbean may be a place to try out such an approach. We have less to lose by the risk."

Harold Shein countered, "As a consultant I don't think you have weighed properly the pressures of profit and growth at home or of instability and corruption in Jamaica. Are you willing in this post-Watergate-Lockheed age to make the necessary payoffs? A corporation advisor would counsel, 'don't exceed your corporate responsibilities for involvement.' However, as an individual I will make a pledge and write a check to Tony for his work. I always wanted to play a flute; this way I can at least buy one."

"The meal is almost over," Dave said. "We seem to have gone in so many different directions I'm wondering if there is any way we can consolidate our efforts in response to Tony."

This case was prepared by Professor Robert A. Evans and Alice Frazer Evans as a basis for class discussion rather than to illustrate either effective or ineffective handling of the situation.

Alice Frazer Evans was educated at Agnes Scott College, the University of Edinburgh, and the University of Wisconsin. She is a Fellow of the Case Study Institute, for which she has written numerous cases. She is the coauthor of *A Casebook for Christian Living* (Atlanta, Ga.: John Knox Press, 1977). She is a ruling elder in the Presbyterian Church, and a member of the faculty of Hartford Seminary Foundation.

Robert Allen Evans is a member of the faculty of Hartford Seminary Foundation. He studied at Yale University, University of Edinburgh, and the University of Basel and received his Ph.D. from Union Theological Seminary, New York. He is the author of *Intelligible and Responsible Talk About God* (Leiden: Brill, 1973), and *Belief and the Counter Culture* (Philadelphia: Westminster Press, 1971) and editor of *The Future of Philosophical Theology* (Philadelphia: Westminster Press, 1971). He is also an editor of *Christian Theology: A Case Method Approach*, with Thomas Parker (New York: Harper & Row, 1976). He is an ordained Presbyterian minister.

Reflections on the Story

The focus of the book is: "Can you be a Christian in the business world?"; or, put another way, "Should one try to bring Christian values into corporate policy?" The issues are not nearly as simple as they may at first appear. One dimension of this question poses itself to the business executive under the rubric, the social responsibility of business.

In contemporary business circles there is much discussion about the social responsibilities of business. This theme emerged from the yeasty social debates of the sixties, and has resulted in a vast amount of literature around two central questions:

1. Beyond providing a product and obeying the law, does business have to attempt to be "socially responsible?" If so, should business limit its concerns to "avoiding social injury," or should broad societal goals be subsumed under corporate policies?

2. If the answer to either facet of the first question is "yes," what would be included in a comprehensive code of social responsibilities?

I. ISSUES FOR DISCUSSION

The leader might open the case discussion by asking the group what some of the basic issues are. Two related issues that frequently emerge are: What is the role of corporate power in a community, and what is the social vision of democratic capitalism?

A. *The Responsibilities of Business.* The leading characters in the case appear to have a different understanding of the role of corporate power. A suggested way of interpreting each view follows. Do you agree, and how would you respond to each?

Harold Shein's stance echoes that of the classic position on the "free enterprise system." Harking back to intellectual underpinnings in the work of such scholars as John Locke and Adam Smith, this position's most prominent spokesman today is Milton Friedman.

Shein's position could be understood as declaring that the primary role of business is to satisfy customers and make a profit. Assuming legal obligations are met, corporations are accountable to shareholders alone. In this scheme of things, business best serves Jamaica by narrowly focusing its concerns on increasing profits and thereby providing more jobs and paying higher taxes to the Jamaican government. In turn, by continuing to maintain a profitable climate for business, the Jamaican government will attract new businesses to the island. Shein is arguing from a perspective clearly articulated by Adam Smith. Smith held that the common good would be best served if each pursued his/her/its own interest. In the long run, then, the best course for business and society is for business to maximize profits. This provides income for individuals and governments to use for social projects, should they desire to do so.

Note that Shein would be happy to give a "personal" contribution. He may be a generous and compassionate individual but his ideological commitments prevent him from endorsing any corporate social involvement. Does this mean he checks his religious values at the corporate door? Is Shein living out at least two separate stories with his life, one for the office and another for his personal life?

George Delaney, while a firm believer in the free enterprise system, presents another characteristic position for the executive today. No slave to any theory, he appears to be open and fundamentally practical. "Will it work?" is George's question. From this perspective the task is to convince the company that its own self-interest will be advanced by becoming involved in social issues in Jamaica. Any company programs that could neutralize hostility between the haves and the have-nots would ensure that business could continue to increase on the island. This "interest group" mentality reasons that the company (one interest group) will thrive only if specific other interest groups (for example, the poor youth of Jamaica) are relatively content. Hence Delaney wants to work out a solution that advances both of their interests.

Frank Palmer summarizes his position: "I am accountable for those in need *because* they are in need. Somehow I must assume responsibility for my influence in my private and corporate life." Frank seems to suggest that corporate decisions ought to be assessed not simply on how they affect the profit and loss column on the balance sheet, but, more broadly, on how they influence the common good. He appears to understand the common good as the community where persons grow into all they are called to be.

B. *The Social Vision of Democratic Capitalism.* An often neglected aspect of the way of life in the United States is the underlying vision of what constitutes the "good life." Is democratic capitalism solely an economic system? Is not the economic system closely intertwined with and dependent on a political and cultural system? Does not our way of life presuppose some important human and religious values, and does not our practice in the "free market" often belie those founding values?

The Constitution and Bill of Rights inspire us with a lofty set of inalienable rights. So often we hear our way of life defended solely in economic terms—the free enterprise system, etc. Yet this free enterprise system presupposes for its operation a moral individual, a spirit of cooperation, a basic integrity, and trust, to name but a few of the values. The economic system, in turn, supports an open political and cultural community where creativity can flourish, where intellectuals can thrive, and where freedom is for all. The genius of the total system is that it incorporates a system of checks and balances that takes into account the ever-present human frailty and weakness. If our way of life seems to rest on a set of important values, should these values not find their way into the conduct of business in foreign lands?

II. AN ANALYSIS

In this case the characters see the same facts, yet they differ in their interpretation of the facts. This difference in interpretation (whether corporations have any responsibility to solve societal problems), is largely a result of a difference in values and hence of diverse frameworks of analysis. One way of conceptualizing the process is as follows.

A. *Ascertaining the Data.*

1. The great mass of people in Kingston, Jamaica, live in abject poverty.
2. Most of the adult population are uneducated and have little hope for employment, and public education is not available for many young people.
3. Tony Robinson has requested funding for a band that he has organized with 100 of his young parishioners.
4. Pastor Dave Hopkins has asked three successful businessmen in his suburban Chicago parish to support Tony's project.

B. *Interpreting and Clarifying the Data.* The facts are being interpreted in diverse ways. We will only consider two interpretations here: Frank Palmer and Harold Shein.

1. Frank Palmer, perhaps being guided primarily by the biblical image of Heir to the Kingdom of God, sees that corporations as well as individuals have a responsibility to contribute to the good of the whole society. For him it is a question of finding the best way to help Tony.

2. Harold Shein, being guided primarily by the business image Company Person, sees that the self-interest of the firm must color the perspective of all its executives if the firm is to thrive. There is much to say for this position, for corporate profits and stability provide jobs to the citizens and taxes to the government of Jamaica. Harold Shein takes this to be the best way that business can contribute to the common good. For him, business has only a minimal responsibility to assist in Tony's humanitarian efforts. Business has the responsibility to advance its own self-interest, where self-interest is narrowly understood as referring to long-run maximization of profit.

C. *Values in Conflict.* The following are some of the values at issue.

1. The value of power as service to the common good. Corporate power has its source in the corporation's ability to meet the needs of the community. Thus where it has competence and power, it ought to have a social responsibility. (Frank Palmer seems to hold this value as number one.)

2. The value of long-run profit maximization. (Harold Shein seems to hold this as his number one value.) This position assumes that if each institution pursues its own interests, then in the long run all will work out for the common good. Adam Smith spoke of the "unseen hand" that would ensure that actions done in self-interest would be beneficial for all in the long run.

D. *Alternatives and Decisions.* In this case Pastor Dave Hopkins is asking for a way to respond to Tony. Perhaps Harold Shein could give from his personal funds, while George Delaney and Frank Palmer might tap corporate resources. In any event, the participants in the luncheon discussion ought to be asked to clarify their values. The significant point here, however, is that this request opens the way for fruitful dialogue on the issue of social responsibility. The pastor might initiate an education program in the church and raise consciousness on these crucial questions for our time.

III. IMAGES OF FAITHFULNESS

The authors see Frank Palmer as an example of one who is guiding his life story with a master image from the Bible, perhaps the image Heir to the Kingdom of God that was discussed in Chapter 3. With this self-understanding certain values become dominant in a life. Such values as justice—entailing that all have the means to a humane life— are reinforced in a person with this sort of master image. Character traits reflecting the values of the Kingdom of God, such as generosity, compassion, and idealism, are accented when a person understands him- or herself to be an Heir to the Kingdom of God. Frank Palmer seems to embody this image in his life story.

Palmer sees that corporate power is a serious responsibility for its holders and that holding power is justified only as far as it is employed in ways that advance the prospects for a humane community. What is not so clear is exactly what is to be done.

If George Delaney sounds somewhat more realistic than Frank Palmer, it may be because Frank is retired and has the luxury of speculating on the way things ought to be. It may be easier for some business people to identify with George. In fact, this book has as one audience business persons similar to George, people who are open and compassionate and would like to find a way to make corporate life more responsive to human need. Perhaps as a result of this event, George will expand his vision and shift his self-understanding to see that self-interest in the long run includes the interests of all persons in the community. Although some would claim that the only responsibility of business is to avoid "social injury" in Jamaica, one might suggest that it should include much more, even to actively seeking broad social improvements when possible.

It is interesting to note that the assumption of Adam Smith that the common good would be served if each pursued his/her/its own interests has often proven faulty. Smith's position is that seeking "his own advantage" was the best way an individual could contribute to that which is "advantageous to society."[1] Smith held that a "hidden hand" would ensure that actions done out of self-interest would eventually benefit all. What is good for the individual is good for society. Over the years it has become clear that this doctrine does not always work so well in practice. The "common good" demands attention to the preservation of natural beauty, public welfare, and so forth, and often these considerations appear to be to no one's individual self-interest. Smith's "unseen hand" is more and more often the very visible hand of government. If business does not assume responsibility for the common life in its area of competence and power, it seems the government will. This area needs much more discussion in order to reach some consensus on a constructive resolution for the future. There is need for a vision that goes beyond the requirements of individual self-interest and looks to what is good for the community of persons and what will enhance its growth.

No matter how Pastor Dave Hopkins might finally resolve the particular problem at hand, the really crucial issue here is to find ways to raise the consciousness of Christians on the social responsibilities of business. There are various angles of vision one could take on corporate life and purpose. One perspective focuses on the good of the whole society. According to this view all the actions of individuals and organizations ought to advance the common good—a good that is not simply the sum of individual goods but includes the formation of a community that enhances our humanity and common dignity. Preserving the beauty of nature and cultivating the arts, as well as job training for the unskilled, are all examples of what is entailed by the "common good." A key task for business is to formulate a vision that includes broad societal goals and to assess individual business decisions in the light of this vision.

IV. SUGGESTED READINGS

(For additional readings in this area see the Suggested Readings for Chapter 11.)

Daniel Bell, *The Cultural Contradictions of Capitalism* (New York: Basic Books Inc., 1976). This book offers a searching analysis of the value conflict between our culture and the techno-economic order, and suggests a new order of priorities for the business world.

Keith Davis, "The Case For and Against Business Assumption of Social Responsibility," *Academy of Management Journal,* Vol. 16, No. 2 (June 1973), pp. 312-321. This article succinctly summarizes much of the current literature in the business community on the question of the social responsibility of business. It lists ten arguments in favor of assuming a broadened responsibility, and eight against.

Richard A. Falk, *A Study of Future Worlds* (New York: Free Press, 1975). The author develops four values as a basis for discussing alternate visions of world order.

Milton Friedman, *Capitalism and Freedom* (Chicago: University of Chicago Press, 1962). Friedman, a highly regarded economist, argues against the social responsibility of business from the point of view of the classical economic doctrine of a free market.

Jon P. Gunnemann (ed.), *The Nation-State and Transnational Corporations in Conflict* (New York: Praeger, 1975). The volume reports on a seminar organized by the Council on Religion and International Affairs (CRIA) to discuss the social responsibility of multinational corporations. Participants included theologians, business executives, and university administrators.

Theodore M. Hesburgh, *The Humane Imperative* (New Haven, Conn.: Yale University Press, 1974). The book presents a vision of what is required for a humane life in the next millennium.

John G. Simon, Charles W. Powers, and Jon P. Gunnemann, *The Ethical Investor: Universities and Corporate Responsibility* (New Haven, Conn.: Yale University Press, 1972). Chapter one has an excellent review of the issues involved in the responsibilities of corporations and their owners. An important distinction between *not causing social injury* and *actively seeking broad societal goals* is developed for the reader's consideration.

Notes

1 Adam Smith, *An Inquiry Into The Nature and Causes of The Wealth of Nations,* ed. Edwin Cannan (Chicago: University of Chicago Press, 1976). For an example of how Smith uses this notion of self-interest, see volume 2, p. 49.

Chapter Eight
Give Us This Day Our Daily Bread

In the judgment of Senator Berg (D-Ala.) sharply differing responses to human extremity loomed behind the dry prose of the bills now before the committee. The conditions addressed were the same to be sure. Witness after witness, thirty-four in all, had profiled a grim consensus: a continuing population explosion until at least the year 2000, declining food production and natural resources, sharply rising costs for energy and critical technology, and a virtually nonexistent international strategy. Senator Berg's conclusion was as clear and certain to him as any piece of history could be: even doing its best the world community in the next decade would experience the death of millions from starvation and from malnutrition-related diseases. The question was how to respond. And on that the bills differed markedly.

By actual count thirteen bills on food aid had been submitted. A number were identical, however, so the content shook down effectively into only two distinct proposals for legislative deliberation. The first as summarized by the Bill Status Center of the Congress read as follows.

Re: S. 455 S. 697 S. 2429 S. 2677 S. 3173 S. 6453 S. 6744 S. 7224 S. 7227 S. 8145.

Bills to prohibit except in cases of extreme emergency assistance under the Agricultural Trade Development and Assistance Act of 1954* to any country which does not make reasonable and productive efforts, especially with regard to family planning, designed to alleviate the causes of the need for assistance provided under such Act.

---

*The Agricultural Trade Development and Assistance Act Public Law 480 is more commonly known as the Food for Peace Program. It consists of Title I, "Concessional Sales" and Title II, "Donations."

The Bill Status Center reported the second set of bills as follows.

Re: S. 610 S. 3033 S. 3121.
Bills to amend the Agricultural Trade Development and Assistance Act of 1954 to provide the United States with flexibility to carry out the national interest or humanitarian objectives of that Act.

The committee staff itself summarized the various amendments of the second set as falling into two categories: 1) amendments providing mechanisms that would have the effect of increasing by approximately 20-25% the U.S. food available for concessional sales and donations; 2) amendments providing stipulations that no less than 30% of the food aid in any given year be allocated on humanitarian grounds alone.

In addition to the bills already submitted for committee endorsement, witnesses representing an alliance of U.S. voluntary relief agencies informed the committee of a proposal for which they were presently seeking congressional sponsorship in the form of legislation. The proposal read as follows.

For each of the fiscal years 1977-80 the Food for Peace Program shall provide commodities and revenues in an amount equal to not less than 1.5% of the U.S. Gross National Product for the respective year.* These commodities and revenues shall be used for short-term relief of, and long-term solution to, world hunger, malnutrition, and their related causes and manifestations. Disposition of commodities and revenues shall be made on the basis of need alone, without respect to race, creed, color, nationality, or political persuasion. Recipients will be selected in accord with the United Nations' determination of Most Affected Nations.

In the Senator's interpretation the first set of Bills, with the stipulation of population policy, could be understood as approaching the course advocated by some of the witnesses, a course coming to be known as "food triage."** No matter how desperate the conditions,

---

*Total foreign aid including food aid comprised 0.21% of the U.S. GNP in 1974.

**"Food Triage" was described to the committee as a policy analogous to medical aid triage. The latter was used in the Allied tents during World War I to determine priority in the treatment of the wounded. Three groups were designated: 1) those likely to die regardless of what was done, 2) those likely to live even without treatment, 3) those

the U.S. would grant food aid only to viable nations willing to make an effective move toward bringing population under control.

Initially the Senator found the population stipulation and all talk of "food triage" repugnant—and certainly unthinkable as national policy. Yet, he reflected, in the face of genuine triage conditions might it not in fact be the necessary course of hard-headed, but genuinely compassionate, responsibility? The witnesses had been compelling in their argument that wherever population is out of control and resources in critically short supply, food only feeds the next famine and aid only multiplies the human tragedy. In any case, the Senator thought, the most moral outcome was surely the policy that produced the most humane conditions for the largest portion of the human family over the long term.

Still, the Senator mused, there was something so utterly, intrinsically right about the second set of bills—and the relief agencies' proposal—in their unqualified response to sheer human need, whatever the outcome. And they weren't oblivious to long-range outcome. It was just that they didn't make probable success or effectiveness or viability or anything else a condition for relief.

These preoccupying thoughts soon became the center of conversation as the Senator hosted the regular Wednesday gathering of the "house church" to which the Bergs belonged. The debate over the amendments had pushed up against issues that were at the core of the faith, or so it seemed to the Senator. Didn't the Gospel mean taking no thought for the morrow, responding without qualification or delay to stark human need? And to those in gravest need first, without expectation of return? Didn't it mean faith as simple trust, doing what one must do as a Christian and leaving the course of history, the long-term, in God's hands? Or did the Gospel mean sitting down and counting the costs, keeping watch on the common good and trying to do what could be done to make history come out right? Didn't it mean faith as stewardship, ourselves as God's agents bearing responsibility

---

who might survive if attended immediately. With limited supplies, facilities and personnel, the third group was the only one treated. Triage meant, then, the determination of who it was that received limited critical resources when demand exceeded all available supply. In the case of the first set of bills, the stipulation on population control was a way, its supporters argued, of moving an overpopulated nation in dire need of food away from the certain fate of the first group to that of the third, and eventually the second.

for the direction and outcome of events? Wasn't the Kingdom to be "built," at least in some measure?

Of course, the Senator noted in passing, the decision on the proposed bills involved considerably more than the answers to these questions. There were other factors besides personal religious convictions. Still, wasn't there a meaning at the heart of the faith that at least set the terms of responsibility here? The query passed unanswered as the group closed with a silent sharing of bread and wine and with the Lord's Prayer: "... Give us this day our daily bread. And forgive us our trespasses as we forgive ..."

As best the Legislative Assistant could judge, Senator Berg's vote might well be the tie-breaker as the committee decided which bill—S. 455 or S. 610—would be placed before the entire Senate. No clear mandate had come from the Alabama constituency; very little mail had been received on this issue. It probably mattered little, however, as the Senator could not help but feel this was one of those issues on which the citizenry expected less a reflection of its thinking than a direction for it. It was a time to lead.

At ten o'clock the Senate Select Committee on Nutrition and Human Needs convened. The roll call began immediately. "Senator Berg." ...

This case was prepared by Professor Larry L. Rasmussen of Wesley Theological Seminary, Washington, D.C., as a basis for class discussion rather than to illustrate either effective or ineffective handling of the situation.

Rasmussen is Professor of Christian Social Ethics at Wesley Theological Seminary, Washington, D.C., and a Fellow of the Case Study Institute. He studied at St. Olaf College, Luther Theological Seminary, and received his Th.D. from Union Theological Seminary (New York). He is the author of *Dietrich Bonhoeffer: Reality and Resistance* (Nashville: Abingdon Press, 1972), and coauthor, with Bruce Birch, of two volumes, *Bible and Ethics in the Christian Life* (Minneapolis: Augsburg Pub. House, 1976), and *The Predicament of the Prosperous* (To be published). He is a member of the American Lutheran Church.

Reflections on the Story

A basic issue that is raised in the case is one that is of concern to all humankind, but particularly to a Christian business person: What is our response to the growing food and resource crisis in developing nations? In light of the fact that those of us in the United States are a part of the 5 to 6% of the world population that consumes more than 40% of the world's total food and nonfood resources, what responsibilities do citizens have? More specifically, considering the biblical values of power as service and justice, can we continue to increase our own standard of living with new products while segments of the rest of the world are near starvation? This sort of focus on world hunger can easily flow from an analysis of Senator Berg's dilemma.

I. ISSUES FOR DISCUSSION

The leader might open the case discussion by asking what others see as the broader concerns facing Senator Berg. Three focal issues often emerge: the role of the local Church in the life of the Christian, the dilemma of limited resources in the world, and the problem of waste in an affluent society. We include here some of the points that might arise in discussion.

A. *The Role of the Church.* Chapter 1 developed the theme that an important role of the Church is to help shape the lives of its members so that their values and intentions reflect the biblical way of life. How well does Senator Berg's Church perform that task? How well do the churches you know function in this regard? How might one make the Church more effective in communicating its vision and framework in the face of powerfully attractive alternatives provided by other organizations? Are there other groups with whom the churches might cooperate? One point that seems crucial here is that the local Church must be a support group, which by its prayer and discussion fosters growth in the Christian way of life.

B. *The Dilemma of Limited Resources.* Today the Christian business person may wish to add to his or her cluster of guiding images that of the small spaceship used by astronauts and cosmonauts. It has become for many thoughtful observers a symbol of our collective, global situation. Barbara Ward (Lady Jackson) was one of the first to see our earth as a spaceship with its life-sustaining ecosystem growing ever more vulnerable to quite limited resources. For her, one of humankind's greatest technical and organizational achievements quickly became a symbol of humankind's fragility and limitations.

Later another Christian writer, Theodore M. Hesburgh, effectively adapts the imagery of the spaceship to dramatize the plight of the global poor:

> To put the case for the poor most simply, imagine our Spaceship Earth with only five people aboard instead of more than 3.5 billion. Imagine that one of those five crew members represents those of us earth passengers who live in the Western world of North America and Europe—one-fifth of humanity on earth, mainly white and Christian. The person representing us has the use and control of 80 percent of the total life-sustaining resources available aboard our spacecraft. The other four crewmen, representing the other four-fifths of humanity—better than 2.5 billion people—have to get along on the 20 percent of the resources that are left, leaving them each about 5 percent to our man's 80 percent. To make it worse, our man is in the process of increasing his portion of these limited resources to 90 percent.[1]

For Barbara Ward, the spaceship is an image of human interdependence and global vulnerability; for Theodore Hesburgh, it is global injustice. One question for the reader is this: If the spaceship imagery is appropriate and helpful, what then is the manifold response of the Christian business person? How, in other words, does one integrate business competence with Christian inspiration and commitment in the context of the new imagery?

C. *The Waste of an Affluent Society.* John Kenneth Galbraith has been increasingly critical of the industrial system for what he calls its manipulation and management of the consumer. In particular, in his *The Affluent Society* and *The New Industrial State,* Galbraith is concerned that many of the material "needs" of American consumers have been instilled by advertising and salesmanship. People are being trained to act as consumers, and their values are altered in order to insure that the production lines are kept in operation. Economic growth is the unquestioned objective.

How does a concerned person raise questions about corporate policy in this area? Are there not moral values at stake in the choice of products a corporation produces? Can affluent countries destroy important values in developing countries by fostering extravagant consumer habits for a select elite in the poorer nations? Is the answer more government regulation?

II. AN ANALYSIS

The case discussion may proceed in any number of ways. The following is one way, using the format presented at the beginning of Part II.

A. *Ascertaining the Data.* One focus of the case would include these as the significant data:
1. There is a food crisis in the world community.
2. There is no international strategy to meet the crisis.
3. Two bills are being proposed as the United States' response to the crisis:
    (1) A bill that gives the food to starving nations without any conditions. (At least 30% of the food would be allocated on humanitarian grounds alone.)
    (2) A bill that gives food to starving nations only if they are willing to take measures to bring their population under control.

B. *Interpreting and Clarifying the Data.* The senator must discern the meaning of the data for himself. His quandary is how to decide which of the biblical images meets his Christian responsibility. The data are interpreted differently depending on which image focuses the investigation.
1. Trust in the Father ("Give us this day our daily bread"). For Senator Berg, being guided primarily by this image means giving the food with no conditions and allowing his "trust in the Father" to cover the purported long-range population problem.
2. Steward of God's World ("Be fruitful, multiply, fill the earth and conquer it" Genesis 1:28). For Senator Berg, being guided primarily by this image means voting for the bill that stipulates population control programs as a condition for receiving the food.

C. *Values in Conflict.* The following are some of the values at issue.

1. The value of the dignity of the human person and each person's right to share in the necessities of life.
2. The value of a nation's right to determine its own policies.
3. The value of stewardship for the earth involving rational plans and policies to ensure the survival of the species.
4. The value of trust in God the Father in light of the fact that ultimately all depends on him.

D. *Alternatives and Decisions.* Here the senator must decide. Given his responsible position and the magnitude of the world hunger problem, he is blessed with a creative opportunity to serve humankind. After the vote, for example, he might find ways to educate his constituency about the gravity of the world food situation and develop legislation aimed at long-range solutions.

III. IMAGES OF FAITHFULNESS

Senator Berg has not adequately grasped the biblical perspective; the two images he is considering ("Trust in the Father" and "Steward of God's world") both lack sufficient breadth to comprehend the problem. As an alternative, assume that the senator understands himself as a Servant of the Lord as this image has been explained in Chapter 3. He might reflect on how Jesus willingly accepted the role of a servant: "the Son of Man himself did not come to be served but to serve, and to give his life as a ransom for many" (Mark 10:45). With the master image of Servant of the Lord, the senator would be disposed to value highly character traits such as sacrifice, generosity, and compassion. His life of concern for the poor might become a model for others who possess power and position.

This central image in the Bible points us to the fact that Jesus' life work was centered on the poor. The account of the Gospel in Luke, which is sometimes called the "Gospel of the Poor," highlights this emphasis. The account continually reminds the reader that insignificant persons were singled out for greatness: two unknowns from Nazareth, Mary and Joseph; the shepherds in the infancy narratives; the old man in the temple; Zechariah and Elizabeth; and so on.

Jesus opened His ministry by reading a text of Isaiah about the poor: "He has sent me to bring good news to the poor, to proclaim liberty to captives and to the blind new sight, to set the downtrodden free, to proclaim the Lord's year of favor" (Luke 4:18) The Beatitudes begin by addressing the poor: "How happy are you who are poor; yours is the kingdom of God" (Luke 6:20).

Finally, the senator might recall how the Old Testament provides a context for Jesus' great concern for the poor. Psalm 72 speaks of how God and *all of his people* regard the downtrodden:

> He will free the poor man who calls to Him,
> and those who need help,
> He will have pity on the poor and feeble,
> and save the lives of those in need. . .
> (Ps. 72:12-13).

Food triage seems to be based on the assumption that in order for the "haves" to continue having all that they are accustomed to having, some of the "have-nots" may have to die. Without glossing over the complexity of the issues involved, it seems fair to say that, no matter what, the biblical perspective has no place for a policy based *solely* on self-interest.

The senator must expand his vision, widen his horizon. In the biblical view, justice demands that all have an opportunity for sufficient food to live. Food is a basic right. No doubt, determining ways to institutionalize this right within our present economic system may be difficult. It has been reported that 95% of the grain reserves in the world are controlled by six United States multinational agribusiness corporations. While most experts believe that part of the solution to critical food shortages is to build grain reserves that could accommodate years when there is a very poor harvest, the private sector depends on a mechanism of scarcity to prevent declining prices.

Even granted that these economic problems are not insurmountable within the present structure, the senator seems to be called to be ever vigilant in monitoring the government's policy on food. Perhaps the most startling statement on the food issue was made by a former Secretary of Agriculture, Earl Butz: "Food is a weapon. It is one of the principal tools in our negotiating kit."[2] The United States often uses food as an instrument of cold war politics. For example, the Food for Peace Program (Public Law 480), which gives food away after all cash sales commitments are met, gave nearly 50% of its food assistance to South Vietnam and Cambodia in 1974. At the same time, countries that were experiencing dire famine received relatively little United States aid.

The International Development and Food Assistance Act of 1975 offers promise for a more humane approach to starving nations. Yet much more remains to be done. As a Christian and a senator, Berg has broad responsibilities to be creative in seeking solutions to world hunger. The authors suggest that he vote for bill S. 610, and then initiate steps for more comprehensive action. Each of us might ask ourselves what we are doing about the dilemma.

IV. SUGGESTED READINGS

Jay W. Forrester, *Toward Global Equilibrium: Collected Papers* (Cambridge: Wright-Allen, 1972). The author is a well-known advocate of the systems-dynamic perspective. The book reflects the Club of Rome's concern for limitation of population and develops a basis for some form of triage.

John Kenneth Galbraith, *The Affluent Society* (Boston: Houghton Mifflin Co., 1958). The book is a searching inquiry into the role of production in the American economy and its relation to national purpose.

Joseph Gremillion, *The Gospel of Peace and Justice: Catholic Social Teaching Since Pope John* (Maryknoll, N.Y.: Orbis Books, 1976). This volume is a collection of encyclical letters and statements. The encyclical "On the Development of Peoples" (p. 387) is an excellent statement of the import of biblical values for the issues of hunger and scarcity of resources.

James M. Gustafson, *The Church as Moral Decision-Maker* (Boston: Pilgrim Press, 1970). The book discusses how the Church might function as a community of moral discourse where persons in community could reflect together on important decisions.

Larry Rasmussen, "Thinking through the Unthinkable: Triage and lifeboat Ethics," in *Hunger in the Global Community* (Washington: Center for the Study of Power and Peace, 1975). This article makes the point that any policy designed to meet the hunger crisis cannot be based on self-interest alone if it is to be within the biblical framework.

John Rawls, *A Theory of Justice* (Cambridge: Harvard University Press, 1971). This is a very scholarly and complex discussion of the concept of justice. The Bible tells us that we ought to be just, but it is not clear precisely what that means. For example, should we all have exactly the same goods of this earth? Rawls develops a substantive theory of justice that readers will want to understand. His "justice as fairness" concept emphasizes society's need to give more attention to those less favorably endowed with ability and social status.

John W. Sewell (ed.), *The United States and World Development: Agenda 1977* (New York: Praeger Publishers, 1977). This publication by the Overseas Development Council provides an assessment of the problems of developing countries and a series of recommendations for action by the United States. There is a good discussion of the world food problem. The volume also contains statistical data on: the global poverty-affluence spectrum; food, fertilizer, energy, and raw materials; world trade; world military expenditures; and resource flows.

Laurence Simon, "The Ethics of Triage," *The Christian Century,* Vol. XCII, No. 1 (January 8, 1975), pp. 12-15. This brief article is a summary of the values at issue in triage and a critique of the policy.

Barbara Ward (Lady Jackson), *Spaceship Earth* (New York: Columbia University Press, 1966). This book tells of the need for all nations to have a global vision and to establish a more equitable distribution of the world's goods.

Notes

1 Theodore M. Hesburgh, *The Humane Imperative* (New Haven, Conn.: Yale University Press, 1974), p. 101.

2 Quoted in Laurence Simon, "The Ethics of Triage," *The Christian Century,* Vol. 92, No. 1 (January 8, 1975), p. 13.

Chapter Nine
The Eli Black Story

"Giving Up: Was Eli Black's Suicide Caused by the Tensions of Conflicting Worlds?" Maura Stevens puzzled over that startling headline from the February 14, 1975 edition of the *Wall Street Journal*. As an assignment for a course she was taking on Values in the Business World, Maura had to research the life story of a senior level executive in a major corporation. She had remembered an article in one of the Chicago papers praising the social consciousness of Eli Black, the president of United Brands, and so she had selected his life story for her project.

As Maura collected material on his life and Black's story unfolded, she learned of his tragic death. She discovered that the story of his life posed a fundamental question for at least one journalist. Over and over again she read one line from the article in the *Wall Street Journal*:

"Can a sensitive person, a person with high moral standards, survive in an uncompromising financial world . . . ?"

Maura knew why the question had touched her so deeply, for it was really her question, and it was that dilemma which had attracted her to the course initially. As she pored over her draft on Black's life for the class presentation, she wondered how she might answer that question for herself.

ELI BLACK'S RISE TO POWER

Eli grew up in a poor Jewish family on the lower East Side of Manhattan. He was from a close-knit religious family that took pride in the fact that they were descendants of ten generations of rabbis. Eli

Black was a brilliant student and graduated *magna cum laude* from Yeshiva University. Mastering the teachings of the Jewish tradition, he was ordained a Rabbi and served a Long Island congregation for a year. He later went on to study business at Columbia University. He was always known as a man of deep religious convictions and, as well, a practical person.

At age 27, Eli joined the investment house of Lehman Brothers. Within a year he moved up to heading the business and industry section of American Security Corporation. From there he joined American Seal-Kap Corporation, and in a short time became its chairman and chief executive officer. From the time he assumed leadership of Seal-Kap in 1954 at age 34, Eli worked at restoring the health and expanding the profitable lines of the company. In 1965, the company was renamed the AMK Corporation, a name that became known throughout Wall Street as the brainchild of Eli Black.

In 1967 AMK acquired the huge meatpacker, John Morrell and Company, with sales of $800 million. Three years later, Black brought his talent to the fruit industry, and the firm became the world's leading banana grower by merging with the lucrative United Fruit Company. The new enterprise was now renamed United Brands Company, and Eli Black was named its chief executive officer. Income of the new conglomerate rose dramatically and by 1973 it reached a figure of over $115 million on sales of nearly $2 billion.

Unusual problems occurring in 1974 brought serious financial problems to United Brands. Up till June 1974, things were looking bright and Eli was quoted as saying at mid-year meeting that he "was quite hopeful that 1974 will prove to be a profitable and satisfactory year." In August banana taxes costing $11 million were levied by Latin American countries for the July-August-September quarter. To make matters worse, hurricane Fifi came to Honduras in September and did damage to company properties estimated at $20 million. At the same time, cost of cattle feed went up; the John Morrell division had a nine-month loss of $40.2 million. To keep United Brands going, Eli Black sold Foster Grant, Inc., a sunglasses and plastics producer held by the company. This sale netted a huge profit and brought some $70 million capital into the operation. "It was Eli Black's last, very brilliant coup," said J. E. Goldman, a high executive of United Brands.

After this setback in 1974, the top executives were convinced that the company was on the way to an even brighter future. Then on February 3, 1975, the 53-year-old Eli Black left his apartment at 900 Park Avenue and, as on every other day, was driven by his chauffeur to his office at the Pan Am Building. He arrived at his office at 9:00 A.M., locked the door, smashed the plate glass window with his attache case, and jumped out the window, falling 44 floors to his death on the Park Avenue ramp.

THE QUESTION

In trying to fathom the tragedy the *Wall Street Journal* put the dilemma this way: " . . . he believed that he could straddle the two worlds successfully by combining business with a social conscience and sensitivity. In the end, the pressure from two worlds split him apart." The *Journal* article, while focusing on Eli Black, continued to note the broader issue for all the business world. At one point the author succinctly stated what he took to be the crucial problem:

"Can a sensitive person, a person with high moral standards, survive in an uncompromising financial world . . .?"*

A friend described Eli Black as "a religious man who believed that life was sacred." In fact, some say that Black's closest friend was Rabbi Jonathan Levine, a 34-year-old Jewish scholar who was involved in creating new Jewish liturgies. As a way of observing the Sabbath, Jonathan and Eli always spent Saturday afternoons together in scholarly discussion. Levine was quoted as saying that Black was "a man who believed that he was living in God's world and that this conviction shaped Black's vision of how to treat people and care for the world."

Eli Black had a keen sense of family. He and Shirley, his wife of 29 years, and Leon, his 23-year-old son, and Judy, his married daughter, were described as a close and devoted family. Shirley is an artist and

---

*Three days after Black's death, two senior vice presidents disclosed the "Honduras Arrangement," a plan that involved United Brands Company paying a Latin American official $2.5 million in return for rolling back the banana tax from $.50 to $.25 a 40-pound box. They maintained that the bribe was made with the approval of Eli Black in Sept. 1974. If indeed that allegation is true, it could, in part, explain Black's behavior. Cf. *The Wall Street Journal*, April 11, 1975, p. 4.

Eli proudly displayed her paintings in executive offices in the Pan Am Building. The weekend before he plunged to his death, Eli was with all the family in their Tudor-styled home in Westport, Connecticut. "On Saturday, I took him to get a haircut, and he took me to a store and bought me a sweater," Leon said. "We all went out to dinner that night. Dad ate a big steak. Then we went to see the movie, 'Orient Express.' On Sunday, I cooked him an omelet for breakfast."

Eli was known as a modest man. His salary was set by himself at a figure half that of presidents of comparable companies. *The New York Times* reported that his office was unassuming for the head of a major company. A former teacher at Yeshiva University who knew him well said of Eli: "He never gossiped against anyone, he never said a bad word against anyone and he had the highest respect for every individual." He contributed to a number of charities but almost always anonymously, according to press accounts published after his death.

THE COMPANY'S SOCIAL CONCERN

A long-time friend of Eli's summed up his observation of Black: "Deep down, he was always measuring himself on a different scorecard from the other fellow. He felt deeply his responsibilities to his shareholders, but he also believed that business was a human operation." He was described by a former teacher and now president of Yeshiva University as a person who "tried to integrate the world of scholars, the world of high morals, and the world of practical affairs." Norman Cousins, publisher of *The Saturday Review* said of Black: "His insight, leadership and sense of conscience created an exciting and new ideal for the multinational corporation."

In 1972, *The Boston Globe* reported that United Brands with Eli Black at the helm "may well be the most socially conscious American company in the hemisphere." *The Globe* was referring to Black's innovations in Latin America when he took over United Fruit. He was determined to rid the company of the image of being a Yankee exploiter. Wages for agricultural workers were raised to nearly six times that of competitors. Housing was upgraded and an alternative was provided for those who did not wish to live in company housing. United Brands built ranch houses and gave employees in Latin America the option of buying them below cost. Electricity was supplied free. When Eli Black was advised by his colleagues at United Brands that the market conditions did not demand that he be so generous with the Latin American workers, he responded that in order to be true to his own convictions he had to be considerate of the welfare of these laborers.

The following excerpt from the 1972 *Annual Report* of United Brands illustrates Black's concerns:

"Companies can no longer deal with their responsibilities at the level of appearances only; they can no longer be satisfied with the treatment of effects. We must concern ourselves with causes and United Brands does . . . In some instances this has meant the deliberate evolution away from traditional policies and practices. And in others, it has entailed creative vigilance to unexpected needs which the Company is equipped to answer (p. 38)."

Cesar Chavez, president of the United Farm Workers, said that, in his opinion, "Mr. Black's life was proof that farm labor and management could work for the betterment of all." According to press reports, Chavez knew Black because United Brands' lettuce subsidiary, Inter Harvest, Inc., was the first grower to settle with the union. Eli Black personally negotiated with Chavez, and after the lettuce agreement was concluded, he invited the union leader to the temple. It just happened to be Rosh Hashanah holiday,** and Cesar Chavez was asked to read a prayer at the New Year's service in Eli Black's home temple in Westport, Connecticut.

Black was known for his concern for others. *The New York Times* reported that he was a well-liked gentleman who often provided financial assistance for employees having family or business problems. People sensed he cared for them. A long-time friend put it this way: Eli Black was a "fiscal giant who remained a rabbi, searching for God all his life." In 1974, when Panama, Costa Rica, and Honduras were in a financial pinch because of higher fuel cost set off by the Arab oil embargo, they instituted a banana tax. This tax cost United Brands $11 million in one quarter alone. Predictably, company executives were upset. Mr. Black's personal lawyer recalls the chief's response:

**Rosh Hashanah holiday is a two-day period of spiritual renewal in celebration of the Jewish New Year. Regulations require abstention from work, lighting the candles for the festival, and reading the Torah. The readings focus on the conviction that God is the creator, Lord of the universe, and ruler of all temporal affairs.

"These people (the Central American governments) are in trouble. We'll have to work something out," said Eli Black.

In 1974, hurricane Fifi caused over $20 million damage to company property in Honduras. Crops and facilities were a shambles and Eli Black's first response was to send relief to the victims of the hurricane.

Black was a recognized leader in his field. The economist, Eliot Janeway commenting on United Brands' sale of Foster Grant, Inc., said Eli Black achieved a "striking financial success." His colleagues were quoted by the *Wall Street Journal* as characterizing Eli as "an executive whose ability lies in uncovering value on a large scale and then getting control of it." John P. Schroeder, an executive vice-president of the Morgan Guaranty Trust Company, his principal banker, said of Black: "he was so bright that many people might have been suspicious of him."

Black confided to a friend some six months before he died that if it were just up to him, he would retire, but that he thought of his job as a public trust.

MAURA'S CONCLUSION

Maura Stevens struggled to find the best way to interpret Eli Black's life story. The lingering question remained: "Can a sensitive person, a person with high moral standards, survive in an uncompromising financial world . . . ?"

This case was prepared by Professor Oliver F. Williams, C.S.C., of the University of Notre Dame as a basis for class discussion, rather than to illustrate either effective or ineffective handling of an administrative situation. It is based on the following sources: *The Wall Street Journal,* February 14, 1975, p. 1, 15; *The New York Times,* February 6, 1975, p. 36; and February 4, 1975, p. 10.

Reflections on the Story

Why did Eli Black take his own life? Of course, we will never know the answer to that question, and no doubt the facts could support any number of interpretations. For the purposes of this book, it is worthwhile exploring the thesis of the *Wall Street Journal* article. The *Journal's* point was that Eli Black was a very unusual person. On the one hand, he was a religious person steeped in the convictions of his community. On the other hand, he was a skilled businessman.

I. ISSUES FOR DISCUSSION

Readers are often struck by the marked contrast between Eli Black's style of operation and that of Harold Geneen as presented in Chapter 4. One way to open the discussion is to consider the list of character traits offered in Chapter 4, and then select those traits that are most applicable to Eli Black. Another major issue of the case is highlighted by asking what the *Wall Street Journal* meant by the reference to the "tension of conflicting worlds" of Eli Black. This can lead to a fruitful discussion of how Black integrated business and religious values.

A. *The Corporation and Character Formation.* Consider the list of character traits below and select the ones that would best describe Eli Black. Cite the basis on which you have made your judgment for each selection by referring to the narrative of the case. Where might Black have cultivated the traits that you have selected?

competence	generosity	persistence
compassion	hardheadedness	rationality
creativity	honesty	self-control
fairness	idealism	spontaneity
flexibility	justice	tolerance
friendliness	loyalty to colleagues	

B. *Integrating Religious and Business Values.* The headline on Eli Black in the *Wall Street Journal* spoke of the tensions caused by these conflicting *worlds.* It may be helpful to explore what they meant by the term "world." The two worlds cited in the *Journal* article had reference to the two different communities that were very significant for Eli Black. On the one hand, there is his religious community with its set of convictions about what is real, firm, and reliable. This community has a model or "story" of what constitutes good performance as well as bad. On the other hand, Eli Black also gave his allegiance to the business world, and this community too has a set of convictions and a "story" of what constitutes good and bad performance. The case enables us to look at Eli Black's life patterns, some of his activity, to see how his commitments to these two worlds actually influenced his actions.

The assumption here is that all action implies a view of the world, and that a person understands his or her actions as fitting into a story or way of life. By looking at a sequence of actions we can glean some insight into just what "world" a person understands himself to be living in while performing that particular sequence. In Eli's case, we see many examples of his religious convictions playing a significant role in his business activity. His love of God and humankind seems to have influenced business decisions. For example, from a business point of view he did not have to upgrade housing or supply free electricity for banana pickers in Latin America. There are no compelling business reasons to provide decent wages to those harvesting the lettuce crop, and he was not required to send assistance to the victims of hurricanes. Can you think of any other examples where Black's religious convictions seemed to influence his business life?

II. ANALYSIS

If a person intends to give serious allegiance to the two convictional communities of business and religion and to participate in their discipline and way of life, he or she is destined for conflict among these warring standpoints. Maura Stevens seems to be struggling with that conflict as she tries to complete her research report on Eli Black. Is it possible to be faithful to religious convictions and still survive in the business world? To assist Maura in answering that question as she has posed it about Eli Black, it may be helpful to outline one way she might structure her analysis.

A. *Ascertaining the Data.*
  1. Black was known to be a good husband, father, and citizen.
  2. He was known as an extremely competent executive: skilled in problem-solving abilities, systematic, cool under stress, creative, flexible, etc.
  3. Black was also known as a person who lived religious values

in his business life: compassion, generosity, concern for others, humility, justice, etc.

4. Black spent time each week in reflection and discussion of the Hebrew Scriptures and in prayer and worship.
5. Black seems to have challenged the corporate system to some extent, according to reports, yet for the most part he appears to have worked within its limits.

B. *Interpreting and Clarifying the Data.*
  1. Black's corporate practices evidenced strong religious convictions nurtured in his religious community.
  2. Black resisted *totally* adapting himself to corporate values of maximum profit and growth. His life shows a full range of character traits: competence as well as compassion, for example.

C. *Values in Conflict.* Some of the chief values that Black was trying to integrate are:
  1. Profit maximization and growth—these are important for the survival of any corporation executive.
  2. Compassion, justice, generosity, etc.—they are necessary values for any religious person.

D. *Alternatives and Decision.* In trying to integrate the two stories (business and religious) with their expectations, there are a number of ways to avoid the question. One could *rationalize* and say that religious values are really not at issue in a difficult business problem. Or one might employ a *double standard* and insist that religious values are for home and church and are not meant to be brought into the office. Another possibility is to *compromise* and adjust value systems for difficult situations. Finally, one can *leave* the business world completely. What course did Eli Black take?

III. IMAGES OF FAITHFULNESS

What dominant images from the Bible might have provided self-understanding for Eli Black? The authors believe that Black may have understood himself as part of a creative minority, a pilgrim people called to be faithful to the Lord in the midst of a society that it does not control. Time and time again the Hebrew Scriptures depict this *Diaspora* situation and the image most often suggested for the guidance of the Jewish minority in an alien land is perhaps best stated by the prophet Jeremiah. Jeremiah is giving advice to the Jewish people who have been uprooted from their native Jerusalem and exiled to Babylon.

> "Build houses, settle down; plant gardens and eat what they produce; take wives and have sons and daughters; choose wives for your sons, find husbands for your daughters so that these can bear sons and daughters in their turn; you must increase there and not decrease. Work for the good of the country . . .; pray to Yahweh on its behalf, since on its welfare yours depends" (Jer. 29:5-7).

The challenge with this image is to improve the present order to make things better for the people. The hope is that the creative minority might, by their religious commitments, bring a new style and sense of value into the existing order. This same self-understanding was that adopted by the early Christian communities depicted in the New Testament.

The significant thing about Eli Black was not that he was a man of religious values, but that when he entered his corporate offices each day, he did not check his religious vision at the door. If we look at the actions of many persons holding religious beliefs who are involved in corporate life, we find that in fact they are living *two* stories. Their actions over a period of time only make sense if the episodes are sorted out into two categories: one set of actions that take place in the business world, and one set of actions that have to do with personal life. Indeed, the personal story that links all extracorporate actions over time may be quite exemplary—at home or in church or community service. Yet when that same person sits in the executive chair a new set of criteria seems to take over, a different understanding of what is really important dominates. For Eli Black, this does not seem to be the case. Like the leaders to whom Jeremiah spoke, Black sought "the welfare of the city" with his corporate power. He tried to integrate his personal story with the business story; he tried for a single comprehensive direction in his life. Needless to say, we think that following the path of Eli Black, the path of integration, is no easy matter.

It is important to note that the Hebrew Scriptures consider charity a *right* to which the poor and downtrodden are entitled. Jews use the word "Tzedakah" for "charity," which literally means "righteousness." Thus, like the Christian Church, the Jewish faith presumes that people are responsible for the poor; charity is not considered a virtue deserving special recognition and praise.

As part of a moral minority *(Diaspora)* living to praise God, Black was not afraid to show compassion, generosity, or a sense of religious justice in the full range of his life. By all accounts, he was a good husband, a caring father, and a socially conscious citizen. And Eli Black seemed to know that keeping religious images and values alive in one's life is no easy matter. To maintain their force in shaping his life, Black dedicated a block of his valuable time each week to discussion of the Bible, prayer, and worship. He allowed the values of the Bible to shape his character, and lived his life with both his head and his heart.

In many ways Black's life story offers us a model. While there is no definitive answer about the cause of his suicide, it certainly seems to have been out of character. In this regard, one might think of Black as a modern Job—a believer, faithful to God, who struggled to do what was right and yet experienced untold suffering. The Book of Job in the Old Testament probes the agonizing question of why the innocent must suffer. It would have been easier to completely forget about the poor and the needy, yet Eli Black was a good man who was schooled by his religious convictions to "see" all that was there. It is probable that Eli Black's study of God made him see that the "real" world is not to be identified with what can be controlled, counted, and predicted. He seemed to see that the "real" world also includes the sacred. To see the world in this light is to have regard for people, for style, for joy in life itself. This vision of things influences how a person deploys energies, directs life, and focuses attention.

While Black made only very moderate challenges to the system, given his situation, he may have done what he could. Each of us must build on the past and work in our own present context. The nineteenth century business leaders appear morally insensitive only if we evaluate them in terms of our present situation and with our expectations. Those leaders appear much more humane in the light of the famine-ridden world of the two centuries that preceded them. The point is that as we advance in affluence, we ought to be more sensitive and aware of human needs.

Today, standing on the shoulders of those who have gone before us, we might ask some hard questions of Eli Black. Why not change some of the rules of the corporate game to avoid molding character in the executive ranks that manipulates and exploits? Why not design corporate life according to social criteria (human and religious values) as well as economic criteria? Chapter 10 explores some of these issues.

IV. SUGGESTED READINGS

Raymond Baumhart, *An Honest Profit: What Businessmen Say About Ethics in Business* (New York: Holt, Rinehart & Winston, 1968). This book has a good discussion of the role conflicts involved in the business world.

Thomas C. Cochran, *Business in American Life: A History* (New York: McGraw-Hill Book Co., 1972). This is a readable and balanced account of the role of business in our time.

Peter F. Drucker, *The Practice of Management* (New York: Harper & Brothers, 1954). A modern classic that analyzes the many tasks of business leadership. It is sensitive to the ethical and humane issues confronting modern business.

Oswald Knauth, *Managerial Enterprise* (New York: Norton, 1948). This volume puts into perspective the role of profit maximization in the spectrum of tasks to be performed by business people.

Juanita Kreps, *Sex in the Marketplace: American Women at Work* (Baltimore: Johns Hopkins University Press, 1971). The author investigates the minority status of women in business and offers suggestions which would insure that women could compete more favorably.

Victor Obenhaus, *Ethics for an Industrial Age: A Christian Inquiry* (New York: Harper & Row, 1965). The book provides excellent chapters on how a religion-based vision confronts the industrial world.

Christopher D. Stone, *Where the Law Ends: The Social Control of Corporate Behavior* (New York: Harper & Row, Publishers, Inc., 1975). By analyzing six cases in business, the author provides a penetrating study of the power of corporations. The book then offers some constructive proposals for increasing corporate responsibility.

Chapter Ten
Bankers Trust Company

BACKGROUND

Founded in 1903 by a group of American financial leaders, Bankers Trust Company was originally established to handle trust business which many existing banks could not accept due to charter limitations. Since its founding the bank had grown steadily in terms of the amount of deposits, as well as in terms of the scope of its activities. In 1905 deposits were $18.5 million; in 1930 they totaled $537.8 million, and by 1970, following two mergers and its incorporation in 1967, the bank had deposits of $7,219 million and it ranked among the top ten U.S. banks in amount of deposits and in terms of permanent capital funds.

In 1970 the Bankers Trust New York Corporation was the second largest bank holding company in the country (based on amount of deposits). Under its organization, Bankers Trust Company was affiliated with six banks in New York State. These banks together had 60 offices located in 42 different communities in 15 counties in the state. Total deposits in 1970 were $493 million. The bank also had several international branches as well as numerous affiliated institutions throughout the world. In addition to the bank and its affiliates, the corporation included a mortgage investment firm and a trust advisory and administrative service.

The bank's headquarters were located in the New York City financial district, with staff and operating units situated in five separate locations in lower Manhattan, as well as over 100 banking offices throughout the city. Plans were underway to centralize the staff and operating units in one facility, while still maintaining the present headquarters. A site had already been acquired for a 40-story building, which would include a spacious plaza and a footbridge to the World Trade Center Building.

COMMUNITY INVOLVEMENT

Bankers Trust Company had taken an active role in various areas of the New York community. Included among its activities were a mortgage lending plan for disadvantaged areas of the city and a special lending service to help businessmen meet antipollution requirements. The bank was also involved in the loan programs of the Small Business Administration. The 11,643 employees at Bankers Trust were encouraged to work with organizations confronting social and environmental problems, and the bank had organized its own volunteer program to facilitate employee involvement and participation. Other employees had benefited from the bank's new programs to improve recruitment and promotion procedures. In 1970 job posting was initiated, and, in order to keep a competitive benefits position, a restructured profit-sharing plan was established for employees, as well as a savings incentive plan where the bank would match a certain percentage of the employees' savings.

Bankers Trust was the first New York City bank to join Plans for Progress, an "organization designed to assist in making equal opportunity a reality for every American." The bank also worked closely with the U.S. Veterans Administration, and, with the added help of other sources, they had found jobs for over 1,000 veterans, 70% of them from minority groups and many of them disabled. As a result of this work, Bankers Trust was the only bank cited by the Veterans Administration for its contribution.

CORPORATE AGENCY DIVISION

The bank offered a wide variety of services to its customers. Along with regular banking features, Bankers Trust performed a stock transfer service for a large number of corporations. This service was carried out by the Corporate Agency Division (CAD) of the bank. Within CAD there were approximately 1,000 employees, 150 supervisors and 33 bank officers. Twenty percent of the division was administrative; the remaining staff were involved in operations. (See Exhibits 1 and 2 for organization charts.)

The Corporate Agency Division had 300 clients, and the service provided for these clients consisted primarily of the various clerical and bookkeeping tasks involved with the transfer of ownership of securities. There were eight account officers who dealt directly with the clients, coordinating the present accounts and acquiring new ones. The major job, however, performed by CAD was the issuance of stock certificates to new holders and the corresponding cancellation of the old certificates of the previous owners. Two related jobs were the maintenance of stockholders' records and the distribution of dividends, stock splits, annual reports, etc., for the division's clients.

ISSUING DEPARTMENT

The bulk of the transfer of stock was done in the issuing department. Several steps were involved and these were performed by different groups of personnel. First the old stock certificates and the appropriate transfer information were paired with the new certificates. Clerks "pulled" and "issued" the new certificates which were located in a large cage in the center of the department. The new certificates were filled out by one set of typists and passed on to another set, the production typists. These employees typed the transfer data onto large sheets. This data was then recorded onto magnetic tapes which would eventually be fed into the computer for the official recording of the stock transfer.

Prior to this official transfer, however, the completed stock certificates were punched and date-stamped by the preparation clerks, or "preppers." The certificates, along with the transfer sheets, had to be reviewed by a checker. There was approximately one checker for each typist. If errors were discovered, the incorrect form or certificate was marked and sent on to a special group of typists who worked only on such corrections. Following a second check after the corrections had been made, the certificates would then be signed by one of the six stock signers who worked among the typists and checkers. Occasionally a few typists were permitted to work as "preppers," when illness or vacations caused a temporary shortage. Any unusual-

Exhibit 1. Bankers Trust Company Fiduciary Departments.

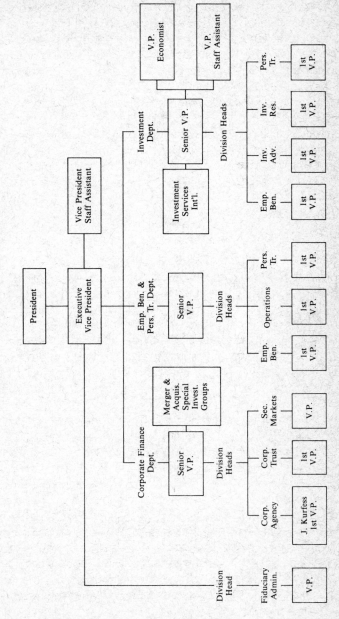

Exhibit 2. Bankers Trust Company Corporate Agency Division—Operations.

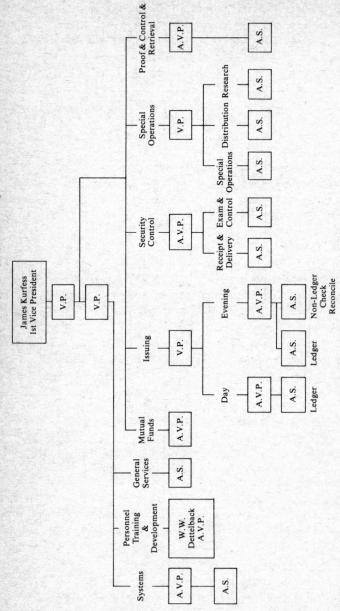

A.V.P.—Assistant Vice President   A.S.—Assistant Secretary

ly complicated transfers, or "specials" as they were called, were assigned to certain selected typists.

The personnel in the issuing department were divided into two
shifts. The typists worked in groups of 14, led by a group leader. The
checkers were organized in the same manner. A group of typists and
a group of checkers formed a section, with a section head in charge.
There were two head supervisors for the ten sections, one for each
shift. An assistant supervisor was assigned to the day shift. The cage
employees, primarily clerks, numbered 18 (14 day, 4 night) with two
supervisors. Finally there was approximately one "prepper" for each
section. All personnel were situated in one large room, with the cage
located in the center. Every member of the department, and of the entire division, had to wear a bank identification card, and there were
security guards at all entrances and exits. The reason behind this was
the millions of dollars of blank stock certificates and negotiable securities in the offices and especially in the issuing department.

The group leaders devoted their time to organizing the work of the
typists or checkers under their supervision. They were in charge of
assigning work to their subordinates, and this was usually done on a
random basis. They were also responsible for changing the computer
input tapes; the typists raised their hands when the tapes needed to be
changed. In addition, the group leaders decided when the group took
its coffee and lunch breaks and the employees had to get their permission to use the rest rooms. Another aspect of the group leaders' job
was talking to their subordinates about any problems or errors.
When these were discovered the group leader would usually get the
entire group together. One leader commented that this was done even
if only one or two of the employees were involved. Leaders also held
meetings with their groups to give out information on changes in pro-
cedure or policy, etc.

Despite the high number of checkers in the issuing department and
the frequency of reviews, division management felt that production
was low and the quality of the work poor. Any errors left unnoticed
created several problems, including incorrect stock registrations
and/or cancellations, misplaced certificates, lost dividend checks
and annoyed customers. Employee attitudes were poor. There was
considerable tension among certain employees and this had led to a
few fist fights in the lounges. Absenteeism and turnover were high.

The latter ran as much as 63% a year and management estimated that this was costing the bank about $1 million. Turnover was not noticeably greater among the minority group employees, who totaled 51% of the work force. While the majority of personnel in the issuing department were women, there were 30 men working in the department, 25 as checkers and five as supervisors. All employees were high school graduates and the average age was 25.

JOB ENRICHMENT

In October 1969, James Kurfess, First Vice President in charge of the Corporate Agency Division, William Dettelback, Assistant Vice President of Personnel and Training, and other division officers had come to the decision that certain measures should be taken to improve the productivity of the issuing department. They were aware of the work that had been done in the area of job enrichment. In an effort to discover if this type of approach would be appropriate, they called in a consulting firm whose work in job enrichment and job design was well known to some of the division officers.

In their investigation of the department and what might be done to increase its productivity, the consulting firm team examined the flow of work, the quality of the work and how to measure it. They were interested in how a transfer was processed and how the issuing department handled over 20,000 items a day. Due to how the work was completed, it was difficult to assess quality, and no method had previously been developed to provide this information for management.

The consulting team wanted to find out how the employees felt about their work. In the course of the interviews, one of the typists expressed her surprise at being asked her opinion. However, others were willing to volunteer their views on their work.

> Employee A: Sometimes I get tired. It's boring. I think it would be better if we could have different kinds of jobs. Sometimes I don't feel like working at all because it is the same thing over and over. I get a headache—the people aggravate me and I don't feel like doing nothing.

> Employee B: I don't see anything good in the job . . . not anything . . . The same thing. What could you learn from typ-

ing stock; typing names and addresses? It is very simple, you don't learn anything from that. I don't see nothing good.

Employee C: How can I explain? What's there to do? There is nothing to do, right? Because that's your job. Typing the stock. You can make no decision because it is there. You have to do it.

Employee D: Same sheeting every day. Don't know when you make errors. Some you are told about, some you are not. Maybe a correction girl will say, "What are you doing over there? You are making twelve errors a day." The work is just routine. I find that this is the main reason for transfers or girls leaving the jobs. You have no say in the programming of the work. Just told to sheet it like this and that's that. You have four or five errors on a sheet that you know yourself can be corrected before the sheets are sent out. Girls just send out —they know they won't get the corrections back so they just let them go that way.

Employee E: Nothing much good except the breaks that we get, which totals three. Outside of that nothing good. I have five bosses to account to; it is ridiculous. I like to be treated like an adult. Not a child in kindergarten. That is exactly the way I feel when I come in in the morning—like I'm going to school.

One typist had put in for a transfer prior to being interviewed by the consulting team. She said that many people had requested transfers but that the supervisors would often "lose" the requests. She added that not very many of these were transferred and if they were, it was after a long wait. While talking about her job she said that most of the typists sat around and griped to each other. They considered their work "a drag," and if a group leader other than their own asked them to help out, they would rarely volunteer. She noted that leaders frequently had trouble getting help from outside their group. At the end of the interview she remarked: "I don't see why I should have to leave my brain on the desk in the morning when I punch in and pick it up on the way out at night."

The consulting team also invited the supervisors in the issuing department to express their views. While many were enthusiastic about the idea of job enrichment when it was presented to them, they did express some reservations about its possible practice in the issuing department. One group leader said: "I don't think it's possible. The employees are still going to need careful supervision and constant checking." She commented that undetected errors could result in a "big mess." Pat had just been promoted from a typist job which she had held for 11 years. In discussing her experiences as a typist she said: "Supervisors didn't have the time to listen. They were very production-oriented and all they thought about was getting the work out." She also remarked that there was little communication between typists or checkers and leaders, or between leaders and section heads. She added that people were secretive and that some of the employees feared their supervisors. According to one of the typists, most supervisors were easy to spot in the department. They were either "little old ladies," she revealed, thirty-year veterans of the office who had spent most of their time as typists, or the supervisors were "aspiring young men."

FUTURE ACTION

As the consulting team reviewed its findings, the members considered the various ways in which jobs in the issuing department could be enriched. They were also concerned with how such enrichment could be assessed after its implementation. At management's request, the team was focusing its attention on the production typist job; however, the members realized that all personnel in the issuing department would be affected to some degree by any changes which were instituted. Other personnel from CAD would be involved as well, specifically the bank officers to whom the head supervisors in the issuing department reported. While division management had given the team its full support, it was unclear what contribution, if any, they would make to a job enrichment program in the issuing department. Concerning this, Mr. Kurfess commented: "Job enrichment is allowing people to contribute as much as they can. We have to be as flexible as we can."

The consulting team was especially interested in the role of the supervisor. In projects for other organizations, first and second level supervisors had made an important contribution in helping determine what could be done and in participating in its implementation. The team had asked various supervisors what they thought might be done to change the production typist job. Most of those questioned mentioned only a few items which they thought might improve the typing job. The consulting team, however, was confident that with encouragement these same supervisors would be able to contribute extensively in planning and implementing an enrichment project. In fact, the team was considering holding a series of meetings with all of the supervisors in order to talk at great length about possible changes in the issuing department.

The team would be discussing the position of the supervisors, as well as several other issues, with division management within a week. While it was not mandatory to present a thorough and detailed proposal at this time, the team nevertheless wanted to clarify its thinking on what changes should be made in the issuing department, and how these changes could best be implemented and assessed.

This case was prepared by Fred K. Foulkes of Harvard Business School as a basis for class discussion rather than to illustrate either effective or ineffective handling of an administrative situation. It was made possible through the cooperation of the Bankers Trust Company, and with help from the following sources: William W. Dettelback and Philip Kraft, "Organization Change Through Job Enrichment," *Training and Development Journal* 25 (August, 1971), pp. 2-6; and W. Philip Kraft, Jr., "Job Enrichment for Production Typists—A Case Study," in *New Perspectives in Job Enrichment,* ed. John R. Maher (New York: Van Nostrand Reinhold Company, 1971), pp. 115-128.

Foulkes is Associate Professor of Production and Operations Management at Harvard University Graduate School of Business Administration, Boston, Massachusetts. He studied at Princeton University and received his M.B.A. and D.B.A. degrees from Harvard Business School. He is author of *Creating More Meaningful Work* (New York: Amer. Management Assn., 1969) and coauthor of *Casebook on Church and Society* (Nashville: Abingdon Press, 1974). He is also a member of the American Management Association Human Resources Council.

Reflections on the Story

This case raises the crucial question of what happens to the person in a large organization. Large-scale organizations are increasingly

becoming the accepted means to mobilize people and resources in today's world. Everything, from government bureaus to business firms,
is growing larger as specialized knowledge and people have to be har-
nessed to handle the manifold tasks that contemporary life requires.
Bigness is *in,* whether it be in government, armed forces, corporations, hospitals, labor unions, or, for that matter, universities.

But what of the person in all this? Size may guarantee the con-
veniences and the knowledge that we all demand as consumers; for
with large scale organizations we can put a man on the moon, or
build ten million cars, telephone around the world, or provide the
academic courses for a bachelor degree. To do all of this, however, we
pay a price. We have to orchestrate people to the organizational requirements. Some critics would use stronger language like "putting
people in boxes" or "rats in a maze." And for the person who is attempting to appropriate the Scriptural value of power as service to
help others develop, the challenge is to put flesh on this value, not
only in one's family or community, but in large organizations like
Bankers Trust Co.

I. ISSUES FOR DISCUSSION

A. *Greyness.* This is a difficult case to master. Unlike some of our
other cases (Caribbean Corporate Strategy or Give Us This Day),
this case presents neither strong personalities nor clearcut issues. Because it portrays something as elusive as the monotony of work, there
is a greyness about this case; things are not going well but then again
not too badly. It is for this reason that the case is a good puzzle, for it
probes the possibility of a religion-oriented business person seeing,
or not seeing very well, issues hidden in a typical organizational
situation. Can this business person, informed by biblical images, see
through the greyness to the significant values that are not operational in this large organization? Most professional people, because of
their success and status, will not experience the kinds of work described in Bankers Trust Co., and they may find it difficult to see and
to judge.

Put yourself in the shoes of the clerk-typist who pulls and issues
the certificates; the same for the "prepper" and the checker; and also
for the group leader, section leader, and supervisor. What does the

world look like from the perspective of these workers? What can people realistically expect, or hope for, from the world of work? Can opportunities for personal growth and satisfaction ever be found in their work? From this exercise in empathy, genuine concerns about the lives and happiness of others in the organization can arise.

B. *Forming Coalitions.* One of the objectives of this book has been to integrate business and biblical values. What has become very clear is that it is not enough to rely on a sentimental religious faith to defend new economic or management policies advanced by theologians. Theologians have to do their homework in economics or management when they seek to integrate biblical values with the business world, and their proposals must be open to a critical assessment by scholars in whose fields they dare to tread.[1]

C. S. Lewis spells out the need for coalition building, and the dilemma of this case.

> I have been asked to open with a few words on Christianity and Modern Industry. Now Modern Industry is a subject of which I know nothing at all. But for that very reason it may illustrate what Christianity, in my opinion, does and does not do. Christianity does not replace the technical. When it tells you to feed the hungry, it doesn't give you lessons in cookery. If you want to learn that, you must go to a cook rather than a Christian. If you are not a professional Economist and have no experience of Industry, simply being a Christian won't give you the answer to industrial problems. My own idea is that modern industry is a radically hopeless system. You can improve wages, hours, conditions, etc., but all that doesn't cure the deepest trouble; i.e., that numbers of people are kept all their lives doing dull repetitious work which gives no full play to their faculties. How that is to be overcome, I do not know. If a single country abandoned the system it would merely fall prey to the other countries which hadn't abandoned it. I don't know the solution; that is not the kind of thing Christianity teaches a person like me.[2]

For C. S. Lewis, the Christian must feed the hungry, but in order to respond to this invitation of Scripture, the Christian must find a good cook—and perhaps, a good economist and manager, to name but a few of the specialists that may be required. Good will *alone* will not suffice. The task then is to combine Bible-based visions of what needs to be done with technical and intellectual competence.

Often these two qualities will not be found in the same person.

Therefore the Christian will have to join with experts in solving problems. Coalition building with others who are operating from different stories and images is a skill that has to be cultivated, if the Christian is to be effective in our complex world.

II. AN ANALYSIS

The executives of the Corporate Agency Division are discovering that there are serious people-problems in their organization.

A. *Ascertaining the Data.*
  1. Bankers Trust has tried to be a good corporate citizen by encouraging community involvement, establishing progressive policies of hiring minorities and veterans, and improving its fringe benefits.
  2. Serious personnel troubles are surfacing in the Corporate Agency Division with its 1000 employees, 150 supervisors, and 33 bank officers.
  3. A consulting firm with a reputation in job design and enrichment has been called in to study the division.
  4. The workers are being encouraged to tell how they feel about their roles in the division.

B. *Interpreting and Clarifying the Data.* It is not unusual for a large corporation to practice corporate citizenship in the community and to have generous benefits "off the job" for its employees. But the design of work is often left to the requirements of the division of labor and job specialization so that work can be done efficiently. Bankers Trust Company is taking a new look at that practice.

C. *Values in Conflict.* The following are some of the values at issue:
  1. The value of providing a climate that encourages human development in organizations.
  2. The value of productivity and efficiency in accomplishing work.

D. *Alternatives and Decisions.* The executives of Bankers Trust Company are reviewing the system of management in the issuing department of the Corporate Agency Division because of low production, poor quality of work, excessive absenteeism, and high employee turnover. They might decide that only a person with a high threshold of tolerance for frustration could be employed in this work and then hire only that sort of person in these jobs. Or they might decide to organize the work in a new fashion, so that a concern for human development takes precedence over "productivity and efficiency" as these qualities had been traditionally understood. This second alternative would be an experiment, and it would entail some risk.

III. IMAGES OF FAITHFULNESS

Bankers Trust Company appears to have developed a commendable social vision, which influences corporate practice. We learn from the case that the firm has "a mortgage lending plan for disadvantaged areas of the city," "a special lending service to help businessmen meet antipollution requirements," "a profit-sharing plan for employees," etc. The image governing Bankers Trust corporate practice could very well be Heir to the Kingdom of God, that is, the firm seems to be attempting to foster a human community where power is understood as service, and justice is taken as concern for the downtrodden, etc.

Yet quite another set of images dominates the practices within the corporation, specifically in the issuing department. For here everything seems to be geared to maximizing productivity and efficiency—to the point where supervisors do not "have the time to listen" to employees. As it turns out, practices thought to enhance productivity and efficiency are apparently not working.

If the image Heir to the Kingdom of God were to guide practice *within* the firm, there would be a new set of priorities. The goal would then be to design a system of management that fosters the development of the person and the community. Such character traits as generosity, compassion, and idealism would be reinforced instead of muted. Every effort would be made to avoid unnecessary anxiety. If persons are taken to be Heirs to the Kingdom of God, (see Chapter 3 for the development of this image), technology can be designed to account for the social implications as well as the economic implications of corporate practice. For this style of operation to be effective, it must permeate the entire corporation from the president to the "preppers." Bankers Trust ought to try it.

IV. SUGGESTED READINGS

Carnegie Samuel Calian, *The Gospel According to the Wall Street Journal* (Atlanta, Ga.: John Knox Press, 1975). This book examines some commonly held values in our time and suggests an alternative set based on the Christian faith.

Barbara Garson, *All the Livelong Day: The Meaning and Demeaning of Routine Work* (Garden City, N.Y.: Doubleday & Co., 1975). An investigative reporter tells of her experiences on the job, with insights about how workers cope with routine work.

Denis Goulet, *The Cruel Choice: A New Concept in the Theory of Development* (New York: Atheneum, 1975). While focusing on development, this book raises some profound questions about the nature of man and the vision of the good society that are commonly assumed.

W. J. Heisler and John W. Houck, eds., *A Matter of Dignity: Inquiries into the Humanization of Work* (Notre Dame, Ind.: University of Notre Dame Press, 1977). This collection of essays by a theologian, a philosopher, a labor leader, and experts in the field of work and workplace reform sketches the critical problems in the world of work and suggests fruitful possibilities for change.

J. H. Oldham, *Work in Modern Society* (Richmond, Va.: John Knox Press, 1961). This is an excellent study by a theologian, prepared for the World Council of Churches, which explores the religious implications for reassessing the meaning of work in our lives.

Harold L. Sheppard and Neal Q. Herrick, *Where Have All The Robots Gone?* (New York: Free Press, 1972). An important book in exploding the myth about Happy Workers by two social scientists.

Louis Terkel, *Working* (New York: Pantheon Books, 1974). A sensitive recording of the feelings of workers in all manner of work situations by America's foremost street historian.

Notes

1 The economist and Roman Catholic priest, Ernest Bartell, C.S.C., succinctly states

the challenge in "Social Responsibility and the New Theology: Comment," *Review of Social Economy* 27 (March 1969), p. 60-62. He notes that: "We cannot have one set of standards based upon a sentimental faith to stimulate motivation and good will and another set of standards (economics, management) based upon rigorous analysis for intellectual honesty . . . (p. 62)"

2   C. S. Lewis, *God in the Dock* (Grand Rapids, Mich.: Eerdmans, 1970), p. 48. C. S. Lewis was a respected teacher at both Oxford and Cambridge Universities in England. Starting out as an agnostic, he later converted to Christianity and became an admired writer on religious themes in his essays, plays, and novels. Quoted by permission of W. B. Eerdmans Publishing Co.

Chapter Eleven
The National Council of Churches vs. Gulf & Western

John and Louise Dayton are two successful people who also have prided themselves on their degree of social concern. John is a real estate broker who has been dedicated to the integration of Chicago's northern suburbs. Louise is an elementary school teacher in the Winnetka public schools. With their three children, Donald, Paula, and Kevin, they live in a comfortable five bedroom house in Winnetka. On their fifth anniversary the Daytons were presented by Louise's father with 25 shares of stock in Gulf & Western Industries, Inc. Since then, they have watched the size of their stocks' dividends grow, but without much interest in the operations of the company.

In the 1975 proxy statement, however, they were asked to consider a stockholder resolution that would be voted at the next stockholders' meeting in December. They were informed that it was sponsored by the National Council of Churches and dealt with the position of G&W in the Dominican Republic. The proposal had been brought before the Securities and Exchange Commission by the company in an effort to remove it from the proxy statement, but the SEC had ruled that it was a valid proposal. Not really understanding the implications of the proposal and not having sufficient information, they abstained from voting on the issue.

When the Daytons received their 1976 proxy statement the proposal appeared again. It had received 4.09% of the vote in 1975—better than the 3% minimum required—and could therefore be placed before the shareholders again. The sponsors this time, in addition to the NCC, were the Adrian Dominican Sisters and the Society of Jesus-Maryland Province (all three holding a total of 495 shares of G&W stock). (The text of the proposal is included in the Appendix.) Accompanying the proposal this year was a series of documents relating the pros and cons of the case. The company brochures explained what G&W was doing in the Dominican Republic.

The Daytons took the proposal more seriously now. They decided to read the material provided, do some research of their own, and discuss what they should do. They began by investigating some pertinent facts about the government and the economy of the Dominican Republic.

THE SITUATION IN THE DOMINICAN REPUBLIC

Since 1930 the Republic has been dominated primarily by two men—Rafael Trujillo and Joaquin Balaguer—both of whom came to power with U.S. aid. Mr. Trujillo came to power in 1930 and through much manipulation and even more outright strong-arm tactics succeeded in making himself and his family the largest landowners in the country. He also controlled a great deal of the industry. No organized or effective opposition to Trujillo was allowed and he was only ousted by assassination at the hands of CIA-backed rebels in May, 1961.

Dr. Balaguer, who was one of Trujillo's lieutenants, assumed power almost immediately. He forced all of the Trujillos to leave the country, but he himself lost popular support and had to flee to the U.S. in 1962. In December of that year Juan Bosch, a socialist professor, was elected president in a relatively free election. However in August of 1963 he was ousted by a military coup backed by the upper classes. The military ruled for twenty months until May 1965, when a revolution supporting Dr. Bosch broke out. The U.S., stating that this was a Communist revolution and fearing another Cuba, sent in the Marines who took complete control. They did not leave until September 1966.

Meanwhile, elections were held in May 1966, in which Dr. Balaguer won over Dr. Bosch by a margin of 4 to 3. He was reelected in 1970 and in 1974. This latter election was hotly contested by the opposition who charged that free elections were impossible since Dr.

Balaguer had the open support of the armed forces. He has ruled in a highly personal fashion and is not in the habit of delegating decisions to others, so that no clear line of succession has surfaced thus far.

Most observers agree that corruption is widespread in the Dominican government. Dr. Balaguer is thought to be honest, but he maintains his power by appointing people to lucrative positions. A person who has done business in the Dominican Republic for years says that it is possible to do business without paying bribes, but that means some delays in the decision-making process.

THE ECONOMY

The Dominican Republic is the second largest country in the Caribbean and occupies the eastern two-thirds of the island of Hispaniola (the other one-third belonging to Haiti). The current population is about 4.7 million and has been growing at the rate of 3.6% per year. (By contrast, the rate in the United Kingdom is approximately 0.5%, in the U.S. 1.1% and in Mexico 3.4%.) In 1970, almost 40% of the people lived in urban areas, including 25% in Santo Domingo, the capital.

During the last ten years the Dominican economy has grown a great deal due to the investments in mining and manufacturing. The GNP in 1971 was $1.6 billion; by 1973 it was about $2.38 billion. However, this comes down to $509 per capita. (Again by way of comparison, in 1973 the GNP in the U.S. was $1.29 trillion, in the United Kingdom $174.8 billion, and in neighboring Haiti $694 million. Their respective per capita incomes were $6,155, $3,120 and $42.) Much of the population suffers from malnutrition and inflation has been very high. From 1971 to 1974 consumer prices rose 38% and food prices 43.6%. Unemployment is also a serious problem, especially among the young. About 30% of the work force is unemployed, although the figure is only 6% for heads of families.

The Balaguer administration has attempted to attract foreign investment by a tax incentive program. Export industries and tourist developments can be tax-exempt for eight to twenty years. Import substitution industries are exempt from import duties and have reduced income taxes. Many investors also want to move into the

Dominican Republic because of the supply of cheap labor. The minimum wage is 40¢ an hour and even skilled workers can only expect to earn $3.00 an hour.

THE SUGAR INDUSTRY

Despite efforts at diversification of the economy, the Dominican Republic is more dependent on sugar production than any other country in the Western Hemisphere. There are three principal sugar producers: the Consejo Estatal de Azucar (CEA), owned by the government and producing 60% of the sugar; the Central Romana, wholly owned by Gulf & Western which has 30% of the production, and Vicini group, owned by Dominican citizens, which produces 7% of the total.

Most of the sugar exported from the Dominican Republic is sold to the U.S. This country's Sugar Act placed quotas on imports of sugar until 1975 when it was allowed to expire. Under the Act, abnormally high prices were paid for sugar. This proved very favorable to the Dominican Republic, since it was granted the second highest quota of any sugar-producing country in the world. Thus the steep increase in world sugar prices in 1974 occasioned exceptionally high profits for the country's sugar exporters.

However, few of the benefits realized through the sale of sugar reached the average worker, despite the fact that the wages of the sugar workers in the Dominican Republic (many of them Haitians brought in to cut the cane) were on a par with or even somewhat higher than those of other countries in Latin America.

G&W'S OPERATIONS IN THE DOMINICAN REPUBLIC

The Dominican operations of G&W are through its agricultural and consumer products division. In 1976 this group had sales of $444.4 million, about 11% of G&W's total. However, pretax operating income was $99.1 million or 25% of the company's total. $130 million or 70% of the company's sugar and molasses revenue came from the Dominican Republic.

G&W is the most significant foreign industrial presence in the Dominican Republic. It has assets there of more than $200 million and it owns more land (2.2% of the land area), employs more people and pays more taxes than any other private entity. The centerpiece of G&W's operations is the Central Romana sugar mill and related facilities which it acquired in 1967. Since then sugar output has doubled and G&W has moved into other areas. It now has more than 60,000 head of livestock and produces furfural, a sugar by-product used in making nylon.

Since 1969 G&W has developed an industrial free-trade zone in the city of La Romana which includes sixteen independent companies employing 3,400 persons. It has also developed a 7,000-acre resort complex in La Romana, and owns two hotels in Santo Domingo and 25% of a cement plant.

Besides its business ventures, G&W has invested heavily in social development efforts. It has organized a charitable foundation which has dispersed $7.5 million in the last three and a half years, supported various health programs (especially in the La Romana area), and undertaken a variety of educational projects. G&W has constructed an agricultural school to train Dominicans and has experimented with various agricultural diversification programs that could help the country reduce its dependence on sugar as an export crop. The company installed a new water system in La Romana in 1975 at a cost of $2 million and will spend several million more to expand it. It has also developed a program to build free housing for cane cutters and their families and invested large amounts to improve the quality of beef production. In addition it has helped develop a method of enriching rice to provide the extra nutrients missing from the Dominican diet.

CONTROVERSY ABOUT G&W

Despite its charitable efforts, G&W has been the target of severe criticism. Some observers feel that the public welfare efforts are politically motivated. *The New York Times* on June 24, 1975, reported that "leftist and even moderate political circles (in Santo Domingo) are genuinely worried that the corporation is gaining an economic stranglehold over the country that is translating into excessive political influence." The criticisms of G&W and the company's responses to them are as follows:

1. *Size and impact.* Out of a total land area of about 12 million acres in the Dominican Republic, only about 1.3 million acres are under cultivation. G&W owns about 271,000 acres—mostly in the area of La Romana—of which 107,000 acres are used for growing sugar cane, 117,000 acres for livestock pasture, 15,000 acres for related activities, 14,000 acres for resort facilities, and 3,000 acres for growing citrus, vegetable, and tobacco crops. That leaves 15,000 acres of undeveloped land.

Critics of the company's activity maintain that it already dominates the eastern portion of the Republic and that it is committed to a policy of expansion that will increase its influence even further. They also point out that the company uses thousands of acres of arable land to grow sugar cane which could be used to grow food for local consumption to offset the widespread malnutrition in the country. The critics further contend that G&W is forced to expand within the Dominican Republic because it can repatriate only 18% of its "registered investment," which means it can take out only $12 million of its current investment of about $65 million. Its earnings are higher than that so the excess has to be spent within the Dominican Republic either in capital investment or in social projects. More capital investment, of course, means more money which can be taken out of the country.

At the company's 1975 meeting, the chairman of G&W's board, Charles G. Bluhdorn, addressed these words to President Balaguer: "We are here, hopefully, as an example of free enterprise as it works in America. We are here to carry the beacon of that which has made America great. The day, Mr. President, that you feel we are not doing the job, which we call the job of self-nationalization . . . you come and take us over. . . . If you think that you can do it better than us, you do it." G&W management feels that the company is committed to the betterment of the country and that it has been very successful in improving the La Romana area.

2. *Political ties.* Many critics feel that G&W has benefitted tremendously from the political marriage of the U.S. government and the Balaguer administration which has occurred since the invasion of 1965. They maintain that the company has warm relations with political figures in Santo Domingo and in the provinces of La Romana

and Higuey where the bulk of their operations lie. One of these people is General of the Police Tadeo Guerrero, who was a central figure in the prevention of the unionization of the Central Romana sugar mill by the Sindicato Unido, a leftist union, in 1967. He was also thought to be responsible for the disappearance of Gildo Gil, one of the better known labor organizers.

In June of 1975 a group of leaders of the Confederacion General de Trabajadores (a nationally organized federation of unions) was placed in jail on various charges. G&W's critics say that these leaders were really trying to organize the cane cutters in La Romana province and that their actions offended G&W officials as well as powerful people in the Balaguer government. The government has urged unions to limit themselves to economic issues and to stay out of politics.

For its part, G&W maintains that it remains neutral in political matters and that it does not wield any improper influence in government circles. It does admit that members of its local management sit on various civic, industrial, and community boards, but, since that is also done in the U.S., there is nothing untoward about it. Recently G&W has admitted to having paid a total of over $400,000 to a sales representative of a foreign-government-owned company and two local union officials, but says that this did not occur in the Dominican Republic.

3. *Treatment of workers.* Many of G&W's critics assert that the company does not pay adequate wages to its workers and attempts to block unions which it is unwilling to recognize. These critics contend that it is impossible for a cane cutter to support his family on his wages and that inflation has actually lessened the buying power of wages received, despite increases granted. Cutters are paid by the ton cut, and the amount cut each day varies with the weather, so that a rainy day could bring only $2 to $3. Critics point out that this income—or even the higher income of $3 to $4 a day under optimal conditions—comes nowhere near meeting the cost of living. Cane cutting is seasonal, providing work for six months at most. The remainder of the year, the cutters are forced to look for other work or to beg. The average Dominican family unit of husband, wife and five children consumes three pounds of flour a day at a cost of 24¢ per pound. Rice, oil, etc., are additional costs. Meat and beans are sim-

ply beyond the means of the average wage earner. The effects of this poverty are devastating, particularly on the children. 75% of the population of the country takes in less than the minimum daily requirement of calories and proteins, which results in physical and mental retardation and even starvation in some cases. In addition, schooling, even at the most elementary level, is beyond the means of the majority of families, thus reducing if not eliminating altogether the prospect of improvement for the upcoming generation. G&W's critics say that the company should share some of its enormous profits with the cane cutters.

G&W management's response to all of this is twofold. First, they say that they are gradually approaching the upgrading of the housing in the "batayas" or groups of cane cutters' shacks. There is a great need for this since they usually have no sewage, water, or electric services. Second, the company points out that there is both a *maximum* and a *minimum* wage in the Dominican Republic, so they could not pay more even if they wanted to. To do otherwise would risk upsetting the whole Dominican economy. The average cane cutter earns $1.31 for every ton cut, plus 15¢ bonus benefits. A healthy man can cut between 2 and 3 tons per day. In addition, the company maintains food stores where workers can get a price break, but these are located only in the city of La Romana, hence inaccessible to many workers.

The year before G&W took control of the Central Romana from the South Puerto Rico Sugar Co., there had been a strike which was won by the company. One union leader was subsequently killed and another disappeared. Critics maintain, though without decisive evidence, that G&W was responsible for these developments, and that the company never spoke out against the violence. They point out that Charles Bluhdorn was on the board of SPRSC at the time. The present administrator of the mill, Dr. Teobaldo Rosell, was also head of the mill when the union was broken and helped establish the present Sindicato Libre which is alleged to have little freedom and autonomy.

G&W says that the labor union is indeed free and denies any involvement in the labor violence or in the bribery of union leaders. It has characterized these charges as "irresponsible," "below the belt," and "totally ludicrous" and adds that the company did speak out against the violence.

4. *Information policy.* In this last area, critics of G&W say that the company's activities in the Dominican Republic are "shrouded in secrecy." They argue that the company has been reluctant to release comprehensive information and that this attitude immediately casts suspicion on their activities and intentions.

Officials of G&W realize that they have had a public relations problem both in the U.S. and in the Dominican Republic, but emphasize that what they are doing will itself counter any criticism. They say that the company will be seen as having acted responsibly when the Dominicans come to realize all the social benefits which the company is providing them and their country.

POSITION OF THE PROPONENTS OF THE RESOLUTION

The various church groups sponsoring the NCC resolution now in John and Louise Dayton's hands, maintain that a full review of G&W's operations in the Dominican Republic is necessary and that concentration on export crops by the company is bound to raise social problems, especially when the poor receive a declining portion of the income. They feel that "corporations must serve larger interests than the maximization of profits and should act responsibly" and that a report "will help stockholders and management assess our corporation's social responsibilities and actions in the Dominican Republic."

Tim Smith, who is head of the NCC-sponsored Interfaith Center of Corporate Responsibility in New York says that the staff received various reports from the Dominican Republic which raised questions serious enough to warrant their resubmitting the resolution in 1976. These reports came from opponents of Dr. Balaguer, academics, trade unions, church groups, and fact-finding teams. Mr. Smith says that one of the areas of greatest concern is whether G&W is dominating the Dominican economy or unduly influencing the government, especially after reports of continued expansion and the sale of G&W land to government officials at low prices. Another area of concern is whether G&W is paying its workers adequately so that they can live above the poverty level and whether the company is dealing fairly with labor unions.

Other representatives of the church groups say that the company is willing to provide them with extensive information regarding its charitable activities but refuses other information necessary to assess the company's overall impact on the economy of the country. They point out the refusal of the company to take part in an "Interfaith Inquiry on Gulf & Western's Role in the Dominican Republic" in September 1976, a fact which seems to confirm the company's unwillingness to disclose information. Various church spokespersons have decried G&W's tactic of equating criticism of its activities with Communist sympathy. They contend that disclosure of information would dispel any false charges against the company.

G&W'S POSITION ON THE RESOLUTION

G&W management opposes the resolution. It maintains that G&W acts responsibly and sensitively everywhere that it operates. Material covering G&W's operations in the Dominican Republic is available to all stockholders, so, management contends, a voluminous special report is not necessary. Officials assert that G&W has a better record than most other multinational corporations, that all of the company's operations in the Dominican Republic contribute to the development of the country, and that they are disappointed by what they feel are groundless criticisms. The company believes it has not been exploiting the Dominican Republic because it deals with renewable resources and because much of its earnings there are put into charitable works.

Spokespersons for G&W state that the "inquiry" which the company declined to attend was no more than an "inquisition" or "kangaroo court" where they had no hope of getting a fair hearing. They question the motives of the National Council of Churches in pursuing this matter and feel that the NCC does not want a real dialogue. G&W believes that it has provided information on its role in the Dominican Republic to those who have approached the company fairly, without "threats, confrontations or other pressure tactics." The company has expressed concern and disappointment at the tactics of the NCC and feels that the NCC should not use the guise of investment in a public corporation to advocate a position on general social conditions in any country.

John and Louise Dayton found themselves more and more captivated by what they read. The Dominican Republic was becoming very real for them even though they had never been there. But they also wanted to be fair; the situation had revealed itself far more complex than they had initially anticipated.

"Well, we still have a few days to work it out," Louise stated with a sigh.

"My feeling is that we shouldn't abstain this year," John added, "even though our vote might not mean that much."

APPENDIX: EXCERPT FROM G&W'S 1976 PROXY STATEMENT*

Certain stockholders have jointly advised the Corporation that they will present the proposal set forth below for action at the meeting.

"Be it Resolved that the shareholders request the Board of Directors to make available to all stockholders within 6 months of the 1976 stockholders' meeting a special report on the role of Gulf & Western in the Dominican Republic. More specifically, this report shall include the following, provided that information directly affecting the competitive position of the Corporation may be omitted, and further provided that the cost of compiling this report shall be limited to an amount deemed reasonable by the Board of Directors:

1. *Factual and historical information:* Give a brief history of Gulf & Western's operations in the Dominican Republic including such things as a list of land held, leased, and in direct contractual agreement; other assets; operating income and revenues from sugar, molasses, and furfural and other major Gulf & Western subsidiaries.

2. *Information about Gulf & Western employees and wages in the Dominican Republic:*

    (a) Provide a chart listing functional job categories and number of employees in each category, along with average wage in that category.

---

*The discussion of the activities of Gulf & Western in the Dominican Republic and the issues raised by the shareholder resolution is based on an analysis by the Investor Responsibility Center in Washington, D.C. I wish to thank them for permission to use the material.

(b) Evaluate whether wages paid to Gulf & Western workers are sufficient to cover basic living costs for workers' families.

(c) Describe how sugar cane cutters are hired, the method of determining their wage scales, the average length of employment and benefits provided.

3. *Union-management relations of Gulf & Western in the Dominican Republic:*

(a) Summarize the history of the company's policy toward unions and their role in Gulf & Western operations since 1967.

(b) List all unions and their officials with which Gulf & Western or its subsidiaries have bargained since 1967 and a description of the terms of the contract arrived at.

(c) List all strikes and other labor disruptions since 1967 commenting on their causes and resolution.

(d) State whether or not any payments, gifts, or any other gratuities or advantages have been offered or paid to union leaders. If so, list them with amount, date, and reason for each.

4. *Relations with public officials and government agencies:*

(a) State whether or not any contributions, concessions, gratuities, stipends, gifts, use of Gulf & Western's facilities, influence or personnel have been given to Dominican public officials and/or political candidates by Gulf & Western, its subsidiaries, or by one or more of the managerial staff of Gulf & Western or its subsidiaries. If so, list them.

(b) State whether or not any advertisements or publicity have been paid for by Gulf & Western, its subsidiaries or employees in favor of public officials or candidates in the Dominican Republic. If so, list them.

(c) Provide a list of all law firms, lawyers, public relations firms or representatives thereof, and lobbyists hired to affect legislation, regulations, sales, or the public image of Gulf & Western or its subsidiaries' operations in the Dominican Republic.

(d) List amount of taxes paid each year in the Dominican Republic and the effective tax rate on operating income that this amount represents. Describe tax agreements and laws under which the sugar, molasses, and furfural operations function.

(e) List Gulf & Western officials who are on any public or governmental boards, agencies, etc."

The following statement in support of the foregoing proposal has been submitted by the stockholders:

"Statement of Security Holder: Our company is mainly involved in sugar operations in the Dominican Republic, is the largest private landholder in the Dominican Republic and has over $200 million in assets there.

We believe a full review of what our company is doing there is necessary. Large investments in export crops (such as sugar) in countries suffering shortages of food staples are, in our opinion, bound to cause social problems. While it is true that sugar products bring much needed foreign exchange in the Dominican Republic, the poor are receiving a smaller portion of the income each year. The U.S. Embassy in Santo Domingo states that 'inflation is rising faster than wages.' Malnutrition has become a severe problem. Gulf & Western sugar workers receive wages so low that it's difficult for them to support their families decently.

As stockholders, we believe that corporations must serve larger social interests than the maximization of profits and should act responsibly. We believe that a report will help stockholders and management assess our corporation's social responsibilities and actions in the Dominican Republic."

A vote "AGAINST" this stockholder proposal is recommended by the Board of Directors for the reasons set forth below.

At last year's annual meeting of stockholders, an identical resolution was overwhelmingly defeated after extensive discussion. 95.9% of the votes cast opposed the resolution.

G & W believes that its role in the Dominican Republic has been open, constructive and conducted with sensitivity to the obligations of a publicly owned American company operating in a developing nation. G&W is committed to human dignity and social justice in the United States, in the Dominican Republic, and everywhere else G&W operates.

Extensive material covering G&W's operations in the Dominican

Republic has been made available to all stockholders. There is no
need to prepare a voluminous special report.

The names and addresses of the stockholders submitting this proposal will be furnished by G&W or the Securities and Exchange
Commission to anyone requesting this information by either telephone or letter.

This case was prepared by David Brooks, S.J., under the supervision of Professor Roger A. Couture, O.M.I., of Weston School of Theology, as a basis for class discussion and is not designed to illustrate either effective or ineffective handling of a
situation.

Brooks studied at Georgetown University and received an M.A. in Spanish from
the University of Wisconsin and an M. Div. from Weston School of Theology. He is an
ordained Roman Catholic Priest of the Society of Jesus.

Couture is Associate Professor of Moral Theology and Christian Social Ethics at
Weston School of Theology, Cambridge, Mass. He holds an S.T.L. from the Univer-
sity of Ottawa (Can.) and received the S.T.D. from the Gregorian University in Rome.
A Fellow of Case Study Institute, he has authored several published cases and has writ-
ten for various religious periodicals. He is an ordained Roman Catholic Priest of the
Oblates of Mary Immaculate.

Reflections on the Story

In this book we take the position that the Gospel has to address
directly the actual situations troubling the world at a particular time.
Often, this new contact with the world will expand humankind's understanding of an issue and increase the fund of ethical wisdom. Certainly the civil rights movement, when finally promoted by mainline
churches, acted as a catalyst in deepening understanding and cultivating sensitivity towards black people in the United States. Theologians often characterize a new development emerging in the world
as a "sign of the times," referring, of course, to the words of Matthew's
Gospel.

In the evening you say, "It will be fine; there is a red sky", and in the morning, "Stormy weather today; the sky is red and overcast", You know how to
read the face of the sky, but you cannot read the signs of the times . . .
(Matt. 16:2-3).

It is suggested that one contemporary "sign of the times" that might be addressed by the Gospel is the accountability for social and political power that accompanies the operation of any large-scale corporation. Although management may quite legitimately claim that its activity is *intended* to be merely economic, it is becoming increasingly apparent that there are always significant secondary effects of economic activity in the political and social arenas. This case might be focused on two important concerns: the secondary effects of business activity; and the role of the personal values of stockholders in corporate decisions.

I. SOME KEY ISSUES FOR DISCUSSION

A. *Accountability.* The instructor might open the case discussion by asking for a list of the major constituencies and their expectations from Gulf and Western Industries, Inc. Some of the following constituencies are generally mentioned:

> G & W stockholders
> G & W cane cutters
> The board of directors
> The chairman of the board
>   (Charles G. Bluhdorn)
> People of the Dominican Republic
> G & W consumers
> G & W critics in the Dominican Republic
> Sponsors of stockholder resolution
>   (National Council of Churches, Jesuits, and the Dominican
>   Sisters of Adrian, Michigan)
> G & W management
> G & W competitors
> United States government
> Dominican Republic government
> General of the Police
>   (Tadeo Guerrero)
> President of the Dominican Republic
>   (Dr. Balaguer)
> Public at large

John & Louise Dayton
Sindicato Unido
Confederacion General de Trabajadores

As one reflects on the probable positions of the various constituencies, it becomes apparent that simply by being present in the Dominican Republic, Gulf and Western has extensive influence in the political and social realms. For example, if Gulf and Western does not want unions, it seems that there will not be unions. The country cannot afford to lose that much capital, and the people in power will do all they can to keep the corporation happy. The corporation can donate money to build the institutions that they choose: schools, hospitals, etc. The management of the company may claim that it is not interfering in the country's internal affairs, and indeed that may be its intention. Yet with assets of $200 million in the Dominican Republic, and 30 percent of the sugar production, the company's presence in itself seems to lend significant support to the *status quo*.

It may be argued that the presence of Gulf and Western has increased the standard of living for the people of the Dominican Republic, and, no doubt, there is some truth to this. Yet there are repeated complaints that the sugar workers still do not earn a salary sufficient to support their families. Remedying the situation may not be a simple task for Gulf and Western management. For example, there are laws in the Dominican Republic limiting salaries, laws that are designed to protect the economy; even if salaries were raised, Gulf and Western would have to ensure that their competitors were following suit, otherwise they could price themselves out of the market. Furthermore, it is not always possible to predict correctly the outcome of remedial steps taken in good faith. One of the major tasks of our time is to devise structures of accountability for multinationals in order to insure that the common good is enhanced.

B. *The Personal Values of Stockholders.* Corporations are in the business of satisfying customers and hence making a profit. Stockholders buy shares in a company in order to increase their income through stock dividends. Is a stockholder responsible for the actions of management in making profits? This is a point of great controversy today. In 1977 a Securities and Exchange Commission panel held nationwide hearings on the advisability of increased shareholder par-

ticipation and on the question of proxy information. Ray Garrett, the
chairman of the SEC from 1973 to 1975, summed up the opposition
position in his testimony: "Giving minority shareholders greater opportunity to push social goals within companies would result in un-
due cost and confusion and unfairly 'disturb and torment' majority
investors."[1] Garrett went on to say that an investor ought to investigate company policies *before* he or she purchases stock. Legislation
allowing minority shareholders access to the process of nominating
directors, or increasing proxy information is strongly opposed by
Garrett and many others in the business community.

On the other hand, those advocating some form of shareholder
participation point to the fact that management must be held accountable to shareholders for its policies. Their contention is that
owning stock is a form of economic power, and, like private property,
its responsible use requires some avenues of accountability. What is
your position?

II. ANALYSIS

John and Louise Dayton see themselves as socially conscious people, and we are told that they live comfortably in a north shore suburb of Chicago. The Daytons learn from the stockholder resolution
that there may be grounds to say that Gulf and Western is not meeting its social responsibilities in the Dominican Republic. They also
know that the company denies any irresponsible activity, and even
points to considerable charitable funding in the Dominican Republic. Consider the following analysis.

A. *Ascertaining the Facts.* Even without the Special Report that
has been requested, the following data is available:
1. Workers are paid two to three dollars a day.
2. Most people in the Dominican Republic do not have a
healthful diet.
3. Gulf and Western concentrates its agriculture on export
crops.
4. Unions are not encouraged and are not present in any Gulf
and Western operation in the Dominican Republic.
5. Gulf and Western has assets of $200 million in the Domini-

can Republic, controls 2.2 percent of the land, and produces 30 percent of the sugar.
6. Gulf and Western has put some of its earnings in charitable works in the country.
7. Gulf and Western sees "no need to prepare a volumious and special report" on its operations in the Dominican Republic.

B. *Interpreting and Clarifying the Data.* In the complexity of the corporate world, it is difficult to assemble adequate information. Without considerable data, stockholders cannot make a conclusive judgment on the responsibility of Gulf and Western management. For example, are the wages adequate to meet the basic costs of supporting a family in the Dominican Republic? What are the company's job benefits, union policy, policy toward the government, and so on?

C. *Values in Conflict.* The following are some of the values at issue:
1. Responsibility. A stockholder is an owner and as such has a responsibility for the consequences of the actions of managers of the corporation. Some shareholders see the secondary effects of economic decisions, effects in the social and political realms, as part of the responsibility of ownership.
2. Profit maximization. Many managers assume that they are exercising their responsibility well when their number one value is long-range profit maximization. Assuming that there are no violations of laws, there is little concern for the secondary effects of economic policies.

D. *Alternatives and Decision.** John and Louise Dayton must weigh the values in conflict and make a decision. They may consider writing directly to the company and to the sponsors of the proxy statement for more information. As socially conscious people they may also want to initiate more discussion of

---

*After this case was written, in December 1977, Gulf and Western Industries, Inc., announced that in response to the stockholder resolution it had "agreed to disclose information on its operations in the Dominican Republic." Gulf and Western said that the comprehensive report "will serve as the basis for constructive criticism and suggestions from interested groups." (See *National Catholic Reporter,* December 16, 1977, p.16.)

this issue in the community, and perhaps begin an adult education program in their home church.

III. IMAGES OF FAITHFULNESS

Assume that both John and Louise Dayton are guiding their life stories with the master image Pilgrim of the People of God. This would mean that they understand their lives as a journey where they are called "to sing the praises of God" who has called them "out of the darkness into his wonderful light" (1 Pet. 2:9). Just as the Israelites were led by Moses to liberation in the Promised Land, so too, John and Louise would be guided into the way of life set out by Jesus, the new Moses. They would see themselves as instruments serving in the task of liberation. First of all, they might serve as instruments of the healing power of God's grace in all the lives they touch. Their voyage through life would also serve a liberating role as they attempt to reform social structures or systems that may be oppressing the brethren.

In the particular case at hand, how would the Pilgrim image guide the Daytons' deliberations on the proxy statement and Gulf and Western's conduct of business in the Dominican Republic? With this master image the Daytons might have been shaped to see that power ought to be an instrument of service and that justice demands that everyone have the necessary means to a humane life. In this light, they would perceive the level of poverty in the Dominican Republic to be inhuman, and they would judge it to be irresponsible to perpetuate that form of life. The Daytons would also have the conviction that stockholders have the right and duty to use their economic power responsibly and that a stockholder resolution is one way to exercise that power.

The Daytons would be very conscious that money can be a great instrument for service, and that inordinate profits at the expense of the poor of the Dominican Republic would go against the grain of all of Jesus' teachings on wealth and property.

A noted Christian philosopher, Jacques Maritain, has neatly expressed the vision of the common good that we take to be the challenge in the Dominican Republic:

... to procure the common good of the multitude in such a way that the concrete person gains the greatest possible measure, compatible with the good of the whole, of real independence from the servitude of nature. The economic guarantees of labor and capital, political rights, the moral virtues and the culture of the mind, all contribute to the realization of this independence.[2]

By being in the Dominican Republic and dominating the economic sector, Gulf and Western has acquired a great responsibility for the welfare of the community. Economic and marketing decisions made by Gulf and Western have a large influence on the island, and becoming aware of these political and social effects is a first step in assessing their impact on the community.

In light of the Christian understanding of power, stockholders are accountable for the policies of their management. By accepting dividends and not voicing any opposition, a stockholder implicitly endorses the major policies of a company. Christians, guided by their values and way of life, would be obliged to speak out against insensitive or unethical management. They might do this by direct communication with management or through shareholder proposals. If it is impossible to influence management, and objectionable policies persist, then selling the stock seems to be the only available course of action.

Corporations are called to do more than avoid social injury by their policies. They also should be creative in finding ways to improve the social conditions of communities they serve. There is mounting evidence that these ideas are finding more and more acceptance in the United States. For example, in 1977 Smith College announced that they were selling almost $700,000 worth of stock in the Firestone Tire and Rubber Company, because Firestone, which operates in South Africa, is doing little to promote equality for the black majority. Significantly, the action was taken by Smith only after gathering sufficient information and talking to Firestone representatives. We think that such measures are essential for those espousing the Christian value of power as service and justice.

Although Firestone might claim that they are only making economic decisions, and that they are most reluctant to meddle in the internal affairs of South Africa, the fact is that the presence of corporate power can be an important force stabilizing a racist government. Corporations have power, and by doing little to promote black equality, they lend credibility to racist values. Sensitized by the biblical understanding of power, justice, and wealth, the Daytons and all Christians will want to discover ways to use corporate power to advance the common good.

IV. SUGGESTED READINGS

(For additional readings see the Suggested Readings for Chapter 7.)

Phillip I. Blumberg, *The Megacorporation in American Society* (Englewood Cliffs, N.J.: Prentice Hall, 1975). The book by a professor of law at Boston University offers an analysis of corporate life today.

George Cabot Lodge, *The New American Ideology* (New York: Alfred A. Knopf, 1976). The book discusses the changes in American society and focus on the move from "individualism" to "communitarianism." "Communitarianism" has much in common with what is referred to in the volume as "the common good."

Milton Friedman, "The Social Responsibility of Business Is to Increase Its Profits," *The New York Times Magazine,* September 13, 1970, pp. 31ff. As the title suggests, this article is a comprehensive statement of the classical "free enterprise" position and highly recommended as an introduction for the understanding of this position.

Jacques Maritain, *The Person and the Common Good* (New York: Charles Scribner's Sons, 1947). This is a sensitive analysis of what constitutes the common good by a Christian humanist.

Charles McCoy and the Staff of the Center for Ethics and Social Policy, *Ethics for a Crowded World* (Berkeley, Calif.: The Center, 1977). The volume is an exercise book designed to educate persons on the need for institutions to be socially responsible. The Center for Ethics and Social Policy is part of the Graduate Theological Union in Berkeley and is dedicated to exploring values and the decision-making process in organizational life.

Charles W. Powers, ed., *People/Profits: The Ethics of Investment* (New York: Council on Religion and International Affairs, 1972). The book is a report on a three-day seminar focused on the social responsibilities of corporations. Participants included corporate executives, labor consultants, church officials, and university professors. The transcripts of some of the seminars provide a good summary of the key areas of disagreement on the issues, and the three papers included in the volume offer some constructive proposals. The final section of the book (Part IV) offers a proposed "Statement of Ethical Guidelines for Social Investment Policy." Parts I and II are helpful in understanding corporate social responsibility.

Mira Wilkins, *The Maturing of the Multinational Enterprise: American Business Abroad From 1914 to 1971* (Cambridge, Mass.: Harvard University Press, 1974). This is a comprehensive study of the development of multinationals and contains an excellent bibliography.

Notes

1   Quoted in *San Francisco Examiner,* November 3, 1977, p. 69.

2   Jacques Maritain, *The Person and the Common Good* (New York: Charles Scribner's Sons, 1947), p. 44..

Chapter Twelve
Bill Clark

"I'm not sure I should send a letter expressing my views on fair housing to the *Riverview Press*," began Bill Clark in early October 1963.

I am worried about what effect it might have on my business since I sense that some people may not appreciate hearing some of my "liberal" ideas. However, I firmly believe that they must be said by someone. Since my experience in the Army I've become quite a bit more outspoken in my church, in the papers, and even at my store.

This is not the first time I have considered taking action of this kind. I have always read the editorial page of the various newspapers of the Midland metropolitan area and in the neighborhood weekly, the *Riverview Press*. I've often found myself disagreeing with what was said by the editors and people who send in their comments. When the fair housing and other civil rights legislation came before Congress this past June, the two metropolitan papers carried a large number of letters from people opposing the legislation. I was really surprised and shocked at some of the reactions people had to the civil rights laws. The editors generally favored the civil rights action being taken in Congress, but I felt they really hadn't answered many of these critics whose letters appeared daily. In the week before the fourth of July this year I finally decided these people must be answered and I wrote the editor of the *Midland Mirror* a letter favoring fair housing legislation.

I heard very little response from people here in the Riverview suburb about this letter. This didn't surprise me too much because in some ways Riverview is removed from the main portion of Midland with other suburbs like Garden Valley and Tanglewood each 4 miles away on our north and east sides toward the heart of Midland.

In this sort of environment people have a pretty good idea of what the next fellow is doing, and grab hold of any local information rather quickly. But a letter like mine to the *Mirror* was just a little splash in a big pond; the ripples don't often travel out here very forcefully.

THE COMMUNITY OF RIVERVIEW

Riverview, a suburb located on the south side of Midland's business district, was approximately 15 square miles in area and had a population of 14,000. Nearly one quarter of the population could be classified as "corporate nomads"—executives who had recently moved there with their families following a job transfer to the area. The rest (predominantly of middle European extraction), had been lifelong inhabitants of Midland's southern suburbs.

Homes in Riverview ranged in price from $20,000 to $80,000, with the average being approximately $40,000. The surrounding suburbs were much like Riverview. With the exception of a small well-ordered Negro community near the outskirts of Midland proper, the entire suburban south side had less than 10 Negro families in residence. Over 90% of Midland's black citizens, who comprised 37% of the total population, lived in two ghetto areas on the north and east sides of the city proper.

BILL CLARK'S HISTORY

After my graduation in 1946 I joined the Army and was sent to Germany as part of the Army Occupation. It's difficult to describe what a great experience that was for me. My outfit served for six months as the guards for the Nuremberg war trials. There I saw a people who had had a civilization very much like ours today, but somehow they fell into a dictatorship which created concentration camps and stamped out freedom. I realized how vital and important for the survival of a nation freedom of speech and action is. I'm stupid or naive enough to believe what our forefathers wrote in the Constitution. Since returning from the Army I've come to see that the Negroes in America just aren't getting a fair shake the way these forefathers felt *all* people in America should. As a veteran I've looked at what my life here would be like if I were a Negro. I'd like to be able to buy a house, travel, join clubs the way a white person like myself can do. These Negroes were equal to all the others in the service but now they're being left out of white society. I feel these people need some support. I'm not overly sympathetic to the Negro cause to the point that they could do no wrong and I'd say they were right; you can't stereotype a Negro by saying he's right or he's wrong. Nevertheless, my father thinks I've become a "nigger lover." A minister friend of mine once told me he'd often been called a "nigger lover" too, but that he didn't see himself as a lover of one particular group but rather as a "lover of all men."

Returning from the army in 1949, Clark decided to join his father who had been in the landscaping business for 40 years. It was not long before Clark's father began transferring responsibility to his son in preparation for his taking over the business.

Bill Clark married in 1950. He and his wife joined his parents in buying a two-family house in Tanglewood. During the course of several years, the landscaping business prospered and enabled the younger Clarks to pay off their half of the $17,000 mortgage. By 1956 business was so prosperous that Clark and his wife decided to set up a retail operation of their own in the neighboring suburb of Riverview. Bill's father who had always done most of his work in the field gave them strong encouragement to take this step. Bill Clark felt that they had chosen a location which afforded their business excellent potential for growth.

In September 1956, we opened the doors of our store on Cortland Road in Riverview. At that time Riverview was officially a "village" with 3800 people. After checking data which the phone company and the electric utility companies had compiled we felt that Riverview really had the greatest potential for growth of any Midland area suburbs. In the first few years we were there we felt a little like pioneers facing the Indians on the frontier; we realized we'd have to work several years at a low return at first, hoping to be rewarded for our efforts when the boom came. Now there are about 14,000 people here and the electric utility company expects 100,000 by 1980.

Ever since we started business our sales and profits have grown steadily, month by month and year by year. The growth in population was only one factor in the growth of our sales, I believe. Over the years we've expanded the business into a total yard-care center. At first we sold only plants, seed and fertilizer. Now we've branched out to sell machines like lawn mowers, clippers, rakes etc. During the summer I have a high school boy work for me, and during most of the year a lady living in Riverview attends the store part-time while I make calls on customers. We made a policy of always giving the proper advice. Since a lot of our business is from do-it-yourself gardeners, the work they do costs them a small amount in materials and a great deal in personal effort; they are extremely disappointed if they don't get the results they expect. I realized from the beginning that if I didn't insist on the job being done properly, it would mean a sale today but a complaint next month. There have been a number of times I have sent people to another store when they have been unwilling to do the job properly. We're the only store in Riverview but some people are willing to go to Garden Valley or 10 miles the other direction to do the job cheaply. I think the real cause of our growth has been that people realize that they are getting good advice from a professional in the field. Sometimes people even call me in the evening to get advice.

Despite the seasonal slump that begins in November and continues into February, we can count on sales of at least $500 per week, with a maximum of $800 per week in the best months. This year we're going to bring in a line of bright artificial flowers to draw people in during the Christmas season. I just committed myself to $500 worth of these flowers; I didn't want to go in too deeply this year until I see how well they sell. The last few years we've been adding some gimmicks like these to keep up some action during the winter; the results have been encouraging in the way they have kept up the customers' interest year round.

We were fortunate in obtaining this store because it is located in a church-owned building which is not trying to make a profit. As a result we pay rent of only $100 a month. Our other overhead exclusive of salaries comes to about $200 per month. With a 50% to 60% markup on most items we have been able to do fairly well in the last few years.

BILL CLARK'S INVOLVEMENT IN THE COMMUNITY OF RIVERVIEW

Bill Clark felt that he had come to know the attitudes of the people in Riverview primarily through his involvement in the Riverview Church where he and his wife were members. Clark was one of 16 out of 300 members in the Church who were active in civil rights and race relations. Among their other activities, Bill Clark and several members of this group had been involved in "dialogues" between whites and Negroes which had been set up by Rev. Bruce Stillwell of the Central Midland Church and the Midland Community Relations

Board which was part of the municipal government. Clark felt the dialogues to be beneficial and expressed regret that the same people always attended. Those who had strong interests in such a program made the effort to attend from the first, while it was very difficult to recruit new participants.

In 1961 Clark was elected President of the Riverview Church's Social Action Committee. The Social Action Committee undertook to inform the members of the church about present civil rights laws and to dispel some of the common myths about declining property values resulting from Negroes entering an area. The group had held several meetings in the church on this subject and had found many people who were quite strongly against the entire civil rights movement. The Social Action Committee had worked to change attitudes at these meetings to make them more favorable to the solution of race relations problems.

Clark felt one of the most important steps accomplished by the Social Action Committee was the organization, with the encouragement of their minister, of a dialogue between Riverview and two Negro churches of the same denomination in Central Midland. One of the Negro churches had been receiving financial aid from the denomination; the other was in a fairly strong financial position. In the last few months, groups from each of the churches had exchanged visits for Sunday services, and in each case had been graciously received. Bill Clark felt that many of these activities were not known in Riverview outside of the churches involved:

> Personally, I haven't been at all outspoken about fair housing or civil rights outside of our church or the civil rights groups I'm in now. I've noticed that not many people have taken note of this black and white pin saying "Let's end discrimination" which I wear on my business suit, with the exception of the Negroes and liberal whites in Midland who are also wearing them.

INTERFAITH FAIR HOUSING ASSOCIATION (IFHA)

Because he was President of his church's Social Action Committee, Clark was asked by his minister to represent Riverview Church in the Interfaith Fair Housing Association which was being formed in all the suburbs around Riverview by a group of concerned laymen in Garden Valley.

During the summer of 1963, a Japanese doctor working for the Defense Department purchased a home in Garden Valley, a suburb of Midland. The residents on that street were successful in petitioning the former owner to cancel the sale, forcing the doctor to move to the other side of Midland. The *Riverview Press* denounced the discrimination and many people expressed their disgust that such a thing had happened. This incident spurred the formation of an Executive Board, the IFHA.

The Board immediately organized four public meetings in various communities to inform people of fair housing practices and to educate them on the existing fair housing laws. It was also hoped that these meetings would help to dispel some of the myths about the effects of Negroes moving into white neighborhoods and encourage people to contact their local and federal legislators in favor of new fair housing laws. With funds raised from private contributors and theater events, the IFHA was able to bring in public speakers from cities which had had successful integration. By September 1963 the organization had nearly 500 names on the mailing list for its bimonthly newsletter (cost: $1.00) which it had been sending out for a year.

Since 1963 was to be an election year for officials in the suburbs of Midland, the IFHA felt that it would be appropriate to poll all the candidates on their opinions about fair housing. The information was then to be made available to the voters. On October 1st, the IFHA sent out 78 questionnaires to the various candidates and requested they be returned within the week. The editor of the *Riverview Press*, while neither a member of the IFHA nor an active supporter of fair housing, had volunteered to print the results of the survey.

At the end of the week, the IFHA had received only 6 responses out of the 78 they had requested. The IFHA Board decided that it would be necessary to contact the other 72 by telephone. However, responses from this additional effort proved to be so meagre that the Board decided against publishing the results. On October 14, the *Riverview Press* carried an article announcing the failure of the survey. In the same issue an editorial appeared that spoke out strongly for fair housing and the necessity for better race relations. Bill Clark expressed his approval of this editorial:

This was the first time the *Press* had expressed such a strong opinion for fair housing, which is encouraging to see. Nonetheless I very emphatically agreed with Rev. Peter Holmes when he expressed his opinions about the apathy and fear of the vital issues among our local politicians. Through my work with church members and others in this community I've often come squarely face-to-face with the whole thing of suburbia: the bridge clubs, the tea parties, the many groups who always have something going or planned to do their good bit for the world. Rev. Holmes wasn't just referring to the politicians, I'm sure. He's also talking about all these "do-gooders" who are not really involved, the ones putting on a show in many cases just to perpetuate their own ends. That letter I'm thinking of sending is really addressed to all these "do-gooders" who do nothing. I feel very strongly about what I've said in that letter but I'm not sure I should send it in; I'm sure some people in Riverview won't appreciate it.

This case was developed under the supervision of Gordon L. Marshall as part of the Program on Business Leadership and Urban Problems at the Harvard Graduate School of Business Administration as a basis for class discussion, rather than to illustrate either effective or ineffective handling of an administrative situation.

Marshall is the president of Wheelock College in Boston, Massachusetts. He did his undergraduate studies at Princeton University and received his M.B.A. and D.B.A. degrees from Harvard Business School. From 1958 to 1971, he was on the faculty of Harvard Business School. He has supervised the writing of a number of cases which focus on the ethical issues in the business world.

Reflections on the Story

"As a Christian, how much must I put myself on the line if I am to be true to my convictions?" Although there are no simple answers to that sort of question, this case provides an opportunity of exploring some of the issues. The case tells of Bill Clark, a thirty-five year old, ex-serviceman, who built a thriving business in landscaping supplies. Up to this point, Bill's story seems to be a genuine Christian businessman's story, that is, he has brought together in one life the convictions of the business world, as well as those of the Christian community. Now he is faced with a dilemma. It may be laudable Christianity to take a public stand on open housing and civil rights, but is it good business? Is it a wise decision for Bill Clark? If so, what kind of letter should he write?

I. ISSUES FOR DISCUSSION

The case can be approached in any number of ways. Before actually analyzing what Bill Clark ought to do, the leader might open the discussion by asking for an enumeration of the key issues in the story. He could then select a few of these issues for further discussion. Three concerns that often occur and merit further consideration are: the meaning of the term "Christian conviction," racism, and the role of the Church in the wider community.

A. *Christian Convictions.* What does it mean to say one has a "Christian conviction?" What is a conviction? It may be helpful to reflect on this question and to share your response with others.

James McClendon, Jr., in an incisive study of religious convictions, defines a conviction as "a persistent belief such that if X (a person or a community) has a conviction, it will not easily be relinquished and it cannot be relinquished without making X a significantly different person (or community) than before."[1] A person *is* his or her religious convictions—they are displayed in words and deeds, in style. Convictions form what we are calling the "character" of a person. Convictions are not appropriated in one snap decision. A person might see the truth of the Christian way of life and understanding of the world, but this "seeing" is only the first step. Convictions are acquired over time and are the fruit of a plethora of minor choices and decisions that give a life a certain thrust and perspective. To change the convictions of a person is indeed to change the person—what he or she sees, takes as real and worthwhile, counts as success and failure, takes as constituting good performance and bad, and so forth.

The purpose of Chapter 3 was to illustrate how religious convictions actually shape lives by means of the biblical images that have the same point as the conviction. These images give substance to the religious convictions, they motivate and reinforce values and traits emphasized in the Bible. Persons who hold the *conviction* that they ought to love others as God loves them could give substance to that conviction, for example, by guiding their lives with the image of the Good Samaritan. They would then understand their lives to be a journey where they must be ever alert to extend help and care.

People go to great lengths to preserve the integrity of their convictions. Sir Thomas More was a man who accepted death rather than violate a fundamental conviction. Robert Bolt in his play, *A Man for all Seasons*, has More reciting his rationale for such a dramatic stance.

If we lived in a state where virture was profitable, common sense would make us good, and greed would make us saintly. And we'd live like animals or angels in the happy land that *needs* no heroes. But since in fact we see that avarice, anger, envy, pride, sloth, lust, and stupidity commonly profit far beyond humility, chastity, fortitude, justice, and thought, and have to choose, to be human at all . . . Why then perhaps we must stand fast a little—even at the risk of being heroes.[2]

Is Thomas More a realistic model for a Christian business person? This is a question that each person must answer for him or herself. If one is considering taking a stand that may be costly (financially, psychologically, etc.), it seems important to weigh the alternatives and calculate the most probable outcome of a proposed action. This sort of deliberation ought to involve all those to whom one owes accountability, for example, spouse and children. Serious dialogue, reflection, and prayer ought to precede any decision. All the while one will want to remember that the Christian life is an invitation to limitless service, and each has his or her unique way of realizing that vocation.

B. *Racism*. Racism seems always to find new avenues to express itself in our growing world. All of us should reflect on our own situations and our stance toward this evil. It is well for those of us in the white majority to remember that black racism is deep in our roots. We have to overcome a 300-year history that has perhaps affected our vision much more than we are aware. Even today with affirmative action and other similar programs, black median income is still only about two-thirds of that of the whites.

The Report of the Fifth Assembly of the World Council of

Churches includes an excellent comprehensive statement of the problem. The challenge is well stated in the following paragraph.

The past years of struggle against racism have shown that we as churches need a more profound understanding of the nature and of all varied manifestations of racism. We need to confront it with the fullness of the Biblical message, to see more deeply its demonic character, and also to comprehend its psychological, economic, and social impact on persons and communities, and its roots in societies. However, although our understanding needs to grow, we already know more than enough to participate in obedience to Christ in the fight against the manifestations of racism in politics and in the Church (par. 59).

C. *Role of the Church.* This case raises a central concern of the book, that is, the role of the Church. We have discussed the Church as a community shaped by the values and intentions of the Bible, which in turn forms its members with these values and intentions. Yet the facts in this case give one cause to question how effective the Church is in this regard. Only 16 of the 300 Church members expressed interest in the civil rights and race relation issues. There is no evidence that the Church rallied to the support of the Japanese doctor or any other victims of racial oppression. In fact, Clark tells us that in the Church he has come to know, he finds "the whole thing of suburbia: the bridge clubs, the tea parties . . . the 'do-gooders' who are not really involved."

It seems that there is a serious problem when the local Church makes no attempt to correct or call attention to violations of human dignity in its midst. The Church is called to be *the model community*, the community animated by the Spirit of Christ, which brings unity to the diversity of humankind in its ranks. By living the values in the Bible and working together for peace and justice, the Church stands as a witness to the future coming of the Kingdom of God.

This book has advanced the notion that corporate leaders ought to develop a social vision as a context for business decisions and that they should be ever alert to advance the common good of the community when possible. Yet executives might well ask how effective the churches are at maintaining these high standards in their own ranks. In many cases, the track record of the churches leaves much to be desired. It helps little to make lofty pronouncements and to organize political lobbies if the local church communities themselves are not witnessing to the values at issue. The members of the Church, as the People of God, are called to be a beacon to all the world, showing by their concern for each other and their lives of prayer and generous service, what human community might be like. Bill Clark should have found his Church to be *the* significant community in which to discuss his conflict of convictions and receive the wisdom and support of his brothers and sisters in Christ. There is little evidence that his local Church rose to the challenge of a brother in need.

Before moving to an analysis of the case, the reader might want to consider what ideas and data should be included in the draft of the proposed letter. What style—reproachful, didactic, generous and openhanded, etc.—should he consider using?

II. ANALYSIS

Bill Clark has focused his attention on events in the community centering around minority families that were refused housing of their choice. He interprets these events in a certain way, and he comes to see the values that are in conflict. Finally, he must decide what his alternatives are, and what he should do. One way of conceptualizing the process is as follows:

A. *Ascertaining the Data.*
1. People of minority races were refused housing in the area of their choice.
2. The local churches did little to assist them.
3. The politicians would not speak out on the issue.
4. The townspeople gave little support to the families who were denied housing of their choice.

B. *Interpreting and Clarifying the Data.*
1. Fair housing rules are not enforced in the area, and this is oppression of the black community.
2. Many people are intimidated by the prospect of angry reprisals and therefore will not defend the rights of blacks and other minorities to housing of their choice.
3. Some people in town are outright racists.

   C. *Values in Conflict.* The following are some of the values at
     issue:
     1. Bill Clark values his business, and it could suffer should he
       take a strong stand for minority families.
     2. Clark also has a strong Christian conviction that the value of
       the dignity of the human person must be respected. Choice
       of housing is part of that value in this context.

   D. *Alternative and Decision.* In this final step Bill finds himself
     torn in two directions. If he sends a letter, he risks angering his
     customers in town and perhaps ruining his business. If he does
     not send a letter, he feels he will have let down his oppressed
     brothers and sisters. As he structures the question, the future
     welfare of his business and the right of minorities for open
     housing are two values in conflict in the person of Bill Clark. He
     must decide what to do!

III. IMAGES OF FAITHFULNESS

Bill Clark is a successful small businessman. He has built up the
business by providing excellent service and developing a reputation
for quality products. He seems to be the sort of person who takes
great satisfaction in seeing a job done well. The business image that is
probably guiding his story is that of the Master Craftsperson. He
seems to have a genuine concern for people, and his family plays an
important part in his life.

As was indicated in the discussion of the Craftsperson in Chapter
3, often this image seems to foster an underdevelopment of character
traits in the area of assertiveness, social consciousness, and flexibility
required to join together with others to stand for a cause. Craftspersons are often reluctant to venture out of their little world because it
all seems so pointless. "After all, what will be accomplished?"

Bill Clark might better guide his life story with a master image
from the Bible, perhaps Servant of the Lord. With this master image,
Bill would understand himself to be one who, like Jesus, bears the
burdens of others. He would not shrink from inconvenience and possible suffering. Indeed, he would see suffering as part of the faithful
life in the community. In Bill Clark's life and circumstance, this

master image would accent the need to be socially conscious, to over-come reticence, and to defend the oppressed against injustice. The master image would highlight the fact that happiness comes with service, and that real power, power that transforms lives, does not reside in the affluent but in the generous and compassionate person.

After discussing the situation with his local Church, conferring with his wife and family, and prayer, Bill Clark must decide what to do. According to the viewpoint expressed here, Bill Clark ought to take some action to bring attention to the plight of the minorities seeking housing, and sending a letter to the press would be one way to do this.

What becomes apparent in the case is that Bill Clark might also have a responsibility to speak much more forthrightly to his local Church. They should not only be supporting minority families denied housing, but perhaps much more importantly, they should be coming to the aid of Bill himself as he struggles with the dilemma. Understanding himself as "a man for others," Clark will find the resources to take a prophetic stance and challenge the complacency of his fellow Christians.

IV. SUGGESTED READINGS

Walter M. Abbott, S.J., ed., *The Documents of Vatican II* (New York: Guild Press, 1966). These documents repeatedly refer to the Church as the people of God in the sense in which we have used the image. See, for example, the decree on the "Dogmatic Constitution of the Church," paragraphs 12, 13, 16, 18, and 44.

Robert Bolt, *A Man for all Seasons: A Play in Two Acts* (New York: Random House, 1962). Bolt's introduction to the play gives further insight on religious convictions.

Stephen MacDonald, ed., *Business and Blacks* (Princeton: Dow Jones Books, 1970). The book contains selected articles from the *Wall Street Journal* on minorities as employees and entrepreneurs.

James Wm. McClendon, Jr., *Understanding Religious Convictions* (Notre Dame, Ind.: Univ. of Notre Dame Press, 1975). The thesis of this book is that one "justifies" a religious conviction by understanding it, and the best way to understand a conviction is to examine the language by which people express it.

Henri J. M. Nouwen, *With Open Hands* (Notre Dame, Ind.: Ave Maria Press, 1972), pp. 138-148. This is an excellent meditation on prayer and its role in the life of service.

David M. Patton, ed., *Breaking Barriers: Nairobi 1975* (Grand Rapids, Mich.: Eerdmans, 1976), pp. 109-113, 118. This reference is to the statement on racism from the Official Report of the Fifth Assembly of the World Council of Churches held in Nairobi, 23 November-10 December 1975. The World Council of Churches is an international organization of 286 Protestant churches representing over 85 nations. Founded in Amsterdam in 1948, the assembly has met five times since then. One of the functions of the assembly is to "set out fully the challenges and tasks committed to the churches" and to provide "a series of recommendations to the churches for future study and action."

John Howard Yoder, "The Biblical Mandate," *Post-American* Vol. 3, No. 3 (April 1974), pp. 21-25. John Yoder is an ordained minister in the Mennonite Church and is well known for his writings stressing the pacifist implications of the New Testament message. This article focuses on the life of the Church as a locus of moral decision-making for the active Christian. See also his *Politics of Jesus* (Grand Rapids, Mich.: Eerdmans, 1972).

Notes

1   James Wm. McClendon, Jr., *Understanding Religious Convictions* (Notre Dame, Ind.: Univ. of Notre Dame Press, 1975), p. 7.

2   Robert Bolt, *A Man for all Seasons: A Play in Two Acts* (New York: Random House, 1962), p. 141. Reprinted with permission. ©1962 by Random House, Inc.

Chapter Thirteen
The John Caron Story

Tom Britt unfastened his seat belt and opened his brief case to find his tape recorder. All around him fellow passengers were stirring, either ordering drinks or selecting magazines for the sixty-minute flight. Tom wanted to use this time to listen to a speech he had just heard.

Tom Britt laughed as he thought about the irony of this trip. His wife, Shirley, and he had decided about eighteen months ago that they ought to join a church. Their children were starting grade school and up to that time the Britts had pretty well ignored religion. But it seemed that it was time to start attending church if the kids were to have any religious exposure.

But church attendance to their amusement soon bloomed to considerable involvement: Shirley in an alcoholic abuse program for teenagers and Tom in an adult education center, both sponsored by their church. At the urging of their minister, Tom agreed to attend a religious retreat to find out its possible use for the members of the church. Tom, an assistant to a corporate division manager, was able to arrange his work so as to attend.

He had mixed feelings about the retreat because much of it didn't seem too helpful for most members of the church, who are mainly business people and professionals. Yet the last talk resonated within Tom. The speaker, John Caron, an apparently very successful businessman, talked about how he related religious values with his business. Tom was struck by the appropriateness of John Caron's subject to his own life. He had just never thought of this possibility.

He settled back and activated the tape.

THE TAPE

Let me start out by giving some of my background. I grew up in Chicago, although I spent summers in a small midwestern town in which my family's wool-yarn-spinning factory was a major employer. I attended the University of Notre Dame, and graduated in 1945 with a degree in chemical engineering. Notre Dame prepared me well, *technically*, to be an engineer, but I had little knowledge in the practical applications of religion to social institutions and social problems.

Later I served in the navy for a year and in 1946 joined the company which was then doing about 4 million dollars in sales. I remember sitting around the home office, cooling my heels. I just couldn't stand the tedium, so I really scratched for something to do. My first job with any sort of responsibility was wool buyer for the company; this was about 100 percent of our raw materials. It was a critical job because wool was world-traded and fluctuated greatly in price. Buying right could have a significant impact on the profits of our company.

To show you the role that chance plays in one's career, the only reason I moved into wool buying was because the principal buyer retired. In any case, it was a great opportunity to understand international problems and markets right after World War II. Boston was the big market where sellers from the Southern Hemisphere came. Australia, New Zealand and South America were represented; I had to learn quickly about these countries in order to judge the price movement in the market.

I had the chance to get a feel for the rest of the industry at the Boston Wool Market and find out where the industry was heading—which was into a slump. The companies that had survived the Great Depression, a managerial feat of considerable proportions, had spent the years of World War II at breakneck speed of production. In the early postwar years our industry found itself with four problems: First, obsolete and wornout machinery; second, competition from new companies in the South with new equipment and lower wages; third, little history of product or machinery research and development; finally, the threat of the synthetic yarns like nylon, orlon, etc.

The chemical companies, like DuPont, that made these new yarns were large, adequately financed, and heavily into research. Old line wool yarn manufacturers had very little going for themselves. To show what happened when I started, there were twenty-eight firms in our industry. Today there are only two of these still in existence.

Later I spent a year visiting the latest textile plants in the South, trying to learn about more efficient machinery and techniques. Could we adapt the idea to our business? Would it help us drive down costs and keep us competitive? And for a company our size, this is the closest we could ever reach anything as sophisticated as research and development. Until enough of our competitors had folded and left the survivors with an adequate market to stay afloat, the challenge was instant improvement in efficiency through innovation and cost-cutting. It can be pretty lonely competing on the one side with the giants with their new plants, and on the other side with marginal competitors who are cutting prices to close an order—hoping to survive.

But we survived, and with the growth of the middle fifties, we found breathing room to look at other dimensions of our operations. I started to examine the financial controls of the company, which needed a lot of work. At the end of the accounting year, we knew we were making an overall profit. But which lines were profitable, and ought to be pushed; or, which lines were costly and profitless, and should be phased out? We found out that we just didn't know. We had to upgrade our concept of budgets, and introduce some hard-headed financial assessments of our operations.

For example, we supplied a manufactured wool yarn to our customers who in turn knitted the yarn into sweaters, socks, and gloves. In the fifties we had a product called Banlon, which was new and had certain aesthetics that were popular with the clothes-buying public. What happened was that a big customer of ours, using Banlon for golf shirts, could make a huge profit. Yet that company felt it could dictate the prices we could charge; since they were a big customer, they could dominate us. And they could, leaving us with relatively little control over our own destiny.

At this time, I was still a bachelor and used to spend the weekends with my sister and her husband. They were very active in the Christian Family Movement, which was an organization for married couples within the Catholic Church. Couples would come together bi-weekly to study a passage from the Scriptures with the help of a priest; this would be about one-half of the meeting. Then they would explore the good and the bad of the world that touches on marriage and the family—which is just about everything.

Since I was hanging around the house, I naturally started sitting in on the discussions. And I learned a great deal about religion in my life. (Later when I was married, my wife and I joined a group.) First, the Scripture is the agenda for social action for Christians, who must transform the family, the neighborhood, the city, and the world into a closer approximation of the values that Jesus Christ taught and lived. Second, the world around us is a complicated place that demands careful observations, hard-headed judgments about what actions to take to transform that world, and then the work. Third and most importantly, at each meeting we had to report on the actions taken since the last meeting.

We could readily see that Christian values could be translated into actions that did change for the better our family lives, neighborhoods and even cities. We found out that we were no longer overwhelmed and frustrated by the world; it could be changed by the concretization of Christian values through the steps of "observe, judge, and act." We found out that we could change the world: "A lot of little things do add up." We found the words and stories of the Gospels coming alive in our lives through the meetings, the commitment and the actions. "To love one's neighbor as oneself," which can be a formalized slogan, becomes a series of action-projects in the family, neighborhood, and community. It was often hard work, but it was worth it.

In the 1960s, some businessmen formed the National Conference of Christian Employers and Managers, but that organization barely got off the ground and did not survive for long. However, it did help me to see opportunities for these values and their implementation in the business world. We had to confront the question: "Is all the power and wealth that we have compatible with religion?" And in Scripture there are some strong statements, like "You cannot be the slave both of God and of money." Or the point about it is easier for a camel to pass through the eye of a needle than for a rich man to get into heaven. These were some difficult problems for us.

My answer is that I don't think that Christ said that having money or being rich was *per se* an evil. I think he was saying that this wealth becomes an evil when wealth obscures all other issues or responsibilities. Now business can have such a hold on the executive that it can very easily obscure all the other issues. Why? Business is exciting; it is interesting; it is all encompassing; and a person can easily get into the situation where business is all he thinks about. In that case, he becomes like the camel.

Now my salary is higher than other executives or workers in the company; I would justify it as a recognition of my greater responsibility. I hesitate to talk about my salary as a reward for talent that I may possess and exercise, but I think you will readily appreciate that there is another justification for higher salaries for some, and lower salaries for others. Our company, and every other company that I am aware of, uses salary as a recognition of talents and responsibilities. The person who really puts out and shows results is entitled to higher compensation than those who don't put out. I see nothing inconsistent with scriptural values in rewarding people for their efforts and abilities.

The image from Scripture that strikes me the strongest is the passage where Christ tells us about the Last Judgment, in which all of us are divided into either sheep or goats, some of us going to heaven and others of us going to hell. The important point is why some are sheep and others are goats. It all pivots on whether we fed, housed, clothed, and took care of the least, or weakest brothers and sisters of Christ . . . which includes everybody. This is the essence of Christ's teachings and the bedrock of the Christian tradition, no matter whether we are talking about five hundred years ago or five hundred years into the future. Now the trick is to figure out how you do this in today's society. For me, it is contributing to the material well-being of everybody by being a competent manager.

But I admit that there can be problems. And I had to face them in my business career. I'll give you a specific example that we faced a few years ago. Our company had a particular division that was always losing money. I finally told my senior executives: "Look, we will have to get rid of the manager of that division and bring in a new one to turn that unit around." Well, the guy they brought in was a tough, hard-boiled manager. I went along with the decision by telling them: "I don't care what style of management he uses as long as he gets that division operating in the black." After a time observing his management techniques and seeing what was happening, I found out that I couldn't be indifferent to his authoritarian style. I found out that I couldn't accept his blindness about people and the environment that he was developing there. I had to struggle with this question for several years, but I finally decided that his style was unacceptable to me and what I thought our organization should represent. We had to get a new manager and struggle in other ways to turn the division around.

In the sixties, we made the decision to change the basic strategy of the company. Up to this time we had been a manufacturer of wool yarn for other companies to make into consumer products; or making consumer products for large retail concerns using their labels. In either case, too many companies could influence our operations by controlling prices and profit margins. We would always be a marginal operation at the beck and call of the giants. To get out from underneath, we had to build up a line of consumer products under our own label.

This meant a new strategy: turning a basically manufacturing organization into a marketing and consumer-conscious organization. We were good at spinning yarn; we became good at making consumer products for somebody else's label; now we wanted to carve out a segment of the market for our own label. But which market? And how do you reach this market? We decided that people had more leisure time, and hopefully, an interest in knitting their own clothes or shawls, bedspreads and rugs. We also felt that helping people use their leisure time creatively would be a small way to improve the quality of life.

Fortunately, there was a viable market to tap. But to reach this market required new talent and people in our organization. We had to learn quickly in a new field where failure might mean financial disaster. But with a "quick learn" by our people and with the help of the new people we brought into the organization, we were successful in reaching and exploiting the growing interest in knitting yarn and do-it-yourself craft products. By the seventies, our company was the leader in this field . . .

Now a question I am frequently asked: "Can a person be both a business executive and a Christian at the same time?"

First, I would like to change the question to "Can you *try* to be a business executive; can you *try* to be a true Christian?" There are immense difficulties in being either of them, let alone mixing them together. Yet I believe it can be done.

Another way of answering this question would be to pose another; "Can you be a Christian in the 20th Century?" After all, it is a century characterized by complex organizations and problems that need executive leadership, and business has been an integral part of the growth experienced during the century. If the Christian can't be a business executive, then he or she will be writing off a big chunk of modern life and responsibility. Do we Christians want to do that?

I reject the argument that one cannot be a Christian and be a successful business person. Likewise I reject the argument that Christianity somehow ratifies whatever the corporate executive does. I see myself living out a synthesis of these two powerful worlds. Sometimes I am pulled toward one, and other times I am pulled toward the other.

Now to get out of this bind, the first thing is for the Christian business person to be constantly seeking and asking: "Is there a Christian value or an ethical aspect to the problem we are considering? Have we missed anything because we are so wrapped up in the proximate, obvious dimensions of the operations."

Maybe a better way to explain this is to talk in terms of sins of omission and sins of commission. I believe that Christ wanted his followers to worry about sins of omission, that is, "what did you not do for the least of your brothers and sisters?" He didn't worry too much about sins of commission like adultery, murder, and breaking the religious laws. These would be taken care of by the authorities. He recognized that his followers would break some of these, and therefore, you might say that he spent much of his time with "sinners of commission," urging them to avoid sins of omission by worshiping the Father more than was required, or serving others *more* and in different ways than was required by law.

To put all this in the contemporary context of business, I think we have to worry certainly about "sins of commission," that is, breaking the law or violating regulations, or briberies, or discredited business practices. There has been much in the media about all this.

But if we just stop there, then we are not giving any weight or emphasis to Christ's concern about "sins of omission." And there are a lot of "omissions" to work on, from racial and ethnic injustice to human obsolescence and waste in large organizations, from consumer rights to the poor in our country and worldwide.

All of this sounds terribly ambitious and heady. Let me put it in perspective. I remember hearing a speech by Crawford Greenewalt, who at that time was chairman of the board of DuPont. He said (and I have quoted it a million times): "The difference between mediocrity and success is not a flash of brilliance or genius, but it is doing many small things a little bit better." And I interpret Christ the same way. I don't think Christ was asking the people of his time or asking us today to have flashes of brilliant action and insight. If you look at the people he spent his time with, many were failures or only modest in ability. But the theme that comes through is to keep asking the important questions and to keep on trying.

Point two is this question of people . . . of having sensitivity and awareness about the needs of people. And in my experience most people fail in business not because they lack technical skills, but because they lack people skills. If you go back into business history to the start of the Industrial Revolution, manufacturing was the emphasis—just produce goods. People were mainly interested in industrial output because the standard of living was so low. Then business evolved into a marketing era; it wasn't enough to simply turn out the goods. The business person had to identify his or her potential customers and create an acceptance of the product. I think it was Peter Drucker who said: "The goal of the business firm is not profits, but the creating and satisfying of customers." These are the marketing functions of consumer research, advertising, pricing, distribution channels, etc.

More recently we have seen a change in emphasis to the financial control of the firm. The road to the top was more and more the financial and accounting aspects of the business but I believe that this emphasis has peaked. I foresee that the new emphasis, the one that's starting, is the people era in business. People working are more educated; foremen have college degrees; managers have MBA's. So all the ranks in business today are better educated, and their expectations are higher. We're talking much about "the quality of life" today. Workers and managers want this "quality of life"—not just for their vacations—but they want it extended to their work environment. I believe the effective managers of the future, the ones who will rise to the top, are those who are very effective in organization and people skills. They will have to be able to answer the question: How can we create an environment in which the talents and skills of working people are being recognized and maximized?

If you follow the literature on the subject you will find that all kinds of experiments are going on in business: job enrichment, flextime, profit-sharing, and job rotation. But there is one common thread that runs through all of these experiments, that is, there must be a high degree of participation and involvement by the workers and middle managers in planning their worklife. This is good business, and can be highly pragmatic because there have been some spurts in productivity. But it is good ethics and consistent with Christian values .

The third priority I made for myself was the need for business competence. There is nothing to me less inspiring than a person who talks Christian values and ethics, but who is a failure in his or her profession or work. A person can talk, but can he or she act? Can he or she accomplish anything? I think the mark of the Christian business person has to be competence in a very demanding profession. When I hear young people say that business is a rat-race, or it is dirty, or "I won't get in the gutter" my reaction is that this is a copout. This is a substitute for the hard work that competence implies. If a person believes that business needs changing or reform, then that person has to get into the action by being competent. He or she will then have the respect of business peers *and* have an influence for reform of business.

This is true through the entire organization. I think that any manager from the foreman up to the chairman of the board can live out these Christian values and principles with his or her superiors, peers, and subordinates. So regardless of the level one holds in the organization, the same principles can apply. I admit that the impact of a decision by the chairman of the board will be greater than that of the foreman. But the impact of the foreman's decision within the scope of his or her job can be just as important and necessary. Any good manager has to ask how he or she relates to the people that he or she works with. I remember an old cartoon about the navy; there would be the Admiral barking at the Captain, the Captain with the Commander, and so forth down the line until the apprentice seaman barked at the parrot. The point that I am making here is that someone should have broken that line of barking. If you get stepped on, the tendency is for you to turn around and step on the other guy. But I believe that there is an opportunity to break that cycle if you are in the type of environment that encourages a different style of managerial leadership and sensitivity to people. You will be especially effective in breaking the cycle if you are competent and respected within the organization. Your superiors and subordinates will start to recognize that you have values and that you can make them work within the organization. That combination is almost always unbeatable.

I also believe that large organizations, in order to survive, will have to be places where people can raise ethical questions. We have had too many examples in the last 15 years of corporations being surprised and unprepared for too many socially important questions like pollution, hiring of minorities and women, the humanization of work, etc. The effective boss of the future will have to signal to his or her subordinates by actions and words: "Bring these problems to me, I want to hear about this. I want these questions raised and argued within the organization." Now I admit that if top management doesn't signal this way, it will be extremely difficult for the middle manager to raise these questions but I think the trend is toward more openness and debate within the organization.

Another problem for us in business is how we handle our family life when we are so busy running companies. Okay, let's face it! This is a tough question that has concerned me for a long time. We have six children growing up quickly. I worry about overcommitting myself to the company at the price of not even knowing our children, of losing contact with them.

The same thing can be said about the husband-wife relationship. It can be devastating for the wife because the husband is in an exciting environment, taking on responsibilities and doing things, and traveling all over the world, while the wife stays at home with the kids, running the house, cooking the meals. She begins to wonder why she went to college, or whether she has any role outside the home. I have seen a lot of divorces growing out of this tension about roles.

We, like most older couples, have not really gotten a handle on this.

The problem with the busy executive is that he or she gets terribly involved in some complex operation or maybe a crisis that eats up one's time and thinking. Before you know it, the family takes a back seat. To counter this fact, I tried to devise some personal rules to follow. For instance, I take a half a day a month from the office to spend with my wife. She will come into the city and we will have lunch, go to a museum or the theatre. Sometimes we simply walk around and talk.

Another rule is that I will never work on the weekends. I used to be away frequently on business in Europe or South America, but now I plan all my trips to be back by Friday night. Last week I was working with our European manager, and he wanted me to stay over the weekend to complete some work we were doing. I told him I would come back again if necessary, but I was committed to being home with the family.

I won't even take home materials to read from the office. I will really hustle while at the office to get the work out in order to be free evenings. When I am not traveling I leave work at 5:15 so that I can have dinner with my family.

Still I worry about all this. My life is sharply divided between work and home. When our home office was in a small town in Illinois, I was five minutes from the office, and I could take the kids to the factory to show them what the company was like. My wife and kids felt an involvement in what I was doing.

Now I am working in New York and living in Connecticut and it is a different world. I have to leave early to commute into the city and come home physically tired. The family has no way to get involved, or to see the exhilaration that comes from managing a fairly large company. All they see is a business environment that must not be attractive if it can drain a person so much. They challenge me as to why I do it.

I have, a number of times, posed to myself this question. I worry that business can overwhelm all of the other things of my life.

To close, I believe my role in business is compatible with my religion. I see no problem there, at least in theory. What I do see as a problem is whether I am doing enough as a religious person in the business world. And I am a little uncomfortable at being held up as an example of a Christian businessman. As I said earlier, it is very difficult to be either a good Christian or a competent business person. And it is infinitely more difficult to be both a good Christian and a competent businessman. If I'm an example of anything, it is that I am trying . . .

TOM BRITT'S QUANDARY

The "Fasten Your Seat Belt" sign went on as the jet started its long descent. Tom switched off his cassette, and reflected on what he had just heard. He liked John Caron and wanted to accept what John had talked about. But could he? Could religious values be used in the demanding business world that Tom knew? And if they could, was Caron's life a successful model of what could be? Or, was Caron right when he worried aloud "whether I am doing enough . . .?"

This case was prepared by Professor John W. Houck of the University of Notre Dame, as a basis for class discussion rather than to illustrate either effective or ineffective handling of the situation.

Houck is Professor of Management at the University of Notre Dame. A former Danforth teaching fellow, he has earned degrees from Notre Dame, North Carolina, and Harvard Universities. He is the editor of *Outdoor Advertising: History and Regulation* (Notre Dame, Ind.: Univ. of Notre Dame Press, 1969), and coeditor of *Academic Freedom and the Catholic University* (Notre Dame, Ind.: Fides Publishers, 1967), and *A Matter of Dignity: Inquiries Into the Humanization of Work* (Notre Dame, Ind.: University of Notre Dame Press, 1977). He is a member of the Roman Catholic Church.

Chapter Fourteen
Writing Your Own Story

"*Perfect, George. The only thing missing is you.*"

I think that the Christian images in my life will serve to guide my decisions, yet I am equally certain that my business experience and career will direct as well. Integrating the values of the business world into the creative context set by my Christian faith is the challenge of my life story.

I just want to live a nice life and have a good family. I do not plan on doing anything terribly wrong and I will raise my children as Christians. What more do you expect? (Excerpts from the stories of two persons who are beginning careers in the business world.)

As is pointed out in the introduction, this book seeks to raise the consciousness of us who call ourselves Christians so that we can become more aware of the implications of our Christian convictions for speech and action. The particular focus of the volume is on Christians in the business world. In order to complete this learning experience, it may be helpful for the reader to take some time to write his or her own story. Putting our stories down on paper not only helps reveal the many self-deceptions that we erect to avoid the painful truth about aspects of our lives that may be difficult to face, but also enables us to possess our values, to make them our own in a fuller way. The very process of putting our values into words helps build them into our life pattern.

KNOWING WHO WE ARE

Most of us generally assume that the really terrible things that are done in this world are perpetrated by persons *fully aware* of their misdeeds but intent on some goal perceived as warranting the behavior. For example, when we think of the deeds of the cast of characters in the Watergate affair or of the executives in a price fixing scandal, we imagine that they were consciously and deliberately reflective about all the havoc (and evil) that they caused in the human community. After all, they knew what they were doing. But did they? They understood what they were doing as bolstering a faltering presidential administration, or keeping a firm safely in the black, but could they step outside their professional role and assess what the limits of that role might be? Did they have a story with a dominant image sufficient to keep them humane through it all, a story that could encompass their professional story and put it in perspective?

It is all too easy to call such people hypocrites. They seem to profess noble ideals of integrity, sincerity, and loyalty while at the same time acting in quite another fashion. Yet, perhaps it is not so simple. Evil is often brought into the world by persons acting quite unwittingly. A good example of the dynamics of self-deception is documented by David Halberstam in *The Best and the Brightest*. Halberstam presents a detailed account of the people and events involved with the war in Vietnam. A central point in the book is that often our failures were compounded because high officials could not face the bitter truth that they had made some mistakes in earlier analysis and decision-making. The book provides some character sketches that reveal to the reader just how easy it is to rationalize and dismiss what we do not want to hear. As Halberstam put it: "A lie had become a truth, and the policy-makers were caught in it; their policy was a failure, and they could not admit it."[1]

The fault of most evil doers lies in their failure to stop to take stock of what they are doing, to assess their words and deeds in the light of consciously appropriated stories and images. Most evil doers (and all of us might find ourselves in that category at one time or another) really did not know all that they were doing when they were doing it.

All of this is not to say that we are not accountable for what we say and do. On the contrary, as responsible human beings we must continually take stock of the story we are writing with our lives, spell out our involvements in the various worlds of which we are a part, and see if our master image still provides coherence to our experience. There is always the danger of self-deception—that we will do or approve things in our corporate "role" that we would never be inclined to do otherwise. For Christians, all this may be caught when we spell out our story, when we stand back to give a coherent account of our lives.

A REVIEW

Being a Christian necessarily implies that key images from the Judeo-Christian Scriptures govern the experience of a life and guide a personal story. Christians, of course, appropriate differing constellations of biblical images at the various stages of life, and hence, each life takes on its own unique pattern. One of the objectives of the book has been to assist the reader in the personal appropriation of the Christian story as an alternative to "falling into" one of the dominant cultural stories of our times, or to appropriating uncritically the images available in contemporary corporations. With the Christian story as a basic story for a life, the other stories are thereby set in an appropriate context. The parable of the Prodigal Son was discussed to illustrate how the scriptures provide images that move us to a new vision and set the stage for "seeing" more profound discoveries of the heights and depths of what it means to be human. The Christian images make a claim to govern all experience. No doubt, everyone has a whole host of nonbiblical images in the imaginative context that forms the basis for understanding his or her experience (for example, The Company Person). Yet the claim of Christianity is that its images are to be the prevailing and controlling influence on a life story. Life ought not be divided in two, one part governed by a set of images from the business world (The King of the Mountain, for example), and another part governed by a set of images from the scripture. Biblical images provide an integrated vision of a life project that includes career achievements, as well as family life, love, laughter, and prayer. They help us organize our hierarchy of values consistent with our religious convictions.

Chapters 1 and 2 contain a summary of one understanding of the Christian story. This entails going to the Bible and reading and reflecting on its stories in order to discern some key values for a Christian. Chapter 3 focuses on the skill of integrating the values of the Christian community into the contemporary business world. The next ten chapters are built around ten cases that asked *you* for a decision.

The decision-making process is outlined in four steps:

1. investigate the case and discern the relevant data.
2. interpret the data, that is determine and clarify the meaning of the facts. Often the Suggested Readings are very helpful in this step.
3. evaluate the data, that is determine what is valued in the situation, and the consequences of the various actions.
4. consider the alternatives and decide what to do. In this final step, one can go only one way.

In each of the ten cases, you made a decision and, because of that decision, you are a different person. In making the decision, placing one value over another, you have opted to change the way you will live your life. (This explains why the theologian, Bernard Lonergan says this fourth step involves a "conversion," that is, a "change in direction.") The purpose of writing your story is to consolidate any "conversions," these "changes of directions," that may follow from your decision.

As an example, consider how these steps would apply in the Bill Clark case (Chapter 12). In that case, you are asked to take the part of the small businessman, Bill Clark, and decide whether to send the letter to the local newspaper—a letter that would boldly support open housing and criticize the citizenry for their apathy. In doing this case, you would first *ascertain the data*: minority families were refused housing of their choice, the churches did little to assist them, the politicians did less, the townspeople gave little support, and so on. You would then *interpret the data*: fair housing is not enforced, many people are afraid to defend the rights of minority persons, some are outright racists, and so on. The third step is *evaluation*: Bill Clark values his business, and it could be hurt if he takes a strong stand. On the other hand, as a Christian, Clark holds the conviction that the dignity of all persons must be respected in the matter of the choice of housing. The final step, *decision*, finds Bill torn in two directions. If he sends the letter, he risks angering his customers in town and perhaps ruining his business. If he does not send the letter, he feels he will have let down his oppressed brothers and sisters, and will be unfaithful to his own integrity. The future welfare of his business and the right of the minorities for open housing are two values in conflict in the person of

Bill Clark. He can only realize one value. (At least the way this case is posed.) He must decide!

In terms of the method proposed here, this process can be outlined as follows: (Assume that he sends the letter.)

1. RESEARCH AND EXPERIENCE   (HE EXPERIENCES)
   Bill Clark ascertains the facts.

2. INTERPRETATION   (HE UNDERSTANDS)
   Bill Clark discerns the meaning of the facts for him; no one will tackle the racist issue in the community.

3. EVALUATION   (HE JUDGES)
   Bill Clark values both the welfare of his business as well as the human dignity of all persons.

4. DECISION   (HE DECIDES)
   A. Bill Clark is pulled in several directions.
   B. He finally decides to send the letter—Lonergan calls this "conversion."

Note that this final step is called "conversion" in order to indicate that in every decision we are changed in the direction of the value that we have affirmed in that decision. In each of the ten cases, by your reading, analysis and decision, you were "converted" or changed as you weighted the values at stake and opted for some and not for others. Yet the crucial point here is that in order to appropriate these "conversions," to ascertain the full implications of these decisions for a life story, a further process is necessary; we call this final step "writing your own story."

Writing your own story entails having an image of God, humankind, and the world. For example, it is likely that underlying Bill Clark's decision to send the letter are some basic convictions about God, the world, and humankind. These convictions are the basis for Clark's evaluation of the situation and his attitudes and intentions. Thus, if Bill Clark were to put the implicit premises of his decision into words, he might say something like this:

> *God* is a gracious father who lavishes unmerited love on all his children.

Humankind, although sometimes irresponsible, is basically good
and will respond well to care and concern. All people are brothers and sisters, and are possessed with human dignity.
The World, in spite of evil, is at root a friendly environment where
good persons can make life more humane.

Bill Clark might see his lifetime as a journey where he enjoys the
good things of creation, develops his talents, supports other persons
in need, and builds the human community—all to the honor and
glory of God. Disagreements on particular actions, (for example, Bill
Clark sending the letter), tend to focus on the level of policy disputes,
when, often, what is at odds is the basic story that underpins the decision. When Bill Clark opted to support the oppressed family against
the racist policies of his community, the values and attitudes that
went into making the decision flowed from his personal story. Rules
are interpreted in relation to a story. For example, Clark might hold
the principle, "always consider self-interest first," yet he would interpret that principle in the context of a Christian story. Thus, he might
see that "self-interest" would dictate helping oppressed minorities,
because we are all one human community, and if some members suffer, all are less happy. In another story, perhaps the one we called The
Millionaire, self-interest might dictate solely *self-centered* activities
and clearly preclude any actions that would jeopardize the Clark
business. In that case, the blacks or other oppressed minorities would
have to fend for themselves. They might be dismissed with the comment that, "After all, the Irish had to struggle *on their own* and made
it to the top; let the blacks do it the same way." Only by knowing the
story a person lives out of, can we understand how he or she interprets principles.

YOUR STORY

These remarks on the Bill Clark story are intended to display the
importance of coming to terms with the basic story that provides the
premises for your life and work. One way to appropriate the Christian story as a basic story is to focus on appropriating a dominant biblical image as the master image to guide the sort of person you are

becoming. A biblical image may evoke the whole constellation of biblical values and other biblical images. It helps instill the attitudes and intentions of the Bible into the intellectual and emotional fabric of the person.

The image of the sort of person one is becoming changes over time; the biblical image that is most appealing to a person varies depending on life experiences. When you are young, Jesus as the Lord of Creation might be attractive. As an adolescent, Jesus seems more like a brother. A young adult might resonate more with Jesus as prophet. An adult often finds Jesus to be primarily a healer. In middle-age, he seems best expressed as savior, for many; while perhaps in old age the best image is the suffering servant. All those images of Jesus are true, yet none of them exhausts the reality that he is. As your dominant image of Jesus changes with life experience, other images from the Bible that are helpful in guiding life stories vary in importance with time and circumstances. A wealthy and talented business executive may see his life and circumstances interpreted best by the image of the Good Samaritan, while a poor monk might find the publican image in the parable of the pharisee and the publican most helpful. The Bible is the sourcebook of master images to guide a Christian story.

STEPS IN WRITING YOUR STORY

1. Imagine that you are preparing to meet an old friend whom you have not seen for a number of years. He asks you to write *three brief sentences* that give as accurate a picture as possible of you.

2. After writing the three sentences, reflect on them for a while, write out the image of God, humankind, and society that is entailed in your self-description.

3. What biblical image best captures the sort of person you hope to become? Write two or three pages focusing on what you believe the master image of your life to be.

4. Write about how your life will probably develop (or has developed) using the master image (step 3 above) as a guide.

A FINAL NOTE: ASSESSING THE
TRUTH OF LIFE STORIES

We have made the point that the challenge of becoming a Christian involves the skill of learning to understand ourselves and to describe and interpret our experience with the great biblical images. The question arises how we can know whether these images (the Cross, Heir to the Kingdom of God, Servant of the Lord, etc.) are *true*. That is to say, is there any way to show that the life-style that flows from biblical images is *truer* than other life styles, for example, the aggressive, hard-charging business life-style?[2] One way to explore the truth of the vision evoked by the Judeo-Christian images is to examine the quality of life evoked by a life governed by biblical images. The truth is assessed by examining the lived life. For example, John Caron has a Christian vision that clearly provides him with a wider perspective on his corporate responsibilities. For John, making a profit will never in itself bring career fulfillment. The Christian vision provides the breadth and depth to see through popular consumeristic culture. It challenges us to find our fulfillment in reverence for the Father and service to the brothers and sisters. And as we are reminded in the parable of the Prodigal Son, the New Testament is ever vigilant, lest we take ourselves too seriously.

In Chapter 2 we examined seven values highlighted in the Judeo-Christian scriptures. Another way of putting our question is, "How do I know the Judeo-Christian values are truer than other contrasting ones that might be attractive in the culture?" Based on our research and experience, we have assumed that the Bible is more realistic about what is humanly fulfilling, and that some values of popular culture hold out a vision of life that they cannot possibly deliver. For example, consider the case of John Ehrlichman. As a top staff officer in the White House he was living a story that no doubt had some degree of truth, limited though it may have been. It was a story that had the master image of problem solver, someone who "makes it to the top" by "getting things done." This Gamesman-King of the Mountain story probably accomplished some good through sheer pragmatism and perhaps brought some degree of fulfillment to Mr. Ehrlichman. However, when tragedy came along, John Ehrlichman's whole world collapsed because his story lacked the resources within itself to account for tragedy. He tells us that his life came apart, and that he is now searching for a more encompassing story.

It is interesting to compare Ehrlichman with Bill Clark. The case of Bill Clark related an actual situation. Bill was a thirty-five-year-old man who had a thriving landscaping supply store. After he spoke out boldly in favor of fair housing legislation in his small community, his business was boycotted by irate citizens. Slowly he lost the whole business and had to sell at a considerable loss. You would think that Bill Clark's world would have fallen apart, that he would be depressed and beaten. Yet, although certainly distressed, he was unshaken in his convictions for the downtrodden and began to plan for new ways to help his ghetto brothers. Bill had a story (the Christian story) that accounts for tragedy and, in fact, says that a full life includes failure as well as success, weakness as well as power, and anxiety as well as confidence. From the Christian story, Bill had images that could help him identify sin and the power of evil both in himself and others and while he was a competent business person, he was also a Christian. He put the two stories together, and continued that path of integration of the stories (he started again in business) after one failure.

The breadth and depth of the biblical vision of life, a vision discussed at length in Chapter 1, is perhaps best said in poetical form in the Book of Ecclesiastes (3:1-8). Recounting a whole range of events and human emotions, the passage proclaims that "There is a season for everything, . . ." There is a realism in this piece from the Bible that says that heartache, weakness, evil, and failure are shot through the joy, power, goodness, and success of a human life. Any view of the "good life" must take this tragic dimension into account. The Bible, as God's revelation to humankind, does this most completely. Often the Bible can clarify ambiguity in popular values, and bring out and highlight all that is good and noble in the culture. With its help a career in the business world—a career that results in a good salary, influence, power, and the enjoyment of the world—*can* be the path of Christian holiness.

CONCLUSION

I think that religious images have continued to dominate my career-planning and decision-making. True, some images are fresher in my mind than others at various times; still there are some that have continued to play upon my consciousness for as long as I can remember.

It sounds so easy to be uncompromising and faithful to my religious values in the future. It is like being brave when no danger exists. I recognize that I may encounter career problems if I do not fit into the business mold. I can't answer with absolute certainty what my actions would be if there is conflict . . . . (Excerpts from the stories of two persons who are in early stages of their careers in the business world.

Being able to articulate who you are, what you think of the world around you, and what you believe God to be like, provides a foundation from which to evaluate new problems and situations. Certain attitudes, values, and intentions flow from a Christian understanding of God, society, and the human person. In putting your own self-image into words, you also become more aware of the hierarchy of values that ought to prevail in your assessment of new situations requiring decision and action. It is suggested that you go through this process of writing your story periodically, perhaps every two years. All of us should try to remember that it is only by the power of the Lord that we are enabled to put our knowledge into action.

One of the objectives of this volume is that those who profess the Christian faith might find in a Christian story the guidance and encouragement to strive for a better world. The ten cases have portrayed the ambiguity and the magnitude of the challenge. Discussions on religion and life often present the Christian values and way of life in such absolute terms that they seem to have little bearing on the institutions most persons know. Furthermore, many middle or lower management people with an exemplary Christian vision have little opportunity to implement their values into corporate life. Because of circumstances apparently beyond their control, some executives seem powerless to realize all their personal values. By focusing on biblical images to guide one's story, and by assessing the values at stake in each decision, there is a way out of that dilemma.

It is true that even those who have the power and influence to work towards a more humane world frequently find themselves reluctant to accept new challenges. Indeed, we can be sure that there will always be missed opportunities and occasional lapses in determination. The only consolation for this prodigal behavior is our belief that God continues to lavish his love on his prodigal sons and daughters!

Notes

1 David Halberstam, *The Best and the Brightest* (New York: Random House, 1972), p. 285.

2 For a good account of how to assess the truth of stories and images, see David B. Burrell, C.S.C., and Stanley Hauerwas, "Self-Deception and Autobiography: Theological and Ethical Reflections on Speer's INSIDE THE THIRD REICH," *Journal of Religious Ethics* Vol. 2, No. 1 (1974), pp. 99-117. This essay is also available in a volume authored by Stanley Hauerwas with Richard Bondi and David B. Burrell, C.S.C.: *Truthfulness and Tragedy* (Notre Dame, Ind.: Univ. of Notre Dame Press, 1977).

Index of Biblical References

Index